FINDING MEANING IN WINE

This book examines controversies in American wine culture and how those controversies intersect with and illuminate current academic and cultural debates about the environment and about interpretation.

With a specific focus on the United States of America, the methods that we use to discuss literature and other art are applied to wine-making and wine culture. The book explores the debates about how to evaluate wine and the problems inherent in numerical scoring as well as evaluative tasting notes, whether winemakers can be artists, the discourse in wine culture involving natural wine and biodynamic farming, as well as how people judge what makes a wine great. These interpretative commitments illuminate an underlying metaphysics and allegiance to a culture of reason or feeling. The discussions engage with a broad range of writers and thinkers, such as Roland Barthes, Susan Sontag, Louis Menand, Michael Pollan, Greg Garrard, John Guillory, Amitov Ghosh, Pierre Bourdieu, and Barbara Herrnstein-Smith. The book draws upon not only a number of texts produced by wine critics, wine writers, literary critics and theorists but also extensive interviews with wine writers and multiple California winemakers. These interviews contribute to a unique reflection on wine and meaning.

This book will be of great interest to readers looking to learn more about wine from cultural, literary, and philosophical perspectives.

Michael Sinowitz is a Professor in the Department of English at DePauw University, USA. His previous publications include *Sex, Drugs and Bodies in Patrick O'Brian's Aubrey-Maturin Novels* (2014) and essays on Graham Greene, Angela Carter, Thomas Berger, and Elmore Leonard.

ROUTLEDGE FOOD STUDIES

Food Education and Gastronomic Tradition in Japan and France
Ethical and Sociological Theories
Haruka Ueda

Finding Meaning in Wine
A US Blend
Michael Sinowitz

For more information about this series, please visit: www.routledge.com/Routledge-Food-Studies/book-series/RFOODS

FINDING MEANING IN WINE

A US Blend

Michael Sinowitz

Routledge
Taylor & Francis Group
LONDON AND NEW YORK

earthscan
from Routledge

Designed cover image: © Getty Images

First published 2024
by Routledge
4 Park Square, Milton Park, Abingdon, Oxon OX14 4RN

and by Routledge
605 Third Avenue, New York, NY 10158

Routledge is an imprint of the Taylor & Francis Group, an informa business

British Library Cataloguing-in-Publication Data
A catalogue record for this book is available from the British Library

Library of Congress Cataloging-in-Publication Data
Names: Sinowitz, Michael Leigh, author.
Title: Finding meaning in wine : a US blend / Michael Sinowitz.
Description: New York, NY : Routledge, 2024 | Includes bibliographical
references and index.
Identifiers: LCCN 2023006920 (print) | LCCN 2023006921 (ebook) |
ISBN 9781032508276 (hardback) | ISBN 9781032505169 (paperback) |
ISBN 9781003399810 (ebook)
Subjects: LCSH: Wine and wine making--United States. | Wine industry--
United States. | Wine tasting--United States. | Food writing--United States.
Classification: LCC TP548 .S6852 2023 (print) | LCC TP548 (ebook) |
DDC 663/.200973--dc23/eng/20230302
LC record available at https://lccn.loc.gov/2023006920
LC ebook record available at https://lccn.loc.gov/2023006921

ISBN: 978-1-032-50827-6 (hbk)
ISBN: 978-1-032-50516-9 (pbk)
ISBN: 978-1-003-39981-0 (ebk)

DOI: 10.4324/9781003399810

Typeset in Bembo
by Taylor & Francis Books

CONTENTS

FIGURES

ACKNOWLEDGEMENTS

So many people have helped me with this project that it has often felt like a communal undertaking. First, let me thank DePauw University, whose help—in the form of both fellowships and sabbaticals—has allowed me to both pursue and complete this work. In terms of individuals, let me start with Tom Chiarella, who once hired me many years ago and who gave me the confidence to pursue this project one sunny day in front of Meyer's Market. Through Tom, the project began with some assistance from Ryan D'Agostino and my first interview, with Wylie Dufresne. Although this project ended up going in a different direction, Wylie's willingness to meet with me on a remarkably humid day in New York was really the first concrete step forward for this book.

I cannot begin to do justice to how welcoming the winemaking and wine-writing community has been towards me and how enormously grateful I am. Notably, Rajat Parr was not only the first winemaker to grant me an interview, but also met with me more than once, connected me with Duncan Meyers and Nathan Roberts and treated me to a very memorable lunch one stormy day in New York. Duncan and Nathan not only provided me with great conversation, but gave me my first magical sip of trousseau and helped me meet Hardy Wallace. I am grateful to Hardy for his generosity, sharing his wines, treating me to lunch, sharing his experiences, and sacrificing his sleep to share some aligoté one night. Justin Smith, thank you for being the first winemaker to talk with me and setting me at ease. In addition, thanks to the kindness of Celia Welch, Hank Beckmeyer, Martha Stoumen, John Kongsgaard, Ted Lemon, Morgan Twain-Peterson, Abe Schoener, Jared Brandt, Cathy Corison, Gideon Beinstock, Michael Browne, Dan Petroski, and Chris Brockway, all of whom you will get to meet in the pages of this book and were liberal with their time, their ideas, and frequently with their wines. Thanks to Elizabeth Vianna who not only granted me time out of her busy day, but shared tapas with me and hosted me at Chimney Rock. Josh Widaman went beyond a conversation and invited me back to Lewis Cellars to explore some of his wines in greater depth. I particularly treasure the generosity shown me by Steve and Jill Klein Matthiasson, who have me welcomed into their home and new winery multiple times. Matthew Rorick was also instrumental in this project, not only spending hours with me in Murphys, and introducing me to Elaine Chukan Brown, but finding time for further conversations over dinners. Lastly, I would like to acknowledge the great generosity of Tegan Passalaqua, who was so kind with his time and who with his wife, Olivia, provided me and my family with two wonderful and memorable dinners.

Among wine writers and critics, I am particularly thankful to Elaine Chukan Brown, Josh Greene, Eric Asimov, John Bonné, and Esther Mobley. Thanks to an email from Matthew Rorick, Elaine dropped everything, met me for dinner, and then proceeded to link me with a host of winemakers who all proved incredibly helpful. Elaine also introduced me to Josh Greene, who not only shared multiple lunches with me, but shared his wisdom and provided me with one of the most indelible experiences of the project, tasting for *Wine & Spirits Magazine*. Eric Asimov and Esther Mobley also met me for helpful discussions and meals, and John Bonné let me share ideas with him over coffee in the East Village.

Once this project began, it probably seemed to my friends that I was always working on it as I never stopped discussing it, and sharing a bottle with friends always seemed like a chance to keep exploring. Two friends and colleagues, Harry Brown and Wayne Glausser, read early drafts of the book and offered great insights. Wayne has shared many wine experiences with me, been a great friend, and served as a mentor, role model, and inspiration. I am particularly grateful to Harry for his guidance with ecocriticism, and, along with David Alvarez, for giving me an opportunity to present some of that material at DePauw. Wayne and Harry also have shared bottles with me over the years as have a number of other friends and colleagues, including Inge Aures, Marnie McInnes, Jeffrey Kenney, Srimati Basu, and Tiku Ravat. I would also like to thank Istvan Csicsery-Ronay for his advice, support, and the many great conversations through the years. Thanks also to Scott Cooper for helping me learn about studio pottery. Two former students, Zach Batt and Vicky Googasian, also contributed to this project, and I am grateful to all the work on transcriptions Vicky provided.

Lastly, I would like to thank my family, including Allen and Maddie Sinowitz, and Louis and Andrea Mendelsohn. Most of all, I want to thank my son Harry, who has already developed a love for California wine country and Robin, my first editor, greatest support, and best friend.

INTRODUCTION

"What exactly is your book about?" The question led to a snicker from the very large man whose body leaned against a wall, thus blocking most of the small, paper-stuffed room.

"I've been riding around with him for hours, and I still don't know," the big man, Tegan Passalaqua, said with a chuckle. Every time I met someone, I inevitably found myself rehearsing a short speech in which I tried to introduce the subject of this book. And inevitably, I had mixed results. Sometimes, I clearly started on the wrong foot. When I met the intense, innovative chef Wylie Dufresne in a coffee shop in New York City on an astonishingly humid day, I nervously babbled for five minutes about literary theory. Over a year later, when I met the academic philosopher-turned-winemaker Abe Schoener at the bar at the Ludlow on Manhattan's Lower East Side, we proceeded via the Socratic method, Abe in the lead.

In between, I found myself in a place I had not in the least expected to be. Although I had already spent a good deal of time with Tegan, I never really got to ask him any of my questions. Instead, the conversation would just take off. Tegan has a legendary knowledge of vineyards. If you are looking for one or want to know about one, he should be one of the first people you contact. In fact, someone had called him during our drive to see if his boss, Larry Turley, might be interested in owning another one. Tegan also spends an extraordinary amount of time behind the wheel of his oversized pickup truck. Located primarily in Napa, Tegan's job as winemaker for Turley Cellars and for his own label, Sandlands, nevertheless takes him to Paso Robles, some four hours south of Napa, or several hours northeast to the Sierra Foothills on a regular basis. Since I had many questions that I still wanted to ask Tegan, I proposed taking a ride with him, perhaps to see some of the old vineyards he worked with in areas like Contra Costa County. As a founder of the Historic Vineyard Society, Tegan had a special affection for these vineyards, some of which date back to the nineteenth

DOI: 10.4324/9781003399810-1

century. Sometime after we visited the Bechthold Vineyard—the surprising home of the oldest Cinsault vines in the world despite their origins in the Southern Rhône and the Languedoc—or perhaps after Tegan's own Kirschenmann Vineyard, though probably earlier, I had completely lost my bearings. By the time we parked in Sacramento, Tegan pulling a bottle of his Sandlands chenin blanc out of the back of the truck and guiding me to a pizzeria, I was simply trying to keep up. After a lunch of two pizzas, a salad, and a bowl of pasta with Bolognese, a visit from the proprietor, some delicious chenin, and some continued arguing over whether winemakers are artists, Tegan said that he wanted to show me something.

We hopped back into the truck and headed a short way down the road to a supermarket, and Tegan began sharing the history of the supermarket and the man who runs it. The pale lime-green awning had white squares spaced across it, and red letters spelled out "Corti Bros." If you have never heard of Corti Bros or its proprietor, Darrell Corti, you might be surprised to know that he, his store, and his work as an importer have had a massive impact on contemporary food and wine culture. Among other things, he gets credit for helping introduce Americans to quality balsamic vinegar, Parmigiano-Reggiano, as well as top Italian wines. His knowledge in this area, as I would find out firsthand, is exceptional. As a profile by Rick Kushman recounts, Corti played a key role in providing ingredients for chefs like Alice Waters, and Ruth Reichl has said that he "knows more about food and wine than anyone else in America."[1]

The store itself, now open for more than sixty-five years, seems somewhat outside of time. The staff and Corti himself wear the kind of blue smocks I associate with the 1950s. The wine selection extends far beyond what you might normally find in a supermarket, even in California, and, above the aisles, one can find a kind of museum of emptied great bottles from around the world and pioneering wines from California. Tegan got particular joy from pointing out the jeweler's cabinet filled with rare, imported balsamic vinegars, including one in the $500 range.

After some initial exploring of the store, which included Tegan introducing me to the sculptor-turned-winemaker Craig Haarmeyer, who also wanted to debate the wine-as-art question with me, Tegan found me and asked me to follow. We headed to the produce aisle at the end of the store, then went back into an employee-only section. Everyone seems to know Tegan, and at around six and half feet tall, he's hard to miss. Rather than getting shouted out of there, we received greetings, as if Norm had just entered Sam Malone's bar. We turned left again and found ourselves outside a green painted wooden door with a doorbell. Tegan rang the buzzer, the door was electronically released from the inside, and we made our way into the narrow stairs to the overflowing workspace of Darrell Corti. Initially, his back was to me as he sat at a computer, papers stacked everywhere.

Short introductions and firm handshakes followed. Then the interrogation began. I tried to carry this off with some academic calm. After all, academics like grilling each other, and it can be friendly ... sometimes. Corti's eyes locked on me, and it was immediately clear that something like a good answer would be necessary. I tried my most basic answer. I am looking at recent controversies and debates in wine culture in relation to similar debates in my own field, literary studies, I said. Silence and a grin from Tegan. "What do you mean exactly?" Darrell asked, somewhat mocking and impatient. "Okay," I said. "So for instance, there has recently been a great deal of interest in California in what some people call esoteric grapes. And this has led to some controversy because folks like Robert Parker have said you can't make great wine out of something like trousseau." "That's ridiculous." "Maybe, but that's not my argument exactly, but when Robert Parker says that only particular grapes, sometimes called the noble grapes or one of the canon of grapes, can make a great wine, he is making arguments that bear a particularly striking resemblance to the ongoing arguments about how novels get included in the literary canon." "But Parker's claims are idiotic."

"Well, would you like me to read what Parker had to say?" I proceeded to read an excerpt of a sort of all-purpose and relatively legendary rant from Parker about how critics and others have tried to dupe wine consumers into buying terrible wines made from ignoble grapes. Corti was having none of it and proceeded to give Tegan and myself an impromptu lecture about particular grape varieties, mentioning some that I don't think even Tegan had encountered. When he finished, I explained that in some ways the very shape of the debate resembled the ways in which the critic John Guillory views the nature of the debate of the literary canon. In Guillory's telling one side consists of the conservative position—a sort of tautological position that texts in the canon are great and that greatness is self-evident—and the other is the liberal critique, which he sees as both viewing the canon as a kind of conspiracy that keeps non-white, non-male representation to a minimum and, in response to that conspiracy, instead seeks to open up the canon. Thus, someone like Parker lines up squarely with the conservative position: Cabernet produces great wines because time has shown that it does (like Shakespeare fulfilling Samuel Johnson's test of time criteria for greatness), whereas many of the winemakers I met in my research—producing California versions of trousseau, ribolla gialla, chenin blanc, and albariño to name just a few grape varieties—seem to be trying to hearken back to a time when an astonishing, often labeled "diverse," number of grape varieties came to be planted in California, carried along with a variety of other things by immigrants and settlers from all over the world.

Now I had Darrell's attention.

★   ★   ★   ★

The germination of this book goes back a long way. Though I could locate it in an early encounter with too much Manischewitz, a more accurate starting place would be the early days of my marriage, living in Miami, attending graduate school, and spending my free time at a local wine shop. While I dedicated hours to trying to make sense of Jacques Derrida and Michel Foucault, I also found myself learning about German Riesling, Spanish rioja, and California Zinfandels. By the time I had earned my PhD in literature, I had acquired a small wine collection, one I managed to largely ruin by packing it into a moving van for a journey to the American Midwest. What started out as something I sentimentally sought to round out a family dinner became a lifelong passion, and I have more than made up for the loss of that initial collection.

Winemakers and connoisseurs can always point to at least one epiphany bottle, a wine that altered their sense of wine's potential or what the experience of drinking a wine could be. For me, it was a thirty-year-old bottle of German Riesling. I had the luck of trying it as I just started to discover wine. Even a winemaker like Morgan Twain-Peterson, who grew up in the trade as the son of Joel Peterson, original winemaker of Ravenswood, can identify some particularly aged bottles of zinfandel that, at the least, illustrated what that grape could produce. Others can recall a variety of wines encountered in a series of sequential steps, opening up different vistas of wine's potentiality, one wine epiphany leading to another.

People often think of the term *epiphany* as pointing to a turning point in one's life. However, I come to the term via James Joyce, who viewed epiphanies as moments of insight, though such insights do not necessarily alter the course of one's life. To think about wine as producing a Joycean epiphany might be to see wine as holding the potential to make one think, to concentrate, to see a break in the everyday. In my mind, as I contemplate these ideas, I keep coming back to one of the final interviews I did for this project with the transplanted New Yorker-turned-winemaker Dan Petroski. His path to a career in wine is a bit more convoluted than most, having left a burgeoning career in publishing with the Time Life corporation to move to Italy and then eventually to California, but wine began to have an impact on him during his initial career.

He talked about ordering a bottle of Chateau Haut-Brion and finding that time stood still as he drank it. There could have been many reasons why Dan felt this way. For one, he already knew that Haut-Brion *should* be a special wine. It's a Bordeaux first-growth, a designation held by only five red wines; in addition, it costs a lot of money (a current vintage might set you back about a thousand dollars). In short, the fact that a bottle like this made the world stop could be attributed to extrinsic factors like cost and reputation, as well as intrinsic factors such as the smell, taste, color, and texture of the wine itself. This project is not concerned with the wine epiphany per se and I raise it here as an example of the notable ways in which wine has been connected to ideas beyond simple consumption. What fascinates me, however, and what can really be seen as a kind of starting point for this project is that the kind of effects wine can produce—even mild intoxication——can often be attributed to art's effects on human beings, and the difficulty of saying whether those effects reside in wine's intrinsic or extrinsic qualities are also ongoing debates within the world of the arts and my particular abode, literary studies, where we can say the same thing about literature. I begin, then, with a very straightforward question: if wine is art, what follows?

This book examines the way in which we make meaning from art—and perhaps the world itself—and based on my initial hypothesis, particularly wine as art. In doing so, I conceive of this process of finding meaning through a few interlocking ideas about interpretation, metaphysics, and what the historian, Tim Blanning, calls "the long-running dialectic between a culture of feeling and a culture of reason."[2]

While Blanning's phrase appears in his discussion of perhaps the most prominent moment of this dialectic in Western culture, that between Romanticism and the Enlightenment, he notes that this dialectic predates this period and has continued to this very day. As we shall see, much of the form of the debates regarding wine reflect this dialectic. This dialectic also might be said to shape, or at the least inform, the history of metaphysics. In *Metaphysics: The Fundamentals*, co-authors Robert C. Koons and Timothy H. Pickavance offer an initial broad definition of metaphysics as an attempt by which "we puzzle and wonder about what exists and what existing things are like, in their most fundamental features and interrelationships."[3] They then divide metaphysics into ontology, "the study of what there is"[4] and the other part of metaphysics they see as "the study of the fundamental structure of reality as a whole."[5] The history of metaphysics the authors sketch out suggests that recurring tensions and disputes have arisen among methods—with that history including the recurring splits among materialists and idealists and ultimately the splitting away of science from philosophy which culminates in what C. P. Snow famously called the two cultures problem.

If we consider that the disputes about methods—that is, the best way to make sense of the world—are essentially a problem of interpretation, that is, how to do we interpret the data around us in order to best understand existing things and the nature of existence, we can see the thread here among these various concepts. As I will discuss further in the first chapter, I will largely be drawing upon two views of interpretation, one framed in opposition to the very notion as applied to art, by Susan Sontag, and one much more pragmatic and favorable, proposed by Steven Mailloux. Mailloux has presented his definition in two venues, one aimed primarily at students in an essay entitled "Interpretation" and the other in *Interpretive Conventions: The Reader in the Study of American Fiction*. The latter arrives at the definition—the same in both sources—by way of trying to examine the nature of the opposition between two very different views of interpretation in literary study—the view of M.H. Abrams and J. Hillis Miller. We might, to some extent, see their views as based in opposing views of a kind of metaphysical project: Abrams sees art as containing "determinate" meanings and thus the goal of interpretations is to "approximate" those meanings as "intended" by an author[6]— though this would extend to all artists. Miller, informed by Deconstruction, the school of analysis developed by the philosopher Jacques Derrida, "has two complementary aspects: interpretation is an unfolding, unraveling, unweaving, of the textual web *and* it is a self-conscious embroidering of its own."[7] In short, "Miller views interpretation, then, as a kind of free yet self-defeating unraveling of a text" because Miller sees all meaning as "indeterminate."[8] Mailloux goes on to make explicit that all definitions of interpretation—and those theories can be both prescriptive and descriptive—-"can be viewed as *argumentative* definitions that promote the user's own hermeneutic theory."[9] Seeking a definition that bridges these views and "does not define one position out of existence," Mailloux arrives at "acceptable and approximating translation."[10] As we shall see, this translation—so vital to understanding or interpreting both art and wine—is what Sontag opposes.

Nevertheless, the arguments and disputes in art and wine that I will explore in this book, I contend, can best be understood in relation to these longstanding debates about how to find meaning, and that those debates often are grounded more broadly in the dialectic Blanning describes, which has historically shaped or been shaped by disagreements about how to both understand the meaning and place of art in culture and the natural world.

To avoid the risk of rehearsing the very awkwardness I described at the outset, let me make clear what debates and controversies I am thinking about and how they can be approached in the ways that I hope to do so in the coming chapters. The start of this process began somewhat far away from wine as part of my own ongoing thinking about arguments in the history of literary studies over the proper way to interpret literature. I frequently teach a course in which I take students through this history, and I have often felt that underlying these debates lay larger arguments about the proper way to describe the world and what counts as significant in that process—a problem of methods and metaphysics. Looking for a more concrete way to describe this process, I realized that a similar problem presents itself when we think about the nature of the debates about the proper way to evaluate, assess, or what I call *interpret* wine.

The first chapter focuses on the basic process of evaluation and interpretation, thinking through what we do when we interpret, how we arrive at the proper grounds for that interpretation, and the critical perspective on what those interpretations both hope to produce but also how they reveal a kind of larger understanding of how reality operates. This may seem a pretty big leap from conventional images of individuals sipping, swirling, and perhaps spitting or a more mundane vision of a bottle of wine opened at a dinner table, glasses partially filled, and conversation flowing, mostly about things other than the wine in the glass. As Jill Klein Matthiasson once said to me over dinner at her house, sometimes wine just helps us wash down our dinner. And I do not deny that sometimes these discussions have left that utilitarian role of wine behind, but it is my hope that thinking about wine in some of the ways I propose sheds light on how wine, literature, and other arts function within our culture.

Thus, the first chapter proceeds from thinking through the nature of interpretation and other related key terms, including what people in literary studies mean when they talk about literary theory. If we begin to consider talking about wine in similar ways, this also implies the existence of a kind of wine theory. The crux of this chapter's discussion, however, revolves around arguments that have developed about how to properly evaluate wine, a process that I argue is akin to interpreting wine. In the recent history of wine writing and wine evaluating, the strongest push has been for the importance of blind tasting—that is, when a taster does not know what he or she is tasting—as a means to best evaluate wine for what it is, to eliminate the extrinsic factors that might color what is exclusively intrinsic to the wine. The example I cited of Dan Petroski's experience with Chateau Haut-Brion speaks to the problem that blind tasting seeks to eliminate. However, I quickly found that some critics, some wine writers, and some winemakers either see blind tasting as inherently flawed—that is, unable to do what it proposes to do—or deceiving in that it puts a value or emphasis on qualities that should not be emphasized in the interpreting or evaluating of wine. In order to see how blind tasting works for those who do it, I detailed my own experiences participating in a blind tasting panel for *Wine & Spirits Magazine.*

The arguments that follow from those who favor or critique blind tasting and that the chapter explores resemble the history of similar debates about the proper means of interpreting literature. Critics we might place under the umbrella term *formalists* have argued that literature is best understood by concentrating exclusively on the words on the page. Proponents of blind tasting might be said to resemble such formalists, for they seek to look exclusively at the wine in the bottle. Each approach then seeks to minimize the importance of the maker, the historical and cultural circumstances of the maker, as well as the learned prejudices of the interpreter or evaluator. In contrast, opponents to these formalists argue that these very factors formalists seek to eliminate are either impossible to eliminate or are in fact the key to properly interpreting or evaluating the object under discussion. When we begin to consider a question such as how important history is, we also begin to see the ways in which these arguments echo larger priorities an individual may have about how to make sense of and describe the world at large.

If the first chapter focuses primarily on the processes of evaluation and debates about how to properly do so, the second chapter focuses more on what we might consider the outcomes of these processes. In terms of wine, the emphasis here is particularly on how wine writers and critics attempt to offer an approximation of their experience of wine in the form of words, particularly tasting notes, and numbers, the hallmark of most American wine critics since the emergence of Robert Parker and his *Wine Advocate.* I consider Susan Sontag's famous essay "Against Interpretation" as both a means of understanding what it is we do when we interpret and also why someone might object to that process. Part of Sontag's objections has to do with taking something she wishes humans to experience emotionally, even viscerally, as it *is,* and instead focusing on translating and revealing its "contents." In some ways, Sontag's view aligns with the way Romantics criticized Enlightenment thinkers and scientists in their attempts to comprehend nature rather than appreciating or simply experiencing it. Sontag's critique then implies a similar distrust for rationalist analysis that sees all trees and no forest. Despite coming at the problem from a differing perspective, similar objections emerged from the American formalists in the twentieth century, mostly now known as the New Critics, who, besides wishing to wall off the poem as an object, felt that translating the contents into other words inevitably lost the beauty of the poem. Thus, one of the most famous New Critics, Cleanth Brooks, became associated with the expression "the heresy of paraphrase."

Similar problems follow the modern history of translating wine into words and numbers. The British wine writer Hugh Johnson recalled his response to first reading Parker's wine scores and objecting to them by noting that we would never append such scores to great symphonies or sculptures. The first section of the second chapter explores those who use numerical scores and defend them, such as the critics from *Wine Spectator*; those who use them but would prefer not to, like the editor, owner, and wine critic for *Wine & Spirits*, Joshua Greene; and those who object to such scoring in principle, like the *New York Times* wine writer, Eric Asimov. The second half of the chapter primarily considers the translation of wine into words. In more recent years, the controversy around tasting notes has to do with how expansive they have grown, the nature of the language employed by wine writers and critics, and the inherent problems in attempting to translate wine—or anything through the process of interpretation—into words. In exploring these questions, I not only draw on some of the arguments of wine writers and critics, but also the world of literary study and its own debates of whether there is such a thing as a literary language that is in some way different from other language, and language's ability to convey determinate meaning.

To explore the way in which language has become central to both understanding wine and also seemingly being at the heart of vexed disagreement, I conclude the section on language by focusing on In Pursuit of Balance (IPOB), an organization of winemakers—founded by sommelier-turned-winemaker, Rajat Parr, and Jasmine Hirsch, of her father's eponymous winery and vineyard—which ignited a controversy over and through the seemingly innocuous word *balance*. In a way, and as the wine writer Jon Bonné suggested in a post-mortem he wrote about the organization, the dispute about what the word meant and what made a wine balanced became the center of a kind of wine culture war. I would also argue that what the organization attempted to do by seeking to define "balance" was control or alter the grounds for interpreting, evaluating, and understanding their wines. In trying to both make sense of this debate and consider the nature of the positions in this culture war, I draw heavily on conversations I had with winemakers from both sides, including interviews with Rajat Parr both before and after the end of IPOB, and winemakers such as Justin Smith from Saxum, Josh Widaman, formerly of Lewis Cellars and currently with Pine Ridge, Elizabeth Vianna of Chimney Rock, and Michael Browne, formerly of Kosta Browne and now with Chev, who could be thought of as being on the opposing side in this contest. Ultimately, this chapter considers how different positions on these questions of words and numbers, as well as the processes by which we arrive at them, stake out a metaphysical position and how the staking out of those positions also resembles the positions implied by the various schools of interpretation that abound in literary studies.

If the first two chapters focus on interpreters, the third might be said to reverse the concern to makers and their intentions. Specifically, this chapter concentrates primarily on understanding how and why winemakers, particularly Californian winemakers, describe what they do—or do not do—in the manner that they do. In particular, this question is at the center of this study: if wine can aspire to be art, should we think of winemakers as artists? Most winemakers, however, tend to describe their work as in some way "doing as little as possible." Because of the broad reluctance of most winemakers I have met to identify themselves as artists, I became fascinated with why they seem so reluctant to do so—often while implying that there are other folks out there who do see themselves that way—and whether at least some winemakers ought to be thought of as akin to other kinds of artists, even if they did not embrace the label. This question really intersects with a number of other issues within the wine world. While it can be thought to have connections with other issues such as the natural wine movement, which I focus on in chapter 4, I primarily wanted to look at it in terms of how winemakers describe the winemaking process, how it connects to their understanding—or at least their discourse—about the relationship between winemaking and the land that produces their medium of creation (a loaded way to describe grapes). While I am using the term *describe*, it might be more apt to consider this an issue of interpretation, since much of the issue here is tied up in how winemakers interpret what they do, and is often informed by leanings either towards reason or feeling. Much of this chapter draws on my interviews with a variety of winemakers, which at some point became a kind of quest to locate a winemaker who would actually see themselves as an artist. In ultimately trying to consider whether we can think about winemakers as artists and to understand the discourse about winemaking shared by many winemakers, I consider the division between art and craft, drawing on some of the philosophy of art, and also try to understand the ways in which winemaking, or at least the discourse of winemaking, can be understood in terms of conception of authorship drawn from Romanticism and from more post-structuralist description of authorship as developed by folks like Roland Barthes.

A similar interest in discourse, then, continues into chapters 4 and 5, which take on the idea of "doing as little as possible" in regard to a number of interrelated movements within the wine world, namely organic farming and winemaking, biodynamic farming, and the natural wine movement. These terms also readily connect the wine world to shifts and trends in the larger culinary culture of the United States (and parts of Europe as well). That is, the interest in moving away from chemical farming and what we might call interventionist winemaking in the wine world can certainly be seen as part of the variety of movements that have influenced both the American restaurant scene and what consumers can purchase at the local Whole Foods. To those outside the academy, it might come as a surprise that the academic world has also developed interdisciplinary movements akin to these same ecologically focused wine and food movements. In the field of literature, this has become known as ecocriticism, which like these food and wine movements, has not arrived without some vexation and with a variety of interpretations regarding what that actually means. In fact, in another tie between the literary world and the wine world, aspects of these movements lie very much in relation to postmodern critiques of science such as those proposed by Jean-François Lyotard. This connection became clear in a conversation with Ted Lemon, a proponent of biodynamic farming, who wanted to show me a French book that questioned the current scientific paradigm, which for him focused too much on individual issues rather than a more holistic ecological approach such as that favored by biodynamic farming. Yet mentioning biodynamics to other winemakers made them immediately shudder and utter words like *cult* and *religion* to describe it. Like the new atheists who tend to see Marx as having undersold the bane of religion when he called it an opiate, these other winemakers wanted nothing to do with an approach that seemed to them based in folklore and mysticism. These divisions—which in many ways echo the recurring paradigmatic shifts between an emphasis on feeling (as in Romanticism) and rationality (as in the Enlightenment)—echo through all these debates.[11] Therefore, like the word *balance*, the word *natural* in terms of wine has sparked the emergence of fierce debates, with its proponents criticized as crusaders or makers of "dirty" wines, and their opponents seen as industrial or chemical winemakers who make confections or, worse yet, chemically made wines that make people sick. If, in the wine world, the word *balance* hung on the percentage of alcohol, the notion of natural could be said to hang on the amount of sulfur introduced to the wine. Almost all of these ideas, however, seem very much tied up in narratives of ways to tell the story of wines and how they are made.

Both in terms of the notions of artistry and of these ecological commitments, winemakers favor—with some notable, often idiosyncratic exceptions—a narrative account of wines being an expression of a vineyard, of a place. In considering the deep structure of these narratives, then, these chapters place these ideas into relation with what noted food writer Michael Pollan, in *The Omnivore's Dilemma*, called "supermarket pastoral" or what winemaker and former philosopher Abe Schoener labeled the sentimentalizing of the vineyard. However, we can also see these movements very much in light of the rise of ecocriticism in literary studies, as both a new way of seeing and talking about literature (and wine) as well as an attempt to take something that could be seen as tangential to real, necessary commitments to altering a negative course humanity has taken in regard to the environment and trying to do something tangible about it.

Advocacy, in other forms, recurs in the final chapter of this book, which focuses on the issues I found myself discussing in Darrell Corti's back office, namely whether only so-called noble grapes can make great wine, and how the elevation of such grapes in the United States squares with the current movement toward—depending on the case or your point of view—the rediscovery or the preservation of the more diverse offerings planted in the United States in the less storied eras of winemaking. Folks that side with Parker would seem to emphasize the role that judgment should play in interpretation. However, the reasons for support on various sides of this debate are not monolithic. Some see it as a chance to particularly preserve historic vineyard sites; some see it as a recovery of a broader diversity of grapes instead of trying to imitate the successful grape varieties of France's most known wine regions; some find themselves championing these varieties because they found them more commercially viable than trying to source cabernet sauvignon from Napa Valley. However, on the other side are those who hold fast to a view that these other grapes are simply not on the same level as the more renowned varieties like cabernet, pinot noir, syrah, or chardonnay that now dominate plantings all through California. Even something like Thomas Pinney's *A History of Wine in America* creates a narrative in which only when California finally moved away from zinfandel, Carignane, and Alicante Bouschet and replaced them with these "noble" grapes did California begin to finally realize its potential as a winegrowing region. Parker's position is more bombastic but certainly echoes the implicit view of most mainstream wine publications in the United States where the focus is rarely if ever on such varieties as trousseau and negrette. These disputes recall the initial disputes about interpretation while hinting at the underlying metaphysical question of whether greatness can be described accurately as a property of art.

Although, as I have suggested, the issues of representation, history, and privilege do not rise to the same level, the issues I have begun to sketch out here have remarkable echoes in the ongoing debates about aesthetics, greatness, representation, and the literary canon. *Wine Spectator's* James Laube has quite literally referred to a canon of grapes, and if we employ the same framework of the literary canon to think about these wine issues, we can begin to see how the discourse around both issues takes on a similar shape and that some of the urgency in both realms are tied up with fairly clear political outlines.

★   ★   ★   ★

Let me draw this introduction to an end by talking a bit about the methodology that informed this book. The issues I have outlined, particularly in the wine world, are not limited to the United States, let alone California. In fact, biodynamic farming derives from the European polymath, philosopher, and mystic Rudolf Steiner; France's government has become involved in the debates about defining "natural wine," and certainly issues about evaluating and describing the winemaking process are global. However, in order to give a shape and focus to these discussions I have concentrated on winemaking in California and wine criticism in the United States.

These choices also connect to the other aspects of my approach in this book in that I spent a considerable amount of time out in California wine country, particularly trying to speak directly to winemakers themselves. In part, this choice came about because, while I found a considerable amount of material that had been published by wine critics and writers on a number of these issues, I noticed that the voices of the winemakers were often either absent or presented in such small doses that I feared that there was much more that was not being said. At some point in my journeys, I found that I followed somewhat upon the road first charted by Jon Bonné in his book *New California Wine* (which also drew upon many articles and profiles he wrote for *The San Francisco Chronicle*); I met many of the folks who emerge as Bonné's heroes in the fight against what he calls Big Flavor (which others might call industrial, commercial, or Parkerized wines). Bonné had chosen wisely in that many of these folks were extremely thoughtful about what they did and the connection of their work to larger cultural trends. However, my questions and concerns largely differ from Bonné. Therefore, I always sought to get multiple perspectives on these issues whenever I could. For instance, in the discussions about balance that take place in chapter 2, I draw not only on multiple conversations with Rajat Parr, founder of IPOB, but also some of his seeming adversaries in these debates like Michael Browne, founder of Kosta Browne. In short, the method that informs the discussions that follow is to draw both on the written accounts and arguments of a number of wine writers and literary critics and theorists, as well as a number of interviews I conducted with a broad array of winemakers and some wine writers. In doing so, I hope to give you a window into the personalities and world of the winemakers as well as a fuller sense of the way in which winemakers talk about the winemaking and their own understanding of the debates and controversies surrounding the winemaking process.

Notes

1 Rick Kushman, "The Tastemaker," *Sactown Magazine* (April/May 2012).
2 Tim Blanning, *The Romantic Revolution: A History* (New York: Modern Library, 2012), xxi.
3 Robert C. Koons and Timothy H. Pickavance, *Metaphysics: The Fundamentals* (West Sussex: Wiley Blackwell, 2015), 1.
4 Ibid.
5 Ibid, 2.
6 Steven Mailloux, *Interpretive Conventions: The Reader in the Study of American Fiction* (Ithaca: Cornell University Press, 1982), 142.
7 Ibid., 143.
8 Ibid.
9 Ibid., 144.
10 Ibid.
11 This history is described well in Tim Blanning's book *The Romantic Revolution*.

References

Blanning, Tim. *The Romantic Revolution: A History*. New York: Modern Library, 2012.
Koons, Robert C. and Timothy H. Pickavance, *Metaphysics: The Fundamentals*. West Sussex: Wiley Blackwell, 2015.
Kushman, Rick. "The Tastemaker." *Sactown Magazine*, April/May, 2012. www.sactownmag.com/the-tastemaker/.
Mailloux, Stephen. *Interpretive Conventions: The Reader in the Study of American Fiction*. Ithaca: Cornell University Press, 1982.

1

AGAINST TASTING

The Problems of Blind Tasting and Interpretation

Summoning the pedantic manner of a professor accustomed to the sound of his own confident voice, Paul Giamatti, playing the role of Myles Raymond, finds himself in the only space he ever feels comfortable: discussing, judging, and speaking about wine. The scene comes early in *Sideways* (2004), a film primarily about middle-aged men suffering the usual middle-aged malaise, but it also famously led to the decline of merlot sales and, even more importantly for me, led perhaps thousands of folks to think it amusing to grab hold of a winery spit bucket and pretend to take a sip.[1] Myles and his former college roommate, Jack, have arrived at Sanford Winery, in the California area known to wine folks as the Central Coast, which lies in the broad stretch of land between Los Angeles and San Francisco.

In a medium shot that moves to a close-up of Myles's wine glass as he begins to talk about the wine, we find Myles and Jack at the typical public tasting room setup, a bar. The wine has already been poured, and Myles begins what can be seen as a mix of instruction—this is how you evaluate a wine—and his assessment of the wine itself. "Let me show you how this is done. First thing, hold the glass up and examine the wine against the light," he explains as the camera zooms in.

> You're looking for color and clarity. Just, get a sense of it. Okay? Uh, thick? Thin? Watery? Syrupy? Okay? Alright. Now, tip it. What you're doing here is checking for color density as it thins out towards the rim. Uh, that's gonna tell you how old it is, among other things.

In the language Myles employs, it is as if the wine remains an unknown, something that needs classification, definition. Myles clarifies that this intense analysis is "usually more important with reds. Okay?" Things then move on to how to smell the wine: "Now, stick your nose in it. Don't be shy; really get your nose in

DOI: 10.4324/9781003399810-2

there. Mmm ... a little citrus ... maybe some strawberry." After some further gesturing and face-making, Myles adds more descriptors: "Passion fruit ... and, oh, there's just like the faintest soupçon of, like, asparagus and just a flutter of a, like a, nutty Edam cheese." Jack, an unserious student in this teaching moment, but still one mildly eager to please, responds: "Wow. Strawberries, yeah! Strawberries. Not the cheese."

This scene seems to exemplify much of the popular imagination regarding wine—and frankly, considering the film's popularity, it no doubt helped shape it.[2] Of course, the scene has been done parodically, but what it parodies has resonance: the seriousness, the intentionality—Myles says, after this lecture, that Jack should "do this with every wine"—and the startling mixture of poetry and ridiculousness associated with attempting to translate the experience of wine into a language certainly has its place in reality. In short, while the scene may read as mere satire, the satire derives not from invention of absurd, imagined procedures but from exaggeration, which in some cases might be considered fairly mild. In fact, we might think of Myles as providing an example of both interpreting wine and providing a prescription for how it is best to do so.

That process and the notion of translation or interpretation will be at the center of what will follow here. This chapter will, first and foremost, be in the manner of Michel Montaigne's notion of the essay. That is, I will use this chapter and the next to explore a basic proposition, and I will do so by linking two seemingly dissimilar things: interpretation—particularly the interpretation of literature—and wine tasting, the process of evaluating, judging, and assessing wine and recording those judgments, whether in numbers or words. Thus, like Montaigne, I am going to grant myself the freedom to wander down paths as they appear, though with the intention of returning to our main one eventually (or seeing how they link up down the road). The proposition that I would like to entertain first came to me while teaching a course on literary theory, which, through the first half, proceeds through a succession of theoretical approaches to literature. We might call these theories of interpretation either descriptions of what people actually do while trying to make sense of literature or prescriptions of what they *ought* to do when doing that task.

For those outside the tight corridors of literary scholarship, one prominent phrase in this book that likely will be obscure is *literary theory*. I'll try to explain. In a *New Yorker* essay called "The De Man Case: Does a Critic's Past Explain His Criticism" from May 24, 2014, literary critic and intellectual historian Louis Menand begins by trying to define literary theory. He suggests that if you view literature as something different from other kinds of written material, "then you have a theory of literature." In expanding on this idea, he offers a further clarification as well as defense: theory

affects the way students will respond to literature for the rest of their lives. But it's also part of an inquiry into the role of art in human life, the effort to figure out why we make this stuff, what it means, and why we care so much about it. If this is not the most important thing in the world to understand, it is certainly not the least.

He feels the need to defend the term because theory, in some circles, has gotten a bad reputation. In some ways, the problem resembles the same implied satire of Myles in *Sideways*, as the world of theory can be mystifying in its abstractions and suggests the same kind of caricature of the fussy, pedantic literary critic. I do not have the space to go into the full reasons why Menand might be defensive, but some of the accusations against theory resemble some of Susan Sontag's problems with the term *interpretation*, which I will touch on shortly. For this chapter, I intend to focus primarily on the "what it means" aspect of theory sketched out above because it most fully aligns with my interest in interpretation. Let me quickly add that while there is not currently a phrase called *wine theory*, the same basic logic and definitions that Menand begins to sketch out can be applied to wine. Therefore, if you think that wine is something other than a simple beverage or one of many ways to alter your mood, then you probably have a theory of wine—or perhaps we might say that you have the ability to develop a theory of wine.

This is one explicit way in which we can say that wine and literature are of a kind by being a type of something—writing, beverage—but thought by many to transcend those pedestrian genres to which they can be said to be a part. In fact, many of those most passionate about wine will insist that wine is in fact not a beverage! And I think that the further clarifications that Menand offers also can be applied to wine: we can ask the same sorts of question about why people ascribe value to wine, what wine means to people, what wine can say about the culture, and, as I wish to get to, what these views about wine can say about a larger understanding of the world. As I hope will become clear, we can also consider that people do not merely drink wine but also interpret it. While I will shortly get to what I mean by "interpretation," let me first offer the proposition I wish to test out. It is simply this: that the means of interpretation one ascribes to—or argues for—also suggests a larger worldview, a metaphysics if you will—what Jim Holt defines as "the project of characterizing reality as a whole" in his book *Why Does the World Exist?*[3]

Now, this framing makes it seem that people remain consistent in this regard; that is, how a person believes you ought to make sense of literature also remains consistent with how a person makes sense of the world. I am not sure that this is the case, and this problem of consistency—or even whether principles or a desired outcome control our interpretive lenses—is one I wish to come back to later. Before I can more fully explain what all of this might have to do with wine, let me try to offer a bit more clarification of what I mean when I use the word *interpretation*. In her famous essay from 1966, "Against Interpretation," novelist and literary critic Susan Sontag sought to distinguish between a kind of everyday interpretation, perhaps akin to American drivers recognizing that a red light means stop, and the kind of interpretation or reading Menand spoke to above. In her attack on "interpretation," Sontag proclaims to "mean here a conscious act of the mind that illustrates a certain code, certain 'rules' of interpretation."[4] Moments later, in a tone of exasperation, she declares that "directed to art, interpretation means plucking a set of elements (the X, the Y, the Z, and so forth) from the whole work." Then, with even more gusto, she seems to shout, "The task of interpretation is virtually one of translation."[5] For Sontag, then, interpretation privileges the idea of taking a work of art and showing, as Menand notes as well, "what it means," and, for her, this process keeps alive the "fancy that there really is such a thing as the content of the work of art [as opposed to just a form]."[6] Implied in Sontag's critique of a certain type of interpretation—the type of interpretation that is part and parcel to about every literature class in the United States—is the implication that not only does it seek to show what is, in her opinion, not there in a work of art, but that such a process will in some way damage the work of art, an approach that aligns Sontag with a culture of feeling. I sketch out these implications here in part because I think those complaints will also be in evidence in some of the debates about wine tasting or, if you will, wine interpretation. I will return to the matter of wine theory in a moment.

Even though Sontag seeks to promote a very different type of reading—or viewing or hearing—than Steven Mailloux, who had been given the task of explaining interpretation in an essay for *Critical Terms for Literary Study* as well as in *Interpretive Conventions*, he also begins with suggesting that "translation" is essentially the starting place in defining what interpretation is, though it does not seem to upset him in the least. In fact, Mailloux suggests early in his essay that "in its etymology, then, 'interpretation' conveys the sense of a translation pointed in two directions simultaneously: toward a text to be interpreted and for an audience in need of interpretation."[7] This might make rather obvious sense if we use a typical example of interpreting a poem in the context of a classroom where a professor attempts to make sense of the poem, to translate its contents or even its words into other language (Sontag's dreaded content), and also to point that translation toward a judging audience (in this example a group of students, who will judge whether the interpretation is accurate or persuasive). However, the notion that this type of interpretation is privileged, different, or purely academic doesn't account for that fact that these procedures take place in all aspects of life, though the audience might be the one who is translating (for themselves) and the object of interpretation much less complex than, say, a poem by William Carlos Williams. Again, the basic procedures here are in operation in interpretations that do not even register as interpretation, like in my previous example of interpreting the signals of a stoplight (though here not much persuasion or judgment is required except of course when you find yourself saying, "But officer, the light was still yellow"—and perhaps that is why Sontag distinguishes it).

The first half of Mailloux's definition seems fairly straightforward; it describes the basic process by which an individual confronts a text and tries to understand that text; however, the second half of his definition suggests a much more controversial claim, namely that "interpretations can have no grounding outside of the rhetorical exchanges taking place within institutional and cultural politics."[8] At the risk of oversimplifying his ideas, I believe Mailloux suggests that interpretation comes down to our ability to persuade our audience of its rightness rather than an inherent rightness or a set of rules that guarantee rightness. Whether we can agree with Mailloux on the absence of a foundation for accurate interpretation, his very point leads us to the fact that much of the excitement that surrounds interpretation has to do with these arguments about how to interpret and the contest between those who do believe in foundations and who like to argue for what they are and why they help create a right or proper interpretation, and those who do not. To those who would object to these criteria, Mailloux would likely respond that if they use rhetoric well, they will have sway, but that is a point for him and not for his opponents—in the larger metaphysical contest. The scariest implication of Mailloux's argument for some people is that it says that there are no right answers; there are just better argued answers.

What, you might rightly ask at this point, does this all have to do with wine? For much of the last 75 years—and arguably much, much longer than that if you want to link contemporary criticism to the ancient Greeks, Plato, and Aristotle as many, like Sontag before me, have done—people have been arguing about how to properly interpret literature, including the occasional voice seemingly arguing that literature or art or music needs no interpretation, a position that still helps keep the debate going. People have probably not been arguing about tasting wine nearly as long, though perhaps increasingly so in recent years In fact, in a blog post titled "Wine Critics—Everything Old is New Again," Justine Vanden Heuvel points out that both Pliny the Elder and Columella argued about wine in their writings and seemed to have developed the concept of *terroir*.[9] These more current debates span so-called expert tasters—essentially wine critics like Robert M. Parker and the primary wine reviewers of *Wine Spectator* like James Laube,[10] Harvey Steiman, and James Molesworth, Joshua Greene of *Wine & Spirits* magazine, or Antonio Galloni of *Vinous Media*—as well as a host of folks in the wine industry and the average wine consumer or enthusiast, to steal the name from yet another wine publication. In what follows, I will sketch out some of these debates as well as to attempt to tease out the implications of these debates. I am proposing that wine tasting—by which I mean reviewing, describing, scoring, as well as the process of consumption—as we will see it, will resemble interpreting literature or other art forms (or even writing) in the ways that both Sontag and Mailloux have sketched it out, and I will also explore whether behind these debates—perhaps not always very far behind these debates—also exists a kind of metaphysics.

Before we go much further, let me offer some brief confession. By trade, I am a literary critic—someone who writes about and teaches literary theory. By hobby, however, I am also a wine lover, a vague description that encompasses the fact that I collect wine, that I frequently read about wine, and that I have spent an inordinate amount of time shopping for wine, poring over wine lists, or visiting wineries across the globe including in Oregon, California, France, and Italy—and even once, Kentucky—not to mention, once being offered a sampling of the best wines India to had to offer while at a private dinner in Jaipur. Of course, on some level, it seems absurd to describe imbibing a beverage—in fact, one that includes a mood-altering substance—as a hobby. Even with all of the legalizing that may happen in the near term, I have a hard time imagining some future professor writing about his *hobby* of smoking marijuana. I'm probably being naive on this point—either about whether this will happen or whether there will be professors in the future. In fact, I know I am, due to columns emerging in Colorado newspapers or articles I receive from friends about "weed sommeliers."

The distinction of wine as a hobby, of course, derives from a few notions:

1. Wine has a rich, complicated cultural legacy.
2. Wine can be a luxury good.
3. There are simply many different types of wine from many different localities. Therefore, if you want to know wine, there is a lot to know.
4. Wine, because of what I have already listed, carries a level of prestige that both makes it attractive as a hobby, but also sometimes opens up the hobbyist to scorn.

In this way, wine can be thought to again resemble literature, because wine and wine knowledge carry with them what the French theorist Pierre Bourdieu called "cultural capital," and wine's relation to cultural capital can be seen as one of the things gently satirized in the scene from *Sideways* with which I began this chapter. While literature can be divided into high and low art on the basis of genre and many elements—some more tangible than others—so too can wine be subdivided. Wine can be used as a status symbol (look at that incredibly expensive bottle of wine at that person's table!); knowledge of wine can be used to gain advantage in the culture or as a sign of where you fit into the class system (or to help smooth your transition into the class system) since wine, especially rare or expensive wine, is a class marker. Water, for instance, does none of these things; it just hydrates!

To return to the issue of wine tasting—that is, the debates about how to properly taste wine—I would begin by suggesting that most of the debates center on a particular type of tasting, the procedure known as blind tasting, which might be the most commonly supported operation for judging or evaluating wine or testing the taster's knowledge. Essentially, three primary types of blind tasting exist. The first has very little to do with the life of the everyday consumer except as a parlor game or as a source for public humiliation. This version consists of the kind of task at which the folks who study to be sommeliers must excel: you essentially taste a wine completely blind—that is, completely unaware of what it is other than wine and its color—in order to identify things like the grape variety, the place of origin, and even its relative age. There is yet another use of this kind of totally blind tasting, which is to determine whether people can actually identify if a wine is red or white when consuming it blindly, something Calvin Trillin wrote about in *The New Yorker* some years ago. But I will not focus on this issue of identification here. Nevertheless, you may be curious to know that apparently, humans are remarkably poor at distinguishing between white and red wine when tasted blind.

I have some experience with blind wine tasting where you know nothing about the wine but what you can see. When I first visited Paris in 2003, my wife and I dined at a restaurant enticingly named Bistro du Sommelier. Along with each course of your tasting menu came a paired glass of wine poured by someone who looked to be still in high school. The server would not tell you what you had, but would instead pour you a glass, let you taste it, and then ask you to guess what it was. After you inevitably failed, the waiter would smirk or laugh openly at your ignorance and then reveal the wine. I would have preferred having to eat off a Twister board, contorting into position to find my French delicacies. Even this model of blind tasting has its critics. Anthony Giglio, writing for *Food & Wine*, worries that it will distract consumers with questions of "which wine is from where" rather than "which wine does each person prefer." "Without answering this question," he adds dramatically, "nobody wins," although I am pretty sure my server won. The goal of this approach is evaluating a wine solely from the wine itself for the purposes of identifying it rather than for the purposes of deciding a wine's merits. In other words, the only one whose merits are judged is the taster. There are two other versions of this type of tasting: those conducted by sommeliers and those conducted by winemakers. For sommeliers, both the sommelier and the wine are being judged, but the emphasis on the evaluative criteria for the wines has to do with typicity. In effect, the wine is judged by how well the wine represents the agreed-upon notions of what a wine from that region ought to taste like, which, in turn, should make it more easily identifiable for a skilled sommelier. What should make up that typicity can become another area for dispute of course, but nevertheless this is a feature of sommelier training, as Rajat Parr describes in his book *Secrets of the Sommelier*. Winemakers, in contrast, at least the ones with whom I spoke, also frequently do some version of this kind of tasting; however, the general consensus of these winemakers was that these tastings were more about learning, for example, thinking about how a wine was made, learning a range of what certain wines can taste like, and so on. In fact, many winemakers participate in tasting groups that do not rank the wines they taste. While this kind of blind tasting overlaps with the other two versions of blind tasting, I will focus primarily on these other versions, which do tend to produce losers but also some winners.

As prolific United Kingdom wine writer Dr Jamie Goode explains in his blog *Wine Anorak*, we can distinguish blind tasting further into what is commonly called single blind, "when the list if [*sic*] wines to be tasted is known, but not the order" or double blind, "when nothing is known about them at all."[11] Many of the leading wine publications in the United States, like Robert Parker's *Wine Advocate,* or its main competition, *Wine Spectator*, employ some version of single blind tasting. In the single blind approach, a taster knows at least one identifying characteristic of the wine even if she cannot see the wine label. Most of the reviewers for wine magazines have particular areas of the world they cover, which tends to set one marker. For example, James Laube formerly reviewed California wines exclusively, so his blind tastings contained only wines for that region, with a few minor exceptions. In addition, these tasters are typically told what the grape variety is or perhaps a more specific region—say, pinot noir from Sonoma County. Note that this differs a little from Goode's definition whereby the taster knows the wines beforehand if not the order in which they will be served. For the most part, the only champions of double-blind tasting for wine reviewing appear to be readers and consumers, such as the many who responded to *Wine Spectator* writer and reviewer Harvey Steiman's column "Blind Tasting and Context" from March 5, 2013. Several pleaded with Harvey and his brethren to employ the double-blind approach. Even double-blind tastings fall short, according to the former *Wine Spectator* columnist Matt Kramer of the "academic gold standard of blind tasting, the narrow and sharply focused 'triangle test,'" a highly complicated methodology used more commonly within industrial food circles than blind tasting of wine.[12]

The case for tasting blind in general can appear pretty self-evident until you examine it with a cold eye. First, however, let's consider the case for it. In an open letter explaining—and frankly defending—their policy, *Wine Spectator* editors Marvin Shanken and Thomas Matthews say that crucial rationale for this approach is to "avoid bias": "Simply put, in a blind tasting, the taster is deprived of information that may bias his or her judgment of the wine in the glass."[13] To support their point, they go on to cite a study conducted in 2001 by a French enologist by the name of Frederic Brochet: the study showed that "confirmation bias" clearly was at work when tasters drank nonblind. The tasters clearly favored the wine given the more famous label no matter what was actually in the bottle. These results certainly seem unsurprising, and Shanken and Matthews claim they are substantiated by many similar studies over the years. The last section of this two-page policy statement, "Building Trust," also suggests part of what is at work here in promoting this methodology. *Wine Spectator* seeks to defend itself against the ready claims that they are in bed with particular aspects of the industry they cover—producers, marketers, distributors—and, rather, that they are serving the people. The name of Parker's magazine, *The Wine Advocate*, tries to advertise the same populist notion up front. Parker offers a similar statement to that of the editors of *Wine Spectator*, though marked by his own idiosyncrasies and some elaboration on possible exceptions:

> When possible all of my tastings are done in peer-group, single-blind conditions (meaning that the same types of wines are tasted against each other and the producers' names are not known). There are exceptions to this policy with respect to (1) all barrel tastings, (2) all specific appellation tastings where at least 25 of the best estates will not submit samples for group tastings and (3) for all wines under $25. The ratings reflect an independent, critical look at the wines. Neither price nor the reputation of the producer/grower affect the rating in any manner. I spend three months of every year tasting in vineyards. During the other nine months of the year, six and sometimes seven-day workweeks are devoted solely to tasting and writing. I do not participate in wine judgings or trade tastings for many reasons, but principal among these are the following: (1) I prefer to taste from an entire bottle of wine, (2) I find it essential to have

properly sized and cleaned professional tasting glasses, (3) the temperature of the wine must be correct, and (4) I prefer to determine the time allocated to the number of wines to be critiqued.[14]

I, for one, am glad that Parker insists upon clean glasses! *Wine Spectator* has some similar exceptions to the blind tasting policy, but they don't try quite so hard to make the case that their tasters spend extraordinary time exploring the vineyards. Parker can allow some mitigation of the ethos gained by way of blind tasting if he can compensate for the lost authority by his accrued knowledge of places through visits, a practice that seems to have grown more regular for Parker over time.[15] A mild controversy emerged on the *Wine Spectator* reader forums when the magazine announced it would no longer have its writers taste in the wine's country of origin. For years, for instance, a former reviewer would review wines from Bordeaux in an office in France. For these readers there is a kind of strange conflation of the objectivity associated with blind tasting—which theoretically can be done any-where—and some kind of authenticity of place achieved by doing the objective tasting on the native soil of the wine. Whatever the nature of these contradictions, to return to Parker's statement, the key passages and claims here line up again with those of Parker's competitors: "The ratings reflect an independent, critical look at the wines. Neither price nor the reputation of the producer/grower affect the rating in any manner." The rest of what Parker lays out here, though, speaks to the complex array of elements a variety of wine writers and experts proclaim necessary in order to taste properly, including, of course, proper glassware.

The case is simple, then. For those who endorse it, blind tasting is the best way to taste because it eliminates the most substantial elements that might prejudice a taster. In essence, the supporters of blind tasting appear to align with attempting to safeguard reason by minimizing feeling. So, if you are what the philosopher Jona-than Cohen—who challenged blind tasting—calls a projector, that is, someone who tries to project how others will taste a wine, you want to defend your ability to project objectively. If you are one of these projectors, you don't want to be accused of promoting wines of prestige or give the impression that you are essen-tially helping to sell particular wines. Instead, you want to come across as a con-sumer *advocate*, which is why Parker derived his name from Ralph Nader's pioneering consumer organization. If you are not a projector but just someone with an overly developed fascination with wine or wish to develop such a fasci-nation (or to increase your cultural capital), you should taste this way in order to experience the wine as it truly is. This point is made in the countless books sketching out tasting procedures in extraordinary detail akin to Myles's from *Side-ways*, including *How to Taste* by Jancis Robinson and *Michael Broadbent's Wine Tasting*.

Implied in this distinction, though, is the kind of division of interpretation made by Sontag, when she distinguishes between everyday interpretation and interpret-ing art. One of the most revered and, as Cohen suggests, most prolific wine reviewers in history, the Englishman Michael Broadbent, calls the kind of drinker who should taste blind "the analytical drinker."[16] Like Sontag, he makes the distinction that all of these arguments have to do with a specific type of tasting (or in her case, interpretation), which he describes as a "deliberate, conscious, and subjective act, the object of which is to assess the quality of wine under review."[17] However, this approach should not just be reserved, according to Broadbent, for "analytical drinkers" but allotted by the nature of the wine itself: "Straightforward, ordinary wines are for drinking, not for philosophical deliberation."[18]

You would not be wrong to recognize a certain chicken and egg problem implied in this disclaimer since the factors that should be excluded from tasting come into play in order to delineate what should be blind tasted. However, somewhat akin to the most interesting man in the world, when Broadbent wants "philosophical deliberation"—which he doesn't always—he drinks blind: "Even the most disciplined taster is biased by the merest glimpse of the label, even by the shape of the bottle." Masking those elements is not enough for Broadbent, as "one can also be swayed by the appreciative—or otherwise—noises and looks of other tasters."[19] We must not just be blinded from the wine—or it blinded from us—but we must taste with a kind of monastic solemnity and isolation.

And so as to not make it seem like the late Michael Broadbent is some kind of passionate outlier, I should add that his younger, fellow countrywoman Jancis Robinson worries, for instance, about the problems of tasting wine in a kitchen in "the presence of strong smells" and notes that "participants in formal tastings are expected to 'come clean' untainted by scent or aftershave."[20] Though Robinson thinks these precautions may be overdone, she goes on to catalog other ways in which competing smells interfere with proper experiences of wines, and she also dives briefly into other competing taste elements like toothpaste.[21] Robinson also makes a case for blind tasting in particular as the best means to "learn how to judge quality in an educated and rational way" and to her credit even makes a case for how quality should be assessed, by what she calls "balance and length."[22] Her take, though sometimes slightly contradictory, is more muted than some, as she concedes that inevitably "wine tasting is above all a subjective sport."[23]

As one encounters these various defenses, pleas, and/or explanations for blind tasting, one might arrive at any number of thoughts; however, I would imagine that the two most popular might be "that seems reasonable" or "people sure get worked up about wine." For the purposes of this discussion, I will focus on the "that seems reasonable" part. Once I came across a phrase that had been associated with certain kinds of expensive and relatively rare Italian wines: "wines of meditation." These would be akin to the wines that Broadbent suggests deserve "analytical tasting" or that might promote "philosophical reflection." I have spent a lot of time as an adult drinking wine, and I have found myself talking about wine—or boring people by talking about wine—and I am not sure that they have ever quite led me to philosophize about the wine per se. About the world, of course. So perhaps deep meditation or reflection is too high a bar, and the fact is that any wine publication is likely to review a broad range of wines, from the everyday to the unimaginably expensive. Broadbent famously has books listing his tasting notes of wines that date to the eighteenth century.

When I have encountered what Broadbent calls "philosophical reflections," they come from the outside world or fiction, such as the long explanation of her love of wine from Maya, Myles's love interest in *Sideways*. In the film, Maya and Myles bond over their shared love of wine (rather than their alliterative names) early in their relationship, and Maya explains to Myles that she "like[s] to think about the life of the wine" and

> how it's a living thing. I like to think about what was going on the year the grapes were growing; how the sun was shining; if it rained. I like to think about all the people who tended and picked the grapes. And if it's an old wine, how many of them must be dead by now. I like how wine continues to evolve, like if I opened a bottle of wine today it would taste different than if I'd opened it on any other day, because a bottle of wine is actually alive. And it's constantly evolving and gaining complexity. That is, until it peaks, like your '61. And then it begins its steady, inevitable decline.

Maya delivers this monologue to Myles with great earnestness. Equally as well known from the film is Myles's explanation about why he loves pinot noir, and it becomes clear that he has come to personally identify with the grape. The rather temperamental, easily flustered, and discouraged Myles says his fondness for pinot noir derives from the fact that "it's a hard grape to grow, as you know. Right? It's uh, it's thin-skinned, temperamental, ripens early. It's, you know, it's not a survivor like cabernet, which can just grow anywhere and uh, thrive even when it's neglected. No, pinot needs constant care and attention." While wine writers will certainly evoke some of these sentiments on occasion—"wine is a living thing because it changes in the bottle" is commonplace—these types of musings simply do not show up in tasting notes of blind tastings and again, in my not very limited experience, they rarely come up in the actual consumption of even the most expressive wines. Instead, you are more likely to hear things like "this wine is awesome" or "amazing" interspersed in and around an unrelated conversation. Perhaps in the dating world of wine fanatics people communicate their inner selves by way of personifying grapes, but I haven't encountered that much either—and people are of course perfectly capable of speaking of themselves indirectly, and wine is not the necessary vehicle for that process (other than alcohol's power to loosen the tongue).

I realize my hesitations about the philosophical reflection aspect of Broadbent's defense are far from scientific, but then again, a phrase like "philosophical reflection" on wine is not particularly scientific either. In fact, this is an unusually feeling-based case for blind tasting. So I am not sure blind tasting is something we ought to equate with philosophy or deep reflection. Nevertheless, to review wines by way of blind tasting seems reasonable because, even though we can all acknowledge that tasting can be subjective as Robinson does, we want our taster to be at his or her most objective best in making recommendations, especially if in the role of recommending wines. Of course, such a position on reasonable objectivity, or reason as Robinson implies, resembles certain kinds of ideas about interpretation—and I hope it is becoming clear that there is a direct element of interpretation involved in assessing wine. The notion relies on the idea that a measure of objectivity is a) needed and b) possible.

If you arrived at the thought, "Well, this blind tasting all seems reasonable," then you would be surprised at how many people have regularly challenged the usefulness, effectiveness, or appropriateness of blind tasting. In fact, in the last several years, these objections have cropped up a number of times, which inevitably leads to the practitioners and supporters of blind tasting to push back again, asserting its value. Let's turn to one of the salvos against blind tasting. In a paper titled "On the Limitations of Blind Tasting," Jonathan Cohen, a philosopher, has provided a pretty systematic critique of blind tasting that sets out several of the key objections. He sees blind tasting as linked to trying to allow tasters to focus solely on "perception" by eliminating the role of a given "taster's preference for or against wines with a particular price or origin (etc.), or other perceptually extrinsic factors."[24] In short, as I have sketched out above, blind tasting appears to make the taster objective or unbiased and thus eliminate the corruptions of experience and feeling. However, Cohen goes on to argue that blind tasting fails to do what it claims to do. He offers two major problems to blind tastings' effectiveness. To explain the first problem, Cohen gives the example—perhaps drawn from the famed prejudices of Myles in *Sideways*—of someone who dislikes merlot going into a tasting; then, Cohen proceeds to suggest that if the person either finds herself able to identify a merlot or qualities in the wine that the taster associates with merlot, then we find that "blind tasting can't control the effects of prior belief after all."[25] In his book *True Taste: The Seven Essential Wine Words*, Matt Kramer describes this same problem in more biblical language. For Kramer, this notion that blind tasting is required to provide objectivity can be seen as the "Original Sin school of wine tasting," which sees humans as "weak creatures so filled with bias as to preclude 'objectivity'." He goes on to describe this as a "simplistic, schoolboy notion of 'fairness'" and ascribes the championing of blind tasting to "its Manichean worldview: the sanitizing light of unbiased, 'objective' blind tasting against the murky, suspicious, twilight of wine tasted with labels in view."[26]

Kramer's rhetoric starts to raise the stakes perhaps a bit too high, and one could be inclined to shrug off these concerns. Like Cohen, whose scare quotes around "objective" give it away—Kramer is skeptical that blind tasting can really do what it purports to do. In fact, Kramer argues that blind tastings can easily be rigged to get particular outcomes and that "our biases go way beyond the prurience of seeing a glimpse of a seductive label sticking out."[27] I want to underscore just how significant a claim Cohen—and, to a certain degree, Kramer—is making. In short, the notion that a blind tasting is the only way to truly taste, assess, or encounter a wine *as it truly is* is undercut by Cohen's argument that no taster arrives at the encounter with the wine a blank slate, and placing a metaphoric blindfold over the experience fails to return the taster to being a tabula rasa.

What's even more remarkable, from my point of view, is how closely this dispute lines up with arguments surrounding what noted literary critic Gerald Graff has labeled the "return to literature" in *Professing Literature*, his preeminent history of literary studies in American universities. As Graff shows, throughout the history of literary studies, there have been periodic movements to return to the literature, to let the student encounter it "unmediated"—to experience literature in some kind of pure, unbiased way, as a counterbalance against the rise of a variety of scholarly apparati that mediate—or even ignore—the literature. As a prime example of this, Graff cites Helen Vendler's 1980 Modern Language Association presidential address, which he says "began in the time-honored fashion with an exhortation to the assembled membership to think back to that primordial experience of literature."[28] As Graff shows, almost every presidential address in MLA's history finds the speaker Eeyore-like, lamenting some facet of the profession.

Vendler laid out some version of this call that has occurred many times, when she asked the gathered professorship to realize that all their learning, scholarship, and "critical terms" had in some ways deadened them to and distanced them from this essential pleasure and experience of literature, and that if the professors insist on all this apparati in teaching literature, students would never get "that taste on the tongue [...] of individual style."[29] I am not only attracted by the metaphor that Vendler employed here, but still! The notion for literary folks, in Vendler's camp, who seek a "return to literature" is that this is the way a "love" of literature is inspired in people, although Graff says that "recent experience shows that bare, unmediated contact with the work itself does not necessarily inculcate that taste either."[30] The repetition of the word *taste* is significant in and of itself and not just, for me, because of the echo with proper *tasting*. It is not so very far from Vendler's phrase suggesting leading students to a first, true taste; even closer to Graff's use is "inculcating" a proper taste. For these literary scholars, the implied argument goes something like this: if young people can just have a fundamental, "unmediated" encounter with a piece of literary greatness, they will get hooked and develop a proper appreciation for great literary art. Vendler's argument derives from feeling in its promotion of love and fears that reason impedes forming that love. While for wine folks the proper taste is thought to have already been developed in the "projector"—and though someone like Robinson suggests that blind tasting helps cultivate the proper taste in the aspirant—the notion is that blind tasting allows for that cultivated taste to be applied properly, that blind tasting ensures the proper application of this cultivated taste.

Graff, at least as far as literature goes, is having none of it! He first dips further into Vendler's address to point out where she concedes that "we all love different things in literature or love literature for different reasons," which sounds like Robinson's caveat about the subjectiveness of wine tasting, and then Vendler admits that "literature is a dense nest of culture and linguistic meanings, inaccessible to the casual passerby."[31] For Graff, as soon as Vendler admits these points, the argument for "unmediated" encounters collapses, for the "need for a contextual and cultural study of literature has been conceded, and there is no point pretending we can revert to a core experience of literary bliss prior to all contexts."[32] Ultimately, Graff's problem with this idealistic notion of a young person's (I'm presuming) romantic encounter with a literary text a reader has somehow happened upon and been so powerfully moved by that he or she keeps seeking out more and more of these experiences, resembles Cohen's first objection to blind tasting: this encounter just cannot happen. For, as Graff says,

> Vendler must surely underrate the extent to which her initial literary excitements (like anybody's) were made possible only by the prior acquisition of cultural and literary preconceptions, ones that were not explicit in the works she read but that she had to bring to the works before they could become interesting or intelligible.[33]

Graff's point would be that however much that reading experience of Vendler's appeared to happen in a vacuum, it most certainly did not—and cannot—and *that* is really what Cohen's first major critique of blind tasting is also claiming.

Cohen identifies a second failing of blind tasting that shows up in the arguments of many other dissenters but usually without the formal categorization that Cohen provides. Cohen suggests that perceptual contrast will inevitably distort the results of blind tasting. To illustrate this idea, he first offers the basic example of placing a black border around two otherwise indistinguishable squares of color, which will lead the viewer to the inevitable conclusion that the one with the stronger contrast—the black bordered one—is darker. The same goes for putting wines of different styles next to each other; certain wines will shine or recede because of the comparison to other dissimilar wines. In what the nephew of the famed science fiction writer and the *New York Times* wine columnist, Eric Asimov, subtitles a "Memoir and a Manifesto," he also argues this point. He gives the example of tasting two wines from the same area and of same varietal, but the one that is "lighter in texture and milder in flavor" will always be likely to lose out to the "heavier, more powerful and vigorous wines."[34] Because blind tasting presumes to identify and assess quality, these side-by-side tastings get played out as a contest or even a fight for the more positive review. Asimov, Cohen, and Kramer all suggest that, in fact, a particular group of qualities will almost always be sought out or praised in the context of blind tasting: "fruitier, more powerful wines"[35] or "depth of color, intensity, oakiness, sweetness, and density."[36] Cohen's language here equates more to sensory responses. However, Asimov's critiques of what happens to the less "powerful" wines seem to have a kind of political language—that the powerful, the "vigorous" will dominate the "mild" and perhaps the meek. Yet I would also say that what Asimov seems to be defending even more here is tradition—that what might appear politically left can also be seen as a conservative defense against the young and robust that would supersede the more traditional styles of wine, which happen to be more muted in the sensory areas that Cohen feels will create the comparative problem in blind tastings.[37]

In a blog column called "Blind Tasting and Context," *Wine Spectator* critic Harvey Steiman acknowledges this comparative problem but says, "Experienced tasters know that. So when I come to a wine that seems relatively insipid, I don't just blow it off. I take a moment to let my palate refresh and go back to it a few minutes later."[38] Steiman's defense actually points to another objection that Asimov gives, namely that he doubts that tasters have "the sheer physical stamina" required to maintain "objectivity" through a lengthy tasting. I should add, though, none of the tasters I have encountered admit to what he claims to have heard—that is, tastings that included over 120 wines. In my own admittedly limited experience, one doesn't need to get even close to 120 wines to start feeling some fatigue. Although almost all such blind tasters claim to spit—swirl the wine around across their palate before then unloading it—such a process can still lead to a certain degree of fatigue, which Steiman seems to admit to, even if you can keep yourself from getting inebriated this way. (This technique also requires the kind of bucket Myles infamously chugs from in *Sideways*.)

Whether fatigue or simply human inconsistency is to blame, a recent study by retired oceanographer and academic, and now winemaker, Robert T. Hodgson, suggests that judges in wine competitions, which feature single blind tasting, do not reliably judge wines with consistency. In "An Examination of Judge Reliability at a Major U.S. Wine Competition," Hodgson claims that "when judges were very consistent, it was often with wines that they did not like"; however, the numbers are worse with wines judges seemed to have liked—at least once.[39] And perhaps even more devastating to the notion that particular tasters might prove more expert or more consistent, Hodgson found that "a judge's superior performance (in consistency) one year does not correlate with the superior performance the next." In other words, the study seems to suggest that no level of expertise or practice is likely to make judges consistent tasters even in blind tasting. The implications of this study provoked Steiman to write another defense of blind tasting, this one titled "Behind the B. S. About Wine Tasting," in which he quotes Hodgson as saying that he's not "intent on debunking the whole idea of tasting and judging wines."[40] However, Hodgson's intentions and the actual implications of his study may be two separate things. Steiman, for his part, offers some concessions such as "wine is personal" and "wine is a moving target [that is, it can taste different at different times, at different stages of being open, etc.—because it is a living thing!]," but then concludes of wine tasting, "It's not perfect, but it's not B. S. either." It strikes me as perfectly reasonable for Steiman to claim that blind tasting—or professional wine tasting overall—falls somewhere in between complete inconsistency and inaccuracy and consistent, objective accuracy. However, if that is the case, then perhaps projectors ought to be more cautious in making the case for their own methodology.

★   ★   ★   ★

The offices of *Wine & Spirits* can be difficult to locate in the crowded and hectic neighborhood of Koreatown in Manhattan. After some confused wandering on their block, I found that their narrow office suite resembles a conventional office space merged with someone's extensive wine cellar. Bottles stood or lay everywhere. I loved it. I was there because I had an opportunity to gain firsthand experience in blind tasting in August 2016 thanks to the generosity of Joshua Greene, owner and editor in chief of *Wine & Spirits* magazine, and Stephanie Johnson, an editor and Italian wine critic for the magazine. Why could they use me for this process, you may ask? *W & S* reviews wines in essentially a two-step process. First, a panel of experts—in this case, experts and me—review wines, and those recommended by the panel then get reviewed by the designated critic of the magazine, who then again narrows down the selection of wines to be included in the magazine. Thus, the wines that readers finally see reviewed are wines that the magazine generally praises; therefore, if, for instance, the panelists and reviewers cannot recommend any Washington state cabernets, no reviews of those wines will appear in an issue of the magazine.

A group of six of us met at ten o'clock on a very hot morning, gathered around a white table in the middle of the office suite. The panel included Josh and Stephanie, as well as an Italian-American wine educator, a sommelier from a respected NYC restaurant, a former *W & S* editor who now works in the business, and an English professor from Greencastle, Indiana. The level of expertise both intimidated and relieved me, seeing as any miscalculations on my part alone would have minimal effects on the fortunes of any of the wines we reviewed. We each received paper to write notes on, as well as another sheet that listed each of our tasting flights and information on what the grape was and from what specific area the wine came. For this day, we were tasting Italian wines from Piedmont: a flight of five Gavi made from the cortese grape, several flights of Barbera from different sections of Piedmont that produced that grape, and then a few flights of the royal wine of the area, Barolo, made from the nebbiolo grape. The tastings work like this:

FIGURE 1.1 Josh Greene among the bottles at *Wine & Spirits Magazine*

1. A very nice assistant comes out of a backroom with a tray of glasses each numbered to correspond to our sheet.
2. Tasters, using their own methodology, taste through the flight and write notes.
3. Stephanie, who ran the panel, then goes around the table, trying to start with a different person every time, asking the panelists whether they would recommend the wine to a friend.
4. If there are mixed responses to a wine, we go around discussing our responses and trying to reach a consensus or at least a judgment.
5. Ultimately, Stephanie makes the call if the wine will be re-tasted by the critic.
6. When we're done with a flight, the process begins all over again.

I had met Josh a few months prior to this tasting at a lovely Portuguese restaurant near his offices, and during the course of our lunchtime interview, he described the *W & S* methodology and approach. Josh is tall, thin, and angular, sporting a well-trimmed beard and glasses. He has both a sense for irony and calm intelligence—one that he doesn't necessarily feel a need to show off but that quickly becomes evident in his ability to move from topic to topic with ease. For him, the priority in judging wines is to find wines that represent some generalized idea of the region from which they came; therefore, typicity matters significantly. In this, he aligns himself with many current and former sommeliers, who are increasingly having an effect in shaping wine buying, and he also stands somewhat opposed to the stereotypical view of *Wine Spectator* and Parker, who seem to favor a very distinct style no matter where the wine is from, and who also, as some of their critics like Alice Feiring contend, favor wines that could be from *any* place. Josh is pretty pragmatic about reviewing, and certainly he doesn't come across as crusading in the way that Feiring, even in her self-mocking style, does to many readers. Josh also doesn't pretend that blind tasting is a perfect model or scientifically sound. However, he does pretty strongly believe that it's the best way we have to judge wines.

When Josh extended the invitation to participate in the tasting, I became first ridiculously giddy—this seemed like a dream come true—then extremely nervous. One can quickly shift from naivete—*Hey, anyone could do this and being a wine critic must be the best job in the world ... I mean they just drink wine all day, right?*—to realizing that maybe there is a lot more to it. I went into training. I knew I would have to spit because we would be tasting approximately forty wines. So to prep for this experience, I got a wine glass, put some water in it, and then found a cup. As my son watched a cartoon in the next room and my wife, nearby, wondered what the hell I was doing, I began sniffing, swirling, tasting, swishing, and then projecting water into a cup. I tried from different heights and different angles, seeing just how close to the cup I needed to be in order to hit my target. I didn't know how close I'd be to my fellow tasters or what manner of spit cup I'd have, but I needed to be ready. I didn't want to be splashing my Gavi on the sommelier across the table to start things off. I confess that while I had previously learned to keep the wine in my mouth for a bit as I tasted, I had kind of avoided the practice of swishing the wine aggressively around my mouth as if I had mouthwash with which I needed to desperately cleanse my breath. It was probably a boisterous Englishman who helped run a winery in Aloxe-Corton who put me off the habit; he swished so fiercely I could hear him across the room. However, knowing that I needed to both judge the wine and spit, I figured I'd better get used to the practice. Now it has become so ingrained—it works!—that I find myself swishing everything, including cough syrup and water during exercise breaks.

Besides the spitting and swishing, I worried about the judging. When Josh had mentioned having me participate in the panel, he said I seemed pretty experienced. I spend a lot of time trying to gain more experience, I replied. But being experienced, I later realized, doesn't mean that you have a good or an educated palate. In fact, for the most part, if you're not a professional, you can pretend to have as good a palate as you like. A friend and colleague of mine once wrote an essay exploring how far away from Michael Jordan he was on a kind of ultimate range of basketball playing ability that included everyone. When I reflected on the fact that Josh was regularly doing these panels—in fact, when I interviewed him, it was between a morning and afternoon session—and that I had never once tasted this many wines in one sitting, I worried I was further away from Josh than my friend was from Michael Jordan.

At the table, we had pitchers of water and some very plain—and a little stale— Italian bread to cleanse our palates. Otherwise, the surroundings remained sparse. Everyone had their own method. Most followed some version of sniff, sip, swish, spit. I quickly found myself dazed. I had to do all this and figure out how to answer the question "Would you recommend this wine to a friend?" Anxiously, I sought further clarification: Do you mean if the friend was shopping for a wine, would I say to get this, or do you mean my friend is at a party and with several wines from which to choose, would you say go ahead and drink this one or avoid that one at all cost? It turned out that they wanted me to focus on the latter. In some ways, it may not have mattered, but it helped to know that the bar seemed pretty low.

I thought, hell, we'll probably be recommending everything. I watched Josh, who sat next to me, as he moved through the wines in roughly a third of the time I needed. Whereas Josh could quickly taste and assess, I found myself going back to my earlier glasses in the flight, sometimes tasting two to four wines at least twice. Sometimes I'd forget to spit and feel embarrassed as if everyone noticed; other times I'd be concentrating so hard on swishing and spitting, that I could hardly remember what a wine tasted like.

I learned a lot during this experience. First of all, this is way harder than it seems in the abstract. It may not seem like it compared to Asimov's notion of 120 wines in a sitting, but forty wines is a lot. While I didn't walk away from the offices at 12:30 feeling buzzed, my brain felt exhausted and the accumulation of acid and tannins—despite spitting—did leave its effects and my lips and mouth felt spent. Therefore, at least for one amateur, I can confirm both mental and physical fatigue.

Let's talk more about brain exhaustion. In my day job, I have to grade essays. Of course, I spend more time on a given essay than I did on any one wine, but the most draining part of that process is deciding on a grade. I usually try not to do more than six essays in a day. Now, I had to judge, come up with a mini end comment in the form of a description or rationale for my judgment, and do it in front of people who I quickly realized knew a hell of a lot more than I did. People like to say things like "You know what you like." However, it is much more complicated than that. With the exception of the Gavis, most of these wines were actually being consumed at a stage that was before their prime drinking window; in the case of the Barolos, it may have been close to a decade or more before. At the tasting, then, we got the Barolos after having tried roughly thirty wines—more on Barbera in a moment—and then we were faced with both the wines I most wanted to try and the wines most difficult to assess. When you'd sip one of these wines, you might feel your mouth pucker, the insides of your cheeks draw back and become roughed up, and then you are navigating a kind of taste maze to figure out what the key flavors of the wine are.

When I smelled one in particular, all I could get was nail polish remover, what winemakers call volatile acidity. I turned to Josh, and asked, "If you can't get past the smell, do you have to try the wine?" He said no. Then, during discussion, the panel split on the wine, which ultimately got recommended. This struck me as telling. I recall legendary winemaker Cathy Corison, who loves Italian wines, suggesting to me that a little volatile acidity can be a good thing. However, the split between me—who couldn't get past the smell of the acetic acid in that particular Barolo—and my fellow reviewer who could, points to the kind of necessarily subjective range of assessment even in blind tasting. That is, I came in having a very low tolerance for both brett and volatile acidity (VA) and blind tasting does nothing to eliminate my prejudices in that regard.

In some ways, the panel worked against subjectivity: that is, no single person's taste got to hold sway. Nevertheless, I could see subjectivity at work not just in how we reacted to winemaking flaws but also in terms of simply deciding whether we'd recommend the wine. Although I occasionally found myself as the complete outlier—the one person to either recommend or fail to recommend a given wine—I often noticed that my descriptions of a given wine overlapped with that of my fellow tasters. I could never articulate the panoply of flavors and aromas as well as, say, Josh could. In fact, he could do it so casually and effortlessly, it made it seem entirely natural to talk about wine that way, whereas I felt like an infant next to him just learning to match words to objects. Moo, says the cow. However, I did often generally view a wine the same way as the other tasters: it had a rich red fruit core, for instance, or it had a lot of acidity. These overlapping descriptions did not necessarily lead us to consensus, though. For one taster, the fruitiness made it appealing; for another, it simply had too much fruit flavors and not enough balance. I also gained some sympathy for Broadbent's desire for tasting in a cloister, for you cannot group six folks around a tasting and expect solitude.

One wine both demonstrated this problem and also undercut the notion of wine reviewing as a dream job. We were in the middle of the Barbera flights, and the first wine of the flight tasted, fairly unmistakably, like fish. Yes, fish. It may have been the single most disgusting wine I ever tasted, in particular because of how unexpected and disturbing the juxtaposition was. I immediately looked up with what must have been my disgust quite evident on my face, and the instructor in Italian wines burst out laughing. Now, this disturbance didn't really alter any results—everyone could taste the fish—but it does suggest how hard it is to prevent basic human responses from intruding upon others. In this particular case, I, again as an amateur, found it hard not to have this first deeply flawed wine not have some effect on the rest of my evaluation of that flight. Hell, if it didn't taste like fish, it was bound to taste good at this point!

★   ★   ★   ★

During our review of the list of producers, there were some expressions of surprise that such and such Barbera was made by such and such producer, but other than knowing basic locale, no other related information had a bearing on our assessment. This leads us to perhaps the most controversial objection made about blind tasting: that blind tasting in effect eliminates the context of wine's creation and that creation matters in tasting, evaluating, and judging the wine. A few different versions of this argument exist. In Jamie Goode's blog post, he offers one of the main concerns often cited by others: "Without knowing the pedigree of the wine, it really is a mug's game predicting how it's going to age."[41] I should add here that to those of you who do not regularly read wine reviews, they almost always feature—when done by "projectors"—an approximate drinking window or at the least a moment when the wines will be at their peak. When I first started drinking wine, I found these to be particularly amazing, especially when I considered that some of the wines being tasted were notoriously difficult to drink when young (e.g., Barolo, Bordeaux, port). Parker will occasionally affix a caveat to his drinking window projections along the lines of "there is no track record for this wine" when he is trying to project a relatively new wine.

Asimov agrees with Goode's complaint that lack of context makes guessing a drinking window difficult, and then goes further: "It's ludicrous to contend that a wine's performance year after year is irrelevant to evaluating it."[42] He goes on to push his position by noting that such context is always deemed relevant in film and literary criticism (not so fast with the literary, I would say—more on that later). In short, Asimov asserts "history and intention count for much."[43] Kramer, though not particularly interested in drinking windows, offers a similar argument that properly judging a wine

> requires not just repeated exposure [to the wine by the taster] over many vintages, but knowledge about what it is you're tasting, the better to evaluate the wine for what you know it should be, rather than trying to figure out what it might be.[44]

These comments about intentions are a fascinating slope I am tempted to slip down, but let's just note it for the moment. Steiman found another related slippery slope in a quote he offers by Jon Bonné, then with the *San Francisco Chronicle*, that I think has strong echoes of Asimov's and Kramer's comments: "I question whether blind tasting … can uncover the most compelling and virtuous wines."[45] Bonné's views here resemble a metaphysical argument: this method will not reveal the true characteristic nature of the object. Later he offers Bonné's explanation that he seeks out the wines of those "that make smart decisions about their cultural values, farming values and esthetic values"—virtue aside, his claims resemble Asimov's "history" and "intention." Of course, not only does blind tasting fail to account for these things, the *virtue* of blind tasting is that it is supposed to exclude these very elements. For the context folks, though, this blindness leads to a failure to appreciate or recognize the merits of particular wines that do not come with the qualities that usually allow them to shine in blind tastings.

I had an experience with two winemakers for whom Bonné has much fondness, Duncan Arnot Meyers and Nathan Roberts of the somewhat eponymous Arnot-Roberts wines, which has influenced my own view of this question. Preparing to head out for an interview with Duncan and Nathan, I decided to try one of their wines beforehand. My wife and I cracked open a 2012 Que Vineyard Syrah (pun intended) with our dinner, and we found ourselves utterly perplexed by the wine. It seemed intensely savory in ways I did not associate with a Syrah from California. All through the meal, my wife and I kept trying to make sense of the wine, which had more acid, more earth, and more pepper notes than I expected. I really wasn't sure what to think, but I leaned toward not liking it. After dinner, I went about researching it and saw that Duncan and Nathan purposely sought out grape sources from areas where Syrah struggles to ripen. They seemed to be bitten by what Edgar Allan Poe calls the "imp of the perverse." Why would you want grapes from areas like that? However, my whole sense of their wines changed during my next encounter with those wines, which was in their company during the interview. I grew to understand what they were after (intentions), why they particularly liked these properties, the problems they found with Syrah made beyond a certain level of ripeness that eliminated some of the flavors they most treasured in Syrah. Duncan told me that if a reviewer were reviewing their wines in a blind tasting, it would make more sense to review them in the *context* of St. Joseph from the northern Rhône in France than California, and my whole perspective changed. Duncan handed me a glass of their Clary Ranch Syrah, and I appreciated—and frankly enjoyed—that wine in ways I struggled to do with their Syrah I tasted without any context. Of course, being in their very pleasant company no doubt creates its own biases. Josh Greene says he would never evaluate a wine for his magazine under these conditions because of the way those circumstances prejudice us.

To make this point about context, Asimov gives the example of J.J. Prüm's Riesling, which he reports always fails to do well in the blind tastings in which he participates (with misgivings, of course) because those wines smell of sulfur when young.[46] My allergy-assaulted nose has failed to recognize this problem; I have always found them delightful whatever the age. At first glance, it appears that Asimov might have chosen a better example. On *Wine Spectator*'s webpage, of the

427 Prum wines they have reviewed, 54 received a score of 95 or higher, and a remarkable 263 received a score of 90 or higher. It is, however, possible that, at least theoretically, a wine's pedigree can affect how it's judged in a blind tasting. That is the initial critique that Cohen raises. This is not dissimilar to how, for instance, knowing a sonnet was written by Shakespeare may affect a reader. Earlier, I had provided Cohen's own example, which is the prejudice against a variety like merlot; however, this can also work the other way around. An experienced taster of German Riesling will no doubt have experience of this wine and know its strong reputation. It is then possible that a taster can recognize characteristics associated with Prum wines and then reward those wines accordingly because of the weight of the winery's success—a strange process in which context reframes the apparent objectivity of blind tasting. While perhaps Asimov's example could be stronger, his general point—that some extremely good wines might not show well young—is still worth considering. I am not sure that Steiman's answer to that complaint holds up all that well. For Steiman, "the character of the wine leads to the context, not the other way around." That is, when he finds a wine that intrigues him in a blind tasting, he seeks out its backstory. However, Asimov might object that a wine that smells of sulfur won't intrigue as much as repel, and the backstory would remain hidden.

★   ★   ★   ★

These debates about not only how and why to taste wine and interpret the experience bear remarkable similarities to the history of literary interpretation over the last 75 years, if not longer. We might, for instance, place the impetus behind blind tasting next to one of the most prominent formalist literary critical schools in America, called the New Criticism. New Critics tried to focus on the literary text walled off from factors that might interfere with a direct interpretation of the lines on the page. This movement did not happen in a vacuum; the New Critics tried to provide an antidote to the dominant faction that Graff identifies as scholars who were accused of spending so much time on literary history and philological minutiae that they ignored the meanings of the texts entirely. This would be the equivalent of wine tasters who spent all their time discussing the winemaker's methods, the history of the vineyards, and viticultural nuance and never saying what a wine tasted like. Thus, the New Critics insisted interpreters focus on the text in isolation, developing the intentional fallacy and the affective fallacy. The intentional fallacy tried to exclude any role the author's history or personal background played and, as its name implied, avoid the mistake of trying to interpret, for example, a poem by the supposed intentions of the artist. The affective fallacy took a somewhat opposite tack and said that any personal or emotive response—any effect on the reader—produced by the text would only distort the interpretation of a given literary text. In short, New Critics strove for a kind of objective criticism—one that avoided distortion from factors outside of the text itself—in much the way that the proponents of blind tasting seek to eliminate prejudice both in the taster and all that comes before the tasting: it implies a taster stripped down to a kind of human tasting machine encountering the wine in isolation. New Criticism suggests a kind of timelessness of the art object; blind tasting almost seeks to freeze the wine in time, though to project, in some cases, its future. And just as blind tasting has reached very specific levels of procedure, grading, and evaluation—and folks even trying to control what language to use in the process—New Criticism also developed its own procedures. Graff's history highlights the fact that for New Criticism to succeed in the academy it needed to become systematized in order for it to be a method that could be reproduced by both critics and students so it could be taught. In fact, New Criticism became so systematic that M.H. Abrams identifies four common procedures for it under his entry on New Criticism in his famous glossary. These included T.S. Eliot's commandment that a poem "be regarded as an independent and self-sufficient verbal object";[47] an emphasis on explication and close reading; an emphasis on "unity"[48] and an opposition to paraphrase; and lastly, the focus on "words, images, and symbols."[49] In fact, this works so well that it can serve as the basis of getting students to write New Criticism by following the script.

However, New Criticism, like blind tasting, has received a series of responses claiming that this kind of reading is either essentially impossible or fails to properly account for factors that are in fact key to proper interpretation. In truth, it is fair to say that many of the differences in schools of interpretation, with the possible exception of the kind of antifoundationalism that Mailloux points to, can be distinguished by what counts as evidence for interpretation or what the interpreter believes should be the foundation for interpretation. For New Critics, like the blind tasters, it should be just the text or just the wine. However, just as certain wines appear—according to critics of the procedure—to stand out in such circumstances, New Critics favored particular schools of poetry, such as Modernist and Metaphysical, that seemed, due to their verbal complexity, to require the kind of close attention that New Criticism sought to apply.

As has happened to the blind tasters, however, many literary critics pushed back against New Criticism. A short survey of these emerging schools finds remarkable echoes in the grounds for objecting to blind tasting. Another famously controversial literary critic, Stanley Fish, led a kind of loosely organized revolt against the affective fallacy, thus helping form a school of thought that came to be known as Reader-Response Criticism. In one of that school's most radical claims, Fish argued that, for instance, readers did not "find" poems, they "made" them; that in fact, not only could you not exclude the reader from interpretation, the reader made the poem through the process of interpretation. While Reader-Response critics differed in the degree they felt the reader played in making meaning, they all concurred with the kind of complaint offered by Jonathan Cohen when he said that blind tasting could not foreclose off prior belief, and thus an account of reading or tasting without acknowledging the subjective role played by the reader or taster is ultimately dishonest. Reader Response would also be the approach that most fully aligns with folks who suggest that all tasting is ultimately subjective (though for Reader Response, again, there is a broad range of views about how much the text controls interpretation).

Other schools emerged that took on the intentional fallacy, and these schools have clear echoes in the kinds of complaints about blind tasting that Asimov, Bonné, and the other proponents of context make. Psychoanalytic critics, for instance, view the keys to reading literature as often found in the author—though unlike someone like Asimov, they worry more about the author's unconscious intentions, whereas he and others like Bonné worry about the winemakers' conscious choices. However, if there is any approach that seems to most line up with the opposition to blind tasting it would be New Historicism. Renaissance scholar Stephen Greenblatt has claimed that he was largely joking when he arrived at that name, but the emphasis on "new" linking it to New Criticism seems quite intentional and obvious. Proponents of New Historicism argued that we can only properly interpret literature by situating it in the history and culture of its creation, much like the arguments that suggest we cannot begin to make sense of a wine without appreciative knowledge of the winery, the locale, the land, previous vintages, and even the kinds of tanks the winemaker chose to employ. As with New Criticism, Abrams can line up a series of procedures to follow. This includes emphasizing the notion that nothing, including literature, can said to be "timeless."[50] It involves seeing a literary text and historical forces as being in "circulation" (i.e., the relationship between cultural objects and history is not in one direction, resulting in a vocabulary including words such as *exchange, circulation, transaction*, and *negotiation*);[51] a de-emphasis, of varying degrees, on human agency; and an emphasis on the notion that not only do texts and authors operate within their historical time, but so do readers. We can see that there are clear links here between New Historicism and those folks who worry that blind tasting fails to take into account how the wine came to be made, how the wine came to be consumed, where the wine was made, how it was made, and even why it was made the way it was made. For both these kinds of wine critics and the New Historicists, blind tasting or so-called objective reading leads to blind interpretations.

I should also add here that it is not just folks in the wine-tasting world—tasters and journalists like Bonné and Asimov—who worry about wines that get too easily dismissed or fail to collect the kinds of reviews that translate into sales, increase prices due to demand, and of course fail to receive recognition they deserve. I recall a tasting at the old Mount Veeder winery, Mayacamas, a few years ago before the winery was sold. This winery had a hold on tradition that few California wineries can claim since its founding dates back to pre-prohibition. (How folks, at that time, found their way regularly up the narrow, twisting slope of Mount Veeder amazes me.) At the time of my visit, the Travers family, who bought the estate during the year of my birth, ran the estate and our tasting was conducted by one of their sons. Even this winery's Wikipedia page mentions, "The estate is known for producing wine of a more traditional style than the Napa trends of recent years that emphasizes power, weight, high levels of alcohol and extravagance,"[52] and certainly this and the winery's failure to get proper respect from folks like *Wine Spectator*'s James Laube became a recurring refrain during both our tour of the old winery and our tasting.

Let me take a moment to explain the problem to those of you who do not regularly drink Napa cabernet sauvignon. (Mayacamas makes other wines, but this is their most noteworthy and the most noteworthy of the county.) Over the years, Napa has moved more and more to a style of wine that is accessible early, with a lot of initial fruit on the palate, perhaps a degree of extraction, and more and more plush tannins. Lewis Cellars or the now controversial Caymus might exemplify these more accessible versions. In other words, it is a version of cabernet that most people will find relatively easy to drink young, will taste and feel smooth in the mouth, and whose most assertive flavors will be those associated with rich, dark fruit.

There are, however, still wineries like Mayacamas—and this one fits the type that I ascribed to Asimov favoring, as Mayacamas is traditional and historic—that make wines in the style of Bordeaux (that is, wines that require a good deal of age before they show their best). These wines typically will seem harsher when tasted young, will have lower alcohol, and will seemingly not show well in blind tastings against more alcoholic, fruitier, and texturally smoother young wines. To help illustrate the problem, I took a quick look at *Wine Spectator*'s archived reviews of their wines, and the results speak to Asimov's and Bonne's worries. In reviews that span from 1970 through 2007, *Wine Spectator* has only given two wines produced by Mayacamas, both cabernets, scores over 89. The highest scoring wine review came for the 1978 vintage, not from an initial review, but from a retrospective done for the November 15, 1998, issue of the magazine. Similarly, the other wine, the 1979 cabernet, received a score over 90 in a twenty-year retrospective in 1999. When many Napa cabernets have declined to the point that you would not want to cook with them, the Mayacamas wines often have reached their peak. However, if you make wines like that, you are likely to make wines that will never be appreciated in initial blind tastings of California wines, or so it seems as most of the reviews on the *Wine Spectator* website bear out.

To just underscore this point briefly, we might compare reviews of Mayacamas and Caymus, which I paired earlier as stylistic opposites, from the same vintage. First, consider James Laube's description of the 2007 Mayacamas cabernet: "Shows a touch of dryness to the tannins and a slight metallic edge to the flavors. More rustic and solid than polished and refined. Ends with dried dark berry, herb and crushed rock notes, with gripping tannins." While it can be difficult to interpret the language of wine reviews (and I will get to this problem in the following chapter), Laube's emphasis on "dryness," "rustic" and "gripping tannins," not to mention the off-putting "slight metallic edge," suggests a wine that is challenging to drink—and no doubt the producers would say that is because it is not made to be consumed young. By comparison, the higher-scoring cabernet of Caymus from the same vintage was described in much more pleasing terms: "Ripe and fleshy, with rich plum, wild berry, spice and savory herb notes that are complex, full-bodied and expansive on the palate, ending with firm tannins and a dash of espresso." Although the tannins may be "firm," the rest of the description emphasizes "ripe" fruit, and instead of metal we get espresso. In short, the Caymus seems almost designed to make the Mayacamas taste unappealing by way of comparison, especially in a blind tasting where considerations of intent have been excluded. While it is possible that Laube at some point made note of the pedigree of the Mayacamas—in fact, the 87 score it received seems a bit generous in relation to the description—he does not present his review in terms of "intentions" or the history of Mayacamas wine. Casually reading through reviews in your newest *Wine Spectator*, using it as your guide, which would you look to buy?

You would have likely chosen the Caymus, and, for reasons I have sketched out above, that choice quite rankles folks like the previous owner of Mayacamas as well as the noted wine iconoclast Randall Graham. His problems with these folks can be found front and center in a wine advertisement he sent out on November 25, 2014. The subject heading reads, "To Serve Mankind," followed by the name of the wine on offer, which, it turned out, had received high scores from wine critics, something that Graham feels he has been slighted from before this:

> In some weird, psychologically, slightly twisted way, I have grown oddly accustomed to being the slightly (or more than slightly) misunderstood winemaker by the likes of the most influential wine media. You know whom I'm talking about; there's no need to name names.[53]

And then he does name names in a footnote! What strikes me most in this opening salvo (of an ad, no less!) is the word *misunderstood*. Like with my comparison of Mayacamas and Caymus, Graham sets up a similar comparison to other unnamed Rhône-style wines from California that "tend to be largely dominated by powerhouse, overwrought *what-would-Barry-Bonds-look-like-if-he-were-a-wine?* competitors; to some extent this style has become normative to the category." His celebration derives from an online review of the wine from a critic who has not "misunderstood" Graham's intent,

> but more to the point, as it were, is that he utterly *grokked* the wine, i.e., seemed to deeply understand the stylistic intention and understood that this wine is exquisitely *balanced*. He got that the wine is all about elegance, finesse and complexity; it needn't be massively extracted (and especially not grotesquely high in alcohol) to be capable of continued development and revelation; this is the gradual unfolding of the lotus blossom, Grasshopper.

Graham's comments could easily stand in for the comments of my guide at Mayacamas about their wines, and they lean heavily in the direction of the complaints lodged by both Asimov and Bonné. While Graham clearly dislikes the style of many of his competitor's wines—he even notes at the end of the email, after an extended bowling/wine analogy (as if the Dude had written this email), that those wines will not last (and they do tend to overshadow his style of wines in blind tastings as Cohen has explained)—Graham seems most upset about the message behind his wines getting lost as exemplified by his hyperbolic excitement at finally being "*grokked*" by a reviewer. And as the subject heading of his wine offer suggests, no matter how tweaked with irony it is, Graham thinks there is a whole lot at stake in his message getting through to people.

The fact that the stakes are so high or can be equated to larger political concerns begins to hint at my sense of the broader implications of these debates. For I would argue that a kind of metaphysics begins to emerge in what folks see as important in assessing, judging, consuming wines. Consider Bonné's talk of virtues or the worries about intentions and contexts. Such language suggests a metaphysics in that it emphasizes how we think about the world, what we should properly attend to about the world, and what we should value. When folks like Bonné or Asimov raise doubts about blind tastings, they do not appear to be just worried that consumers will be shortchanged or that some winemakers will fail to make a proper living. Instead, they are often talking about human beings failing to place emphasis on the proper things in life and failing to celebrate folks who do—and folks like Randall Graham seem to agree with them.

Let me close this section by mentioning one more objection that can be found in many places, including Cohen's essay and Asimov's book: that blind tasting of several bottles of wine almost never resembles the way most people consume wine. Cohen sees this as an inherent flaw in the projectionist model since the projector and the consumer do not approach wine in a directly comparable way. Although Robinson talks about setting up blind tastings for one's dinner parties and how fun that is to do—and yes, I have even done this once or twice, and yes, Jancis is right that it's fun—everyday wine consumption comes most commonly in the form of a couple or individual opening up a single bottle of wine, perhaps as they begin to cook dinner (with all those interfering smells!), and then sit down to a meal where, in perhaps one of humanity's most civil undertakings, the couple or individual begins to gradually sip away over conversation and dinner. The elaborate apparatus of blind tasting is never like this, of course—and remember that Broadbent wishes it to be an extremely nonsocial occasion. I have always remembered an anecdote shared by former *Wine Spectator* reviewer James Suckling of coming across a bottle so good during a blind tasting that he had to stop what he was doing, close the door, and enjoy it. I am sure that the fact that it was among the most expensive wines Bordeaux produces was a mere coincidence.

We should also bear in mind that many critics and writers also note the problems inherent in Steiman's concession that wine is a moving target—that blind tasting, especially as a means to project wine experiences in the future, cannot always accurately see the future or evaluate a wine when it is not tasted at the right moment. Asimov even mentions the fact that reviewers could wait with certain wines, like his beloved J. J. Prum, but then those reviews will not help anyone when they read them since the wines will no longer be on the market.

Theoretically, blind tasting as a means of projecting also stands in opposition to the commonplace conception that since wine tasting cannot be separated from the

FIGURE 1.2 Jill Klein Matthiasson leads a professional tasting in her former backyard tasting area

experience, a given experience, for instance, a convivial tasting at a winery, may prove as deceptive as a projector for what is to come. In other words, to give a common example, sometimes the wine you bought because you enjoyed it so much at a winery with a lovely view and an engaging host somehow seems flat and less enticing four months later drinking it alone at home. And this is simply the most mundane of reasons, for folks like Bonné and Asimov, as well as the New Historicists: context matters. If wine changes all the time, one initial experience may not be ever terribly accurate to project the wine in the future. Although this is a matter of the context of consumption, whether drinking or reading—that is ironically far more ever-changing than the context of the wine or art objects' creation. And let's not forget that if you yourself are a projector, you—unless you have powers that I do not—will not be the same when you taste that wine again either.

Notes

1 An analysis of the film's impact on wine sales can be found in Stephen S. Cuellar and Frederick Acosta, "The *Sideways* Effect," *Journal of Wine Economics* 4 (2009): 219–232. Recently, there has been a backlash to the backlash—either attempts to promote merlot once more or accusing Myles's grape darling, pinot noir, of having become California's next merlot.
2 In fact, a recent beer campaign seems to be satirizing wine consumers in a similar way and concludes with its tagline, "Bud Light for the many, not the few," underscoring the elitist associations with wine consumption.
3 Jim Holt, *Why Does the World Exist? An Existential Detective Story* (New York: W.W. Norton, 2012), 28.
4 Susan Sontag, *Against Interpretation and Other Essays* (New York: Farrar, Straus & Giroux, 1966), 5.

5 Ibid.
6 Ibid.
7 Steven Mailloux, "Interpretation," in *Critical Terms for Literary Study*, ed. Frank Len-tricchia and Thomas McLaughlin (Chicago: University of Chicago Press), 121.
8 Ibid., 133.
9 Justine Vanden Heuvel, "Wine Critics—Everything Old is New Again," *Huffpost* (June 7, 2016). www.huffpost.com/entry/wine-critics—everything_b_10345502.
10 Since the beginning of this project, James Laube has stepped down from his role as the most prominent critic of California wine for *Wine Spectator*.
11 Jamie Goode, "Understanding a Wine: Where Blind Tasting Fails," *Wine Anorak*. Online blog. www.wineanorak.com/understanding.htm.
12 Matt Kramer, *True Taste: The Seven Essential Wine Words* (Cider Mill Press 2015), 25–26.
13 Marvin Shanken and Thomas Matthews, "Why We Taste Blind," *Wine Spectator* (April 30, 2012).
14 Robert Parker, "Tasting Notes and Ratings," *The Wine Advocate*.
15 Parker's role in his own magazine has been reduced a great deal recently due to health issues.
16 Michael Broadbent, *Michael Broadbent's Wine Tasting* (London: Mitchel Beazley, 2003), 63.
17 Ibid., 6.
18 Ibid., 12.
19 Ibid., 11.
20 Jancis Robinson, *How to Taste: A Guide to Enjoying Wine* (New York: Simon & Schuster, 2008), 59.
21 Ibid., 62.
22 Ibid., 86.
23 Ibid., 87.
24 Jonathan Cohen, "On the Limitations of Blind Tasting," *The World of Fine Wine* (2013): 3.
25 Ibid., 4.
26 Matt Kramer, *True Taste: The Seven Essential Wine Words* (Kennebunkport: Cider Mill Press, 2015), 27.
27 Ibid., 28.
28 Gerald Graff, *Professing Literature* (Chicago: University of Chicago Press, 1987), 254.
29 Qtd. in ibid.
30 Ibid., 255.
31 Ibid.
32 Ibid.
33 Ibid.
34 Eric Asimov, *How to Love Wine: A Memoir and a Manifesto* (New York: William Morrow, 2012), 35.
35 Ibid., 37.
36 Jonathan Cohen, "On the Limitations of Blind Tasting," 9.
37 The younger or robust wines would typically be linked to the New World and the traditional to the Old World, though these designations can also be linked to styles of wines rather than simply points of origins.
38 Harvey Steiman, "Blind Tasting and Context," *Wine Spectator* (March 5, 2013).
39 R. Hodgson, "An Examination of Judge Reliability at a major U.S. Wine Competition," *Journal of Wine Economics*, 3, no. 2 (2008): 108.
40 Harvey Steiman, "Behind the B. S. About Wine Tasting," *Wine Spectator* (July 3, 2013).
41 Jamie Goode, "Understanding a Wine: Where Blind Tasting Fails," *Wine Anorak*. Online blog. www.wineanorak.com/understanding.htm.
42 Eric Asimov, *How to Love Wine: A Memoir and a Manifesto* (New York: William Morrow, 2012), 36.
43 Ibid.

44 Matt Kramer, *True Taste: The Seven Essential Wine Words* (Kennebunkport: Cider Mill Press, 2015), 29.
45 Qtd. in Harvey Steiman, "Behind the B. S. About Wine Tasting," *Wine Spectator* (July 3, 2013).
46 Eric Asimov, *How to Love Wine: A Memoir and a Manifesto* (New York: William Morrow, 2012), 37–38.
47 M.H. Abrams, *A Glossary of Literary Terms* (Stamford: Cengage Learning, 2014), 216.
48 Ibid., 217.
49 Ibid.
50 Ibid., 220.
51 Ibid., 221.
52 https://en.wikipedia.org/wiki/Mayacamas_Vineyards.
53 This was sent as a direct email advertisement to previous customers on November 26, 2014.

References

Abrams, M.H. *A Glossary of Literary Terms*. 11th ed. Stamford: Cengage Learning, 2014.

Asimov, Eric. *How to Love Wine: A Memoir and a Manifesto*. New York: William Morrow, 2012.

Broadbent, Michael. *Michael Broadbent's Wine Tasting*. London: Mitchell Beazley, 2003.

Cohen, Jonathan. "On the Limitations of Blind Tasting." *World of Fine Wine* 41 (2013).

Cueller, Steven S., Dan Karnowsky, and Frederick Acosta. "The Sideways Effect." *Journal of Wine Economics* 4, no. 2 (Winter 2009).

Goode, Jamie. "Understanding a Wine: Where Blind Tasting Fails." *Wine Anorak*. Online blog. www.wineanorak.com/understanding.htm.

Graff, Gerald. *Professing Literature: An Institutional History*. Chicago: University of Chicago Press, 1987.

Hodgson, R. "An Examination of Judge Reliability at a Major U.S. Wine Competition." *Journal of Wine Economics* 3, no. 2 (2008): 105–113.

Holt, Jim. *Why Does the World Exist? One Man's Quest for the Big Answers*. New York: W.W. Norton, 2012.

Kramer, Matt, *True Taste: The Seven Essential Wine Words*. Kennebunkport: Cider Mill Press, 2015.

Mailloux, Stephen. "Interpretation." In *Critical Terms for Literary Study*, edited by Frank Lentricchia and Thomas McLaughlin. 2nd ed. Chicago: University of Chicago Press, 1995.

Parker, Robert. "Tasting Notes and Ratings." *The Wine Advocate*.

Robinson, Jancis. *How to Taste: A Guide to Enjoying Wine*. New York: Simon & Schuster, 2008.

Shanken, Marvin and Thomas Matthews. "Why We Taste Blind." *Wine Spectator*, April 30, 2012.

Sontag, Susan. *Against Interpretation and Other Essays*. New York: Picador, 1966.

Steiman, Harvey. "Blind Tasting and Context." *Wine Spectator*, March 5, 2013.

Steiman, Harvey. "Behind the B. S. About Wine Tasting." *Wine Spectator*, July 3, 2013.

Vanden Heuvel, Justine. "Wine Critics—Everything Old is New Again." *Huffpost*, June 7, 2016. www.huffpost.com/entry/wine-critics—everything_b_10345502.

2

ON BALANCE

Numbers, Words, and Wine on a Page

In the beloved children's allegory, *The Phantom Tollbooth*, Norton Juster imagines a world divided by words and numbers. Wisdom has been rent by two warring brothers, King Azaz the Unabridged, who rules the land of words, Dictionopolis, and the Mathmagician who rules the land of numbers, Digitopolis. In the absence of the princesses, Rhyme and Reason, the two fight over the preeminence of words or numbers. The quest in this allegory—besides fostering curiosity for his world in the boy, Milo—involves an attempt to bring balance between these tools for understanding the world. This split between words and numbers has a long history in human culture. The Pythagoreans, for instance, placed an emphasis on numbers and geometry in particular as a means of locating "the principles of order in the universe" and as a "means of escape for the soul."[1] Linguist Benjamin Whorf popularized the notion that language forms a "conceptual grid," wherein language provides a means and limit to understanding and describing a world. The split between numbers and words also recalls C.P. Snow's famous distinction between the humanities and sciences as Two Cultures.

One of the few places, however, where numbers and words come together on a regular basis—though whether in harmony is another matter—is wine reviewing. If we recall Stephen Mailloux's definition of interpretation as centering on translation, then this process has directly led to the highly problematic and now highly widespread practice of translating a wine into words and numbers, often in the service of evaluation. Wine critics might be said to interpret a wine for the purposes of judgment, working within Mailloux's sense that this process gets shaped through rhetoric (though the wine writer Matt Kramer feels that judgment needs re-emphasizing). For whether one gets there by way of blind tasting or some other interpretive process, the experience of wine—and often the evaluation of wine—follows a path of tasting and then finding a means of translating that experience, in which the wine taster interprets his or her own experience into words and

DOI: 10.4324/9781003399810-3

numbers for a listener or reader. Whether the princesses of Rhyme and Reason need to be restored to this particular Kingdom of Wisdom, I will leave you to decide.

In this chapter, then, I would like to explore the scoring of wine and writing of tasting notes—and to some extent the words used to understand wine—for these are the spaces where wine tasting might be said to most obviously resemble interpretation, because both scores and tasting notes require what Susan Sontag most hates about interpretation: they require a translation of the contents of the glass into something other than those contents, whether numbers or words. We will then move to focusing on one word, *balance*, that has become a source of debate as well as an aesthetic ideal before returning to the question of metaphysics with which I began the first chapter. That question, as you recall, was whether commitments to theories of interpretation can be considered as implying a metaphysics, a conception of the nature of reality.

Wine reviewing as a form of interpretation has clear similarities with aspects of literary analysis but also can be differentiated in some notable ways. The most obvious departure from literary analysis has to do with the process of judging or scoring. Literary reviews—with the exception of a few sites like the A.V. Club or crowdsourced popular reviewing like Goodreads—tend not to assign scores or grades. The development of a *Rotten Tomatoes*-like site on books revealed, however, that if you did translate book reviews to grades, those grades would be remarkably high. While it is somewhat beyond the scope of this chapter to provide an extensive history of how this separation arose, I would note that one factor has been the movement away from overt judgment in academics., as well as a tendency for academic literary critics to write for their own exclusive community. As a result, there has emerged two spheres: literary reviews such as those that appear in the pages of *The New York Times* and the somewhat misleadingly titled literary criticism, the purview of academic journals and presses. Literary criticism, while analytical and sometimes quite critical (and judgmental!) does not engage in the process of projecting, or letting you know whether you might like this or that book. Projecting has been given over to nonacademic venues, but most book reviews have not quite fallen into the exact path of how most magazines and newspapers review films with stars or thumbs pointed skyward.

It has not always been the case with wine either. While the choice to rank wines in some way via a numerical score might now seem an obvious method to use, it appears to be a relatively recent development in wine reviewing. In Ellen McCoy's book, *Emperor of Wine*, about Robert Parker, she recounts the story of how either Parker or his tasting mate, Victor Morgenroth, "came up with the 100-point idea."[2] As someone who has spent a lot of the last 25-odd years trying to decide where an essay fits along a similar scale, I am not sure how innovative this approach is, and some of the disputes about it—Parker and *Wine Spectator* using 100-point scales whereas some like Jancis Robinson favor 20-point scales—seem rather overblown. For example, some members of the British wine press seem particularly displeased by the apparently American notion that you essentially get something like fifty points for showing up or, in this case, having actually made a wine that can be poured into a glass. However, it's clear that the scale did take people like the wine writer Hugh Johnson by surprise. He recalls first reading Parker and asking, "But what are these numbers—70s, 80s, 90s—in the margin?"[3] Like another user of the 100-point scale, *Wine Spectator*, Parker even offers a grading rubric with phrases like "90–100 is equivalent to an A and is given only for an outstanding or special effort." I am not sure Parker intends to suggest this, but "effort" strikes me as an odd choice when you consider, in light of our discussion in the prior chapter, that effort suggests a knowledge and value of intentions.

Nevertheless, it is not so much the type of scale as the scale itself that leads to most of the controversy. After a series of seemingly systematic, evaluative maneuvers, one stops, reflects, and says that yes, that wine is an 88. The appeals of the system of scoring wines are readily visible: they continue to present the notion, built from blind tasting, that an objective assessment of a given wine can be had, and grading rubrics further suggest a set of objective criteria by which the wine has been scored. (And yes, folks who use those rubrics to assess essays also hope to convey to students their objectivity.) In addition, these numerical scores provide an easy—and for many, *too* easy—reference point for consumers to recognize a good one. Typically, the line is a 90, an "outstanding wine." The website for the popular online wine merchant Wine Library, for instance, has a search category called "90+" wines. As Kramer suggests, "the 100-point scale brings order to chaos," by which he means both the chaos of the tasting note (more on that in a bit) and the chaos created by the seemingly enormous quantity of wine now available to both the critic and the consumer. He also notes that these "scores are instantly intuitive."[4] That is, as the consumer looking for 90-point wines at Wine Library can attest, those wines simply are better than those that received a score lower than 90. Defenders of such a system, like Kramer's former *Wine Spectator* colleague, James Laube, provide this rationale: "One big benefit of the 100-point scale is that it has given winemakers a target. It's one way for critics to show vintners where their strike zone is."[5] Although winemakers had been "skeptical and cautious" in their view of such scales, Laube finds that many winemakers now use them "to calibrate their excitement about a wine," though that wine would seemingly be their own wine. Tellingly, however, he does not cite any winemakers by name.

By way of praising this system, Laube seems to simultaneously introduce one of the main fears of such systems: that winemakers make wines to please critics. In fact, one of the ongoing complaints about the role Parker played in wine is just that: he encouraged winemakers to make Parker wines, and as you have likely guessed, Parker wines resemble those that Randall Graham disparages, as I noted in the previous chapter. As we will see, this role of the critic has also led to the controversy over the word *balance*, for that controversy derives from a suspicion of what Parker has wrought. While it is both as playful and surprisingly earnest as the title implies, Alice Feiring's *The Battle for Wine and Love: Or How I Saved the World from Parkerization*, for example, catalogues heroic vintners who have resisted making wines aimed at pleasing Parker, but they repeatedly stand alone amid the large-scale homogenization of wine, as Feiring details it.

After several readers responding to Laube's blog post "Grading the 100-Point Scale" brought out this complaint of wine being made to please the critic, Laube

FIGURE 2.1 Advertisement at the entrance to Beringer Vineyards

tries to clarify his own initial comments, saying, "I'm not suggesting winemakers aim for a critic's strike zone, but being aware of where it is can be useful. I consider I [*sic*] have a pretty wide strike zone, as a wide range of wines and styles appeal to me." I am not certain that Laube has really revised that initial impression here. Why, for instance, do winemakers need to know where a critic's "strike zone" is unless they're aiming for it? Presumably, they are not purposely aiming away from it! Yet many winemakers I met might be said to do so, if inadvertently. In the same sequence of exchanges, Laube finds himself also defending the apparent rise in scores—wine's version of grade inflation—and suggesting that the scale and evaluation remain sound: "One reason ratings are higher is wines are better, that and vintners know where to aim if a score is a goal."[6] Laube probably does not help himself much here if you are in the Feiring camp.

I should also concede that, as the Mathmagician would certainly agree, numbers are extremely powerful. When I talked with the winemaker Josh Widaman, then of Lewis Cellars, about wine reviews, he talked about a kind of tension between words and numbers:

> There are ratings where if you took the number away and read what the critic had to say, I wouldn't want to ever taste that wine. But then you put the number there and you go, oh, well, that's gotta [be good and] how different the tasting notes sound from what they score is something that I have a hard time understanding sometimes.

Certainly, when it comes to marketing, numerical scores come first and can influence both producers and consumers. In fact, Steve Matthiasson detailed his struggles when starting out to simply get visibility for his wines, which were not made in the style favored by powerful critics like Robert Parker:

> And so it was like, so here [is] an unknown person with no pedigree, so you need to score. So it was pretty common: submit to Parker, [and] I'll consider carrying your wine once you have a score. You know, that was fairly common, and so you know, it's a lot of, as soon as you submit to Parker, as soon as you have a score, then we'll talk. Because you have nothing else going for you, I can't sell your wine. I can't say you were the winemaker at Colgin or whatever, so I can't use that, I can't use that—the wine doesn't blow me away, it's not rich and ripe, and so I got nothing.

Without the proper scores, then, Matthiasson found little access to wine stores, top restaurant wine lists and consumers.

Wines with high scores, however, come at consumers with the scores leading the way. As a wine consumer and regular purchaser, I receive offers for wines every day. Seemingly every one of them has received a score of 90 points or higher … from someone. And as wine critics have proliferated—in recent years, for example, two well-known writers, James Suckling (from *Wine Spectator* at the time) and Antonio Galloni (formerly from Parker's *The Wine Advocate*), have gone out on their own—I have become struck by the distinct impression that critics are giving out high numerical scores for wines in order to gain publicity. When I asked Joshua Greene, owner and editor in chief of *Wine & Spirits Magazine* about this, he said,

> Grade inflation is one of the obscene things that's going on right now in the wine industry. And it's true. I won't name names, but there are any number of publications and critics, because they know that if they give the wine a high score, the winery will use it, [and] they'll get their name out there. They are using it as a marketing tool for themselves.

They are, to borrow Laube's metaphor, expanding their strike zones so as to get their names attached to more and more wine advertisements and thus increase the traffic to their sites. This is not necessarily a new strategy; Parker built his reputation in a somewhat similar manner by famously going against the grain of opinion in his praise of the 1982 vintage from Bordeaux.

Many of the folks who oppose blind tasting also have concerns with these translations of wine into points. Joshua Greene finds himself exasperated by the 100-point numerical scale and scoring:

> It's ridiculous. It's completely absurd. But if you give wines one, two, and three stars, nobody cares. I'm serious, nobody cares. And there's something about the numerical scale that works really well in this country. People respond to it. I mean, literally, there's not a day that goes by when I'm not thinking, how the hell can we come up with a different scale?

So far those ruminations have not borne fruit, and Josh remains as trapped in the system as anyone. "I do hate numerical scoring," he confessed. "It's perverse. We score wines because otherwise we would not have a business." To illustrate his point, Josh explained his continued practice of releasing an issue every year without scores. When he does so, the sales go down. This problem of advertising is another particularly knotty element of wine reviewing, as there is no doubt that advertising dollars from wineries can be tied to some fear of conflicted interests, and of course there is much documentation of how much impact giving a wine a score of 90 or higher can have on wine sales. I asked Josh if that weighs on him as he's deciding between, say, an 88, 89, and 90, but he said, "No, I never think about that, actually. It has to do more with your reaction to the wine. And psychologically, an 89 wine is a wine that just doesn't make it. And an 88 is a wine you sort of like." What Josh points to here is that while on the surface, numerical scores stand for objectivity and the reason side of the dialectic, they may also mask a much more emotional underpinning. In a podcast interview with *I'll Drink to That*'s Levi Dalton, former reviewer for Parker and now for his own site, *Vinous*, Antonio Galloni talked about his trepidation and anxiety over both high scores and low scores. Since Galloni does not regularly evaluate wines blindly, part of the consequence is personal: he claims that he no longer receives invitations to taste at Bruno Giacosa after giving lower scores than previously, for example. With high scores, Galloni suffers anxiety when revisiting them because, as Hugh Johnson says of Parker, "If it scores more it's worth more."[7] In other words, Galloni fears that a wine won't continue to live up to the kind of value and investment his high score has originated.

Not surprisingly, Eric Asimov also takes some umbrage with this scoring system, but not for dramatic reasons—which he ascribes to others—such as scoring wine being like scoring "works of art in a museum."[8] For the record, Hugh Johnson sits in that camp when he asks, "Who would think of trying to rate Manet or Monet, or Hemingway and Fitzgerald, or *Aida* and *Lohengrin*?"[9] Those complaints clearly resemble Sontag's concerns about interpretation: that to translate art into analytical contents into other language is to reduce and demean the art. While folks like Johnson hold those complaints about the 100-point scale, Asimov dislikes the fact that scores offer too little "information" and thus "are too often misleading."[10] He also cites similar concerns he has about blind tasting—human fatigue, what kinds of wines earn high scores, and so on. For Asimov, then, these problems are of a piece, for often numerical scores derive from blind tasting (though, significantly, not always, as there are reviews that are done non-blind at the wineries themselves like much of Parker's and Galloni's).

How can this scale be thought of as misleading? Consider that the clear boon and bane of the 100-point scale has to do with certainty. Recalling the impact that Parker has had, Johnson observes that "he had invented a system that supposedly took the mystery, the guesswork out of choosing wine. This guy will not only tell you that it's good, but how good."[11] Johnson's first impression of Parker, "very sure of himself," then can be shared by anyone who uses the 100-point scale in evaluating wines. When wine writers evaluate wines from barrel—that is, before they have been bottled—they often offer scores in a range, for instance, 92 to 94. By doing so, wine writers acknowledge that it's early to judge and what you get in the bottle may not match what the wine reviewer tastes at this time. However, most of the major reviewers in the United States eliminate the use of a range when they review the wine in the bottle. Although almost all of them would likely admit that the review occurred as one snapshot in time and that a wine might taste quite different at a different time and place (following the wine-is-alive school of thought), the implication of the scoring system is that now we know for sure. Numbers do not appear to have the same kind of interpretive wiggle room as words. However, one person's 90 would certainly be, upon inspection, as loose as a bag of bones as someone's "good."

★   ★   ★   ★

While the 100-point scale certainly has its detractors, it's arguable that its skeptics have more concerns about its application than its design. However, no area of wine criticism has elicited more discussion than what usually accompanies the scores of wine when you encounter them in a magazine: the tasting note, or the attempt to describe the experience of a wine in language. And perhaps no other element of wine tasting—besides the pomp and facial gestures—has been more open to parody, such as the litany of smells Myles observes in the scene from *Sideways* with which I began the previous chapter. These complaints range from the professional tasters to the amateurs who post tasting notes on websites like Cellartracker and *Wine Spectator*'s own forums. In fact, a recent forum conversation was titled "Things people say in tasting notes" and has 239 entries and over 39,000 views the last time I checked.[12] And here, perhaps more than anywhere else, we can see most overtly the ways in which wine tasting rides sidecar to the kind of interpretation sketched out by both Sontag (for appropriation) and Mailloux (for definition). When I started this book, I had never scored wines myself, so I could shrug that off, but even though I don't write tasting notes, if you ever drink wine with people serious—even mock serious—about wine, you will find that you must summon a vocabulary to express what a given wine smells, looks, and tastes like. Recently, I had a private tasting in the caves of a small-scale winemaker and producer. It was a lovely occasion, and he opened three bottles of his Syrah at a section of his cave designed for such gatherings. I peppered him with questions about many of the issues in this chapter and the previous one, but when we got to the point where we actually tried the wines, I attempted to maneuver him into describing them first—with the hope that he would establish the vocabulary for our discussion. He somewhat forcefully declined, and I found myself introducing all my descriptions with the unwieldy phrase, "what I would call," as in, "It has what I would call a plush texture."

The key part of my earlier phrase to describe wine tasting notes, that they attempt to "express what wine smells, looks, and tastes like" raises the difficulty.

My ending phrase "like" identifies the inherent problem, which is that this language must be figurative. We inevitably describe wine by way of comparison. Unlike a literary critic, a wine critic cannot directly or literally cite the text itself. In *Michael Broadbent's Wine Tasting*, he spends several pages guiding the reader ("analytical taster") through this murky terrain. In a section titled "Use of Similes and Analogies," he seems to get a bit tangled up. He suggests that the degree of reliance on figurative language might be cultural ("The French ... tend to be more poetic than the English, for instance"); he stresses the fact that similes and analogies will be reliant on the familiarity of the audience. (For example, if you've never smelled a truffle, what good is it for you to read that a wine smells like one?) Or as the winemaker Dan Petroski, who grew up in Brooklyn, expressed to me, "What the hell does a honeysuckle look like?" Broadbent then asserts that "analogies add extra dimensions and help other tasters to memorize aspects."[13] Elsewhere, he finds himself defending the use of words—"words are needed"—and suggesting that the words will be "factual or fanciful" before undermining that claim by saying that "facts very often turn out to be opinion."[14] Indeed. Similarly, Kramer finds himself also defending "why words matter," for they are only a means to "speak insightfully about whatever it is that you may find in your glass." Yet Kramer also suggests that "flavor descriptors are—however odd this may sound—not really language" because they lack "inherent meaning."[15]

Wine & Spirits seems to go about constructing their tasting notes in ways that differ from other publications. When I asked Josh Greene about their notes, he said,

> From my point of view of a note [... it] should be 80 percent information and 20 percent experience. Because your experience in tasting that wine is going to be different from my experience, but the information is the same. So the note is there basically to say, in my experience this was an awesome thing to taste. I hope it will be for you. If it is for you, this is what will help you get some traction as to why. And it's not about whether you taste the blueberries like I tasted them.

Winemaker Morgan Twain-Peterson suggested something very similar to me. He argued that wine descriptions should focus on more objective categories like structure and tannin and not on particular fruits since he concurred with Josh that those fruit descriptors are highly subjective, and so Josh's reviewers eschew the usual litany of descriptors.

Matt Kramer does not see the source for the expansive tasting note as deriving from Parker, as many see the problem of numbers as having started there. Parker's approach to notes might instead be seen more as a symptom. In Kramer's view, the real source—and in fact the real problem—of the current state of tasting notes has to do with the rise of wine programs in academics, particularly the famed enology and viticulture program at the University of California, Davis. And with this, we find wine placed in a new version of the Two Cultures problem. The origin of the problem, for Kramer, aligns with his sense that the academics also promoted blind tasting as a means of both seeking out the "Holy Grail of objectivity"[16] but also for the purposes of "trying to achieve in their tasting methodology ... a statistically valid replicability of results."[17] I will return later in the chapter to some of this history, but for now, let's note that Kramer sees the modern tasting note as an outgrowth of what became the academic impulse to create a limited, specific, scientific, and objective vocabulary and one that would eliminate words that are subjective and vague. Kramer implies this problem arises from the culture of reason promoted by academia.

Thus, Kramer feels that following the use of those vocabularies led to what we have now: "At the professional level, with thousands of wines a year to review," writers would inevitably become bored and boring if they used the same phraseology over and over again, "so you get more specific, summoning up black cherry, wild cherry, pie cherry, maraschino cherry, cherry jam and cherry liquor" rather than just "cherry scented."[18] Because Kramer sees these litanies of descriptors as emerging not so much from a desire to interpret—remember, he claims these descriptors are without meaning—but to categorize and replicate. He argues that "an abundance of flavor descriptors in a tasting note tell us surprisingly little about a wine's actual quality."[19] Part of the problem here, then, is the absence of judgment.

Kramer's view certainly runs against the grain of how many folks look at the tasting note and its history, and I will return to his ideas of how he would improve it in a bit. Others might see Broadbent as the starting place for the modern-day tasting note. (You can have fun reading his reviews of wines that you will never, ever see, let alone taste.) Ellen McCoy, in contrast, argues that Parker is the person most responsible for shaping the way people talk about wine today. Some people call this language *winespeak*. McCoy's book provides an excellent account of Parker's transformation of winespeak and its effect, which altered "the way people perceived wine, what they looked for, and how other people wrote about it."[20] She explains that how to talk about wine has been a long-standing problem; like Kramer, she notes the several failed attempts to provide a definitive vocabulary from folks at places like UC Davis—home to America's premier enology program—such as professor Maynard Amerine's "approved list of words" or Ann Noble's "Wine Aroma Wheel."[21]

Amerine wrote several books including *Wines: Their Sensory Evaluation* with Edward B. Roessler. In the conclusion of the book, the co-authors provide a glossary of wine vocabulary, which includes suggestions of what terms to use. Here's a telling example of their style: "**coarse**—Although this is intended to describe an unbalance of flavor components, it is so weighted down with various other meanings that it is best avoided"[22] or "**earthy**—an unpleasant odor perceived *in the mouth*; difficult to recognize or describe."[23] From these you can get a sense of Kramer's concern that Amerine sought to eliminate any word that might produce what the literary critic, Thomas Mclaighlin, might call an "excess" of "meaning."[24]

Noble's wheel can still be purchased. A given wedge of the wheel begins at, for example, "Floral" and then subdivides to "Geranium," "Violet," "Rose," and

"Orange Blossom," which can create the impression that one needs to tour the world's botanical gardens before being able to properly describe the "aroma" of one's favorite sauvignon blanc. When I did a tasting with Josh Widaman in the mannered boardroom space Lewis Cellars has in the front room of their facility, I pestered Josh on how we would describe his sauvignon blanc. Of course, like a good teacher, he turned the question back to me and, echoing Noble's aroma wheel, I said that the wine seemed floral to me. Josh promptly asked, "But what kind of flower?" I had gone as deep as I could, whereas Josh continually trains his nose by testing himself in spice shops and trying to expand his own olfactory vocabulary. Petroski's honeysuckle remark derived from his experience taking a course from a perfumer, which focused on lessons in aromatic identification for winemakers. Kramer says that Noble, like Amerine, sought an "unwavering rejection of all subjective or 'hedonic' terminology in favor of specific, replicable, repeatable terms."[25] Josh and Petroski's experiences suggest that, with proper training, one can come to use these very specific terms in repeatable ways.

Sometimes, though, the language of wine can seem much more charged than issues of specific flowers. McCoy observes that Parker's notes moved away from classist and sexist descriptors. Perhaps. A visit to Burgundy a few years ago, for example, taught me that one part of the region produced "masculine" wines and, you guessed it, the other area, "feminine" wines. Why? Fill in responses from your gender stereotype handbook: they are more "soft," "seductive," "lighter in style." As a brief aside, let me add that it would seem that this language is not just gendered, but gender biased. In Burgundy, the red wines of the Côte de Nuit are described as masculine, and they are more highly regarded and considerably more expensive. Instead of the sexist language, according to McCoy, Parker "included dozens of concrete terms, especially words for fruit and texture," using "just about every fruit ever eaten."[26] In addition, he used a "cornucopia of texture words" and, perhaps more noteworthy, his "testosterone-charged vocabulary to describe the horsepower of wines" such as "big," "hefty," and "massive."[27] If these aren't suggestive enough, McCoy recounts the fact that over the course of ten years, he used the word *hedonistic* "836 times" (271). Sometimes, he skipped the euphemism and simply made direct relations between a given wine and sex.

To illustrate my point, let me present a quick excerpt from Parker's review of the 2010 Château Angélus, which the score suggests he loved:

> Rich, layered and built like a skyscraper, this multi-dimensional Angélus has lavish concentration and moderately high tannin, but it is sweet and well-integrated, as is the oak. Just enough acidity provides focus and delineation to this exceptionally well-endowed wine, which should hit its prime in 7–10 years and last 30–40.

While McCoy may be right that Parker moved the wine vocabulary away from overtly sexist discourse, it's not really clear that he moved it away from a gendered discourse, for the "testosterone-charged" language Parker has used to describe wines he likes reinforces a kind of gendered division of wines, and that division seems somewhat biased. In his praise of the Angélus, for example, he says it is "built like a skyscraper" and calls it "well-endowed." Clearly, then, good wines are associated with other masculine stereotypes or simply are equated to the phallus, and it is these very same kinds of wines that tend to "overpower" wines that have a greater delicacy (it's hard to avoid falling into this kind of gendered language) that Asimov seeks to defend from the effects of blind tasting. While this kind of discourse itself opens up wine notes to scrutiny and parody, it is also the litany of descriptors that some like Kramer feel are empty or that others simply mock. In that same review of the Angélus, for instance, Parker says, "The opaque bluish/purple 2010 Angélus offers up a beautifully sweet smorgasbord of aromas ranging from blueberry pie to espresso roast, white chocolate, crème de cassis, licorice, truffle and a touch of lead pencil shavings." Pencil shavings, while clearly the oddest descriptor here, is more common than you might imagine. On a wine discussion board, one of the livelier recent debates was about whether graphite or saline should be used to describe a wine; this same site has another forum tracking critics' favorite tasting note phrases. What is clear from this list, though, is that Hugh Johnson certainly got it right when he noted Parker's confidence. And, of course, Parker's tasting notes can be extraordinarily long—even compared to probably the most verbose of *Wine Spectator*'s writers, James Molesworth. As McCoy argues, the overall effect of his new vocabulary was to produce a new lens for looking at wine, and with his influence, new desires for wine: "vocabulary is never neutral; it carries an implication of quality"—and much more, I would add.[28]

Before we go any further, I think it would be useful to look directly at some other tasting notes. I have selected two tasting notes, one from a former *Wine Spectator* writer—and now independent reviewer—James Suckling, and another from Parker. The wine is the 2001 Château Rieussec, a wonderful wine I once consumed—almost any expert would tell me—far too young. First, here's Suckling:

This is the greatest Rieussec ever. Technical director Charles Chevallier has finally reached his goal of perfection here. Like lemon curd on the nose that turns to honey and caramel. Full-bodied, very sweet with fantastic concentration of ripe and botrytized fruit, yet balanced and refined. Electric acidity. Lasts for minutes on the palate. The finish really kicks in. This is absolutely mind-blowing. This is the greatest young Sauternes I have ever tasted. Best after 2010.

Now, here's Parker at far from his most loquacious:

A monumental effort, the 2001 Rieussec boasts a light to medium gold color in addition to a fabulous perfume of honeysuckle, smoky oak, caramelized tropical fruits, crème brûlée, and Grand Marnier. The wine is massive and full-bodied yet neither over the top nor heavy because of good acidity. With intense botrytis as well as a 70–75-second finish, this amazing Sauternes will be [at] its apogee between 2010–2035.

Oddly, one can be stunned into silence by these kinds of reviews. I love Parker's second-by-second count of the finish. Suckling's synesthesia, and the usual tendency to find that the only way to explain wine is by other foods (in the case of Parker, even other alcoholic beverages) seem very common practices. (More on this in a bit.) Even as someone who has tasted this wine and many others, I have no notion of claiming I would identify all of these elements in my own inelegant quaffing of the wine at the end of a joyful meal. Wine experts consider this wine, a sauterne, perhaps the greatest type of dessert wine in the world; thus, reviewers describe it by using foods associated with dessert (as both are typically sweet). Some facts get mixed in here, but some of those are self-evident; by its definition, sauterne gets produced by way of the "noble rot" botrytis, so I am not sure that it needs identifying. The smell of lemon curd, though, needs some encouragement. If you jump back to the previous chapter's description of the scene from *Sideways* with Myles's nose deep in a glass, you may wish to reconsider if that scene is more realistic than parodic.

That said, these examples are not in any way outliers and strike me as really quite muted for such an extraordinary wine according, at least, to the numbers: Suckling scored it 100—a perfect wine, and Parker, a marginally flawed 99. Asimov, reliably contrarian in his views of modern wine tasting and writing, offers his critique of these kinds of notes in a chapter titled "The Tyranny of the Tasting Note." He begins the chapter suggesting that writing about wine used to be far less effusive and colorful—and, well, indulgent. At the heart of his critique, he compares what writers like Parker do to a music critic who wrote reviews emphasizing "wattage, intermodulation, and impedance" and argues that "the flowery litany of aromas and flavors does little to capture the experience of a fine glass of wine." I recall tasting with a winemaker who clearly favored Asimov's stripped-down language. When I asked him what he thought the wine he had just sipped tasted like, he said simply, "Blueberry." Such responses, however, remain harder to come by these days, although I had a sense that more experienced winemakers like Cathy Corison and Celia Welch—both, not coincidentally, trained at Davis—certainly favored a limited and specific language. And because of the pervasiveness of the more effusive tasting notes, Asimov worries that "people assume that they are the proper mode of thinking about wine, too."[29] Since the writing of his book, Asimov has not at all softened his view. Over lunch on a steamy Manhattan afternoon, he reiterated his dislike for poeticized and overly detailed wine descriptions.

This objection, though, begs the question of how language shapes thoughts or sets a parameter for thoughts. If highly elaborate language actually distorts or mystifies the experience of wine—in essence, doing the opposite of what that language seemingly intends—then are the times when, as Asimov claims, wine writers use "a series of agreed-upon characteristics" to describe a wine, like "gunflint," any better? As Asimov proceeds with his argument against current tasting note style, he grows more impatient: "At best, tasting notes are a waste of time. At worst, they are pernicious."[30] Essentially, he wishes to champion the notion that wine writers should "speak plainly," but it's also hard to get past what comes out of this section—namely, that he suggests that words fail to provide an accurate experience of what tasting the wine can do. However, pointing to a different vocabulary seems to invite similar complaints, even if that vocabulary was unadorned and less effusive. You will likely side with these objections of Asimov's if you believe certain words can convey proper meaning—that is, translate the experiences of our body's sensations—and others cannot. Although Josh Greene of *Wine & Spirits* can describe wine in an amazing amount of detail as he showed during the blind tasting I did by his side, he remains firm that much of the descriptions in reviews are problematic. The problem, for Josh, is that

> everyone perceives flavors and scents differently. There's very little unanimity, especially in our culture here in the States about what's a positive or negative flavor or scent. There is very little unanimity about whether you taste black cherries or I taste blueberries or someone else tastes raspberries, and whether that means anything at all. So, in order for any of that kind of flavor description to be relevant and useful, the critic needs to use it in a consistent way, and can't just gather information from the panel that says, well, this guy says it tasted like raspberries, and that person said it smelled like onions and that person—it doesn't, it's completely random observation, it doesn't have any value at all.

During my research, the winemakers Steve Matthiasson and Cathy Corison both encouraged me to get on Delectable, a wine-reviewing application where people in and outside the wine trade post wine reviews (both numerical and written). I can see Josh Greene's influence on my own reviews, because I hesitate to ever go beyond something like "red fruit" or "blue fruit." Even that, I suspect, Josh might argue goes to a level of specificity that does not translate readily to everyone. With about every winemaker I met with, I presented them with reviews from multiple wine writers about one of their wines. Some hated it. Ted Lemon acted as I would if I had just been asked to read my student evaluations in the company of a relative stranger. His only comment was to correct one writer's speculation about a winemaking procedure. So distinct are some of the critics that Chimney Rock's Elizabeth Vianna could identify who every critic was after I read the review aloud. Many ignored the kinds of variable uncertainties and poetic fancies I spotted and instead, as in the case of both Cathy Corison and Celia Welch, focused on a pattern of overlap. For them, things like blueberries or blackberries amounted to more or less the same description, and the poetics or oddities like "band-aid" became almost invisible.

While Asimov in many ways can be said to follow the tradition of the UC Davis folks in seeking a stable, limited set of wine descriptors, Kramer, who argues that the UC Davis folks have in fact produced the proliferation of descriptors, whatever their intentions, proposes an entirely different set of keywords to both combat this trend and to reinstate the judgment he feels has been lost. Because of Kramer's anti-scientistic position, his goals seem, with perhaps a few exceptions or contradictions, to provide a vocabulary that could be said to favor a more humanistic and culture of feeling approach to wine. He seeks to find a means to redress the "inappropriate intrusion of scientific parameters upon fundamentally aesthetic matters".[31] In order to do so, Kramer sets out a kind of step-by-step approach for tasters, but the vocabulary he seeks to promote can often seem remarkably close to ones that already exist, as when he seeks to replace "balance" with "harmony" (a phrase to which I will return later), "texture" for "mouth feel," "layers" for "complexity," as well as "finesse," "surprise," and "nuance." The problems with the first two can be the semantic differences between those words and those that they replace; the problems with the last three can be found in just how obscure they can seem. Take, for example, Kramer's understanding of "finesse," which in many ways stands for his anti-scientistic approach. Simply trying to offer a definition for "finesse" seems to give him difficulties. He begins by offering something akin to the famous pornography definition: "It's one of those 'you know it when you see it' things." He then tries to distinguish them by way of a basketball analogy—despite being "no sports fan myself"—as the difference between a finger-roll layup and a dunk. After a return to its French etymology, "fine-ness,"[32] Kramer concedes that "establishing finesse is a matter of judgment and far from an exact science" because "it can't be measured."[33] Then, after invoking the Shaolin priest in *Kung Fu*, Kramer admits that "finesse cannot be rationally proven as real."[34] Yet for Kramer, this is a mark in its favor, for those folks like Amerine and Roessler who would ban its use hold a "willfully blindered view of quality in wine, a form of narrow-mindedness justified by an abiding belief in scientism".[35] So after saying he cannot prove its existence, Kramer concludes, "Finesse exists. It's real. And not only does it exist, but what's more finesse is an [sic] foundational element of all truly great wines anywhere in the world".[36] This ultimately leads Kramer toward some of the issues in the wine culture wars regarding alcohol and ripeness.

Kramer seems to be waging war on two fronts: one in opposition to what he calls scientism and the other against aesthetics. In a blog post titled "Wine Terroir is All Just Myths, You See," he critiques Mark Matthews's *Terroir and Other Myths in Wine Growing* for the same flaw and cites a definition of scientism provided by *Scientism: The New Orthodoxy*, which involves applying natural science methodology to non-natural science studies, "an exaggerated confidence in science" as a cure to what ails humanity, and the need to replace humanistic methodology with scientific methodology, feeling instead of reason. While Kramer then has grounds to try to fight for aesthetics, a form of humanities methodology, he may not do himself favors by relying so heavily on abstraction, analogy, some tautologies, and a sense that to believe in finesse is a matter of faith. While I will return to the question of metaphysics, I think we can see that Kramer makes the matter of the very types of words and methods he uses quite clearly a metaphysical fight about how we should best *know* the world.

Kramer, who for a long time held a prominent role in the wine world as a featured columnist for *Wine Spectator*, however, does not—at least on the surface—hold a very typical viewpoint, though his sense of wine culture as divided among science and humanistic aesthetics would anticipate some of the divisions wine-makers see between artists and craftsmen that I will discuss in the following chapter. In his critique of science—particularly what he calls the scientistic—Kramer is a strong proponent for interpreting and judging wine through the prism of a culture of feeling. As for finding a common language, most critics and winemakers have hoped to secure a more limited, almost essential vocabulary so that descriptions of wine become somehow more stable or more objective or, as Kramer would say, more scientific. However, not everyone would likely buy the reasoning that this process is possible. Even Kramer seems to suggest it is by claiming that wine descriptors that follow from the work of folks like Noble and Amerine do not produce meaning.

In contrast, from the point of view of literary interpreters influenced by the French philosopher Jacques Derrida, such as J. Hillis Miller, who I mentioned in the introduction, the stability of this agreed-upon language is an illusion. Language inherently slips in its meanings. In the words of literary critic M.H. Abrams's glossary and its attempts to describe Derrida's ideas: "We must always say more, and other than we intend to say."[37] Some might be tempted to push back against this claim and suggest that some wine terms really are pretty straightforward and—importantly, in light of these ideas—limited in their meaning. This would align with say Abrams himself who says we interpret by way of the author's intentions. In an essay titled "Can Wines be Brawny?: Reflections on Wine Vocabulary," Adrienne Lehrer mentions some of these more definite words early on, listing "*sweet, sour*, and *bitter*."[38] As Lehrer observes, however, "much of the wine vocabulary is value laden."[39][40] That is, even words that seem fairly neutral or limited in their meanings often come packed with connotations that begin the process of expanding their meanings. Lehrer uses the word *pure* to attribute a wine word with no value judgments attached; she gives the example of "A *light wine* is neutral or good, but a *thin wine* is bad, and a *watery wine* is even worse."[41] While Lehrer makes the case that there are few "pure wines," Derrida would likely argue that there are no pure words, if by that we mean words that fail to carry some kind of expanding sense of meaning or value. As Abrams's gloss informs us, Derrida argues that not only is it the case that "metaphors cannot be reduced to literal meanings but, on the other hand, that suppo-sedly literal terms are themselves metaphors whose metaphoric nature has been for-gotten."[42] Lehrer's example of "thin" fits this bill because, after all, the reason why "thin" fails to be "pure" is because it is essentially metaphoric when applied to wine. Lehrer, a linguist, seems not as troubled by the metaphoric effect; she suggests it is more of a problem in poetry![43]; however, I would contend that whether one takes this notion as far as Derrida and literary critics who subscribe to his ideas (Deconstruc-tionists), we can see that wine vocabulary, like any vocabulary, cannot quite be as fixed as one would hope. (Lehrer distinguishes between "scientists" and other kinds of wine writers and suggests scientists require a more controlled vocabulary).

While I am skeptical that Asimov's well-intentioned call for a more limited, standardized vocabulary will work to make tasting notes more useful or that Kramer's shift in terminology will rekindle a more aesthetic and "insightful" means to properly judge a wine's value, I am somewhat sympathetic to both their frustrations that tasting notes can seemingly complicate wine to such an extent that it becomes off-putting. It strikes me that we might categorize some of the problems into three groupings: the use of references that seem foreign to the reader, the use of a bewildering litany of descriptors (however we arrived at that tendency), and the use of descriptors that rely on a kind of metaphoric application.

Let's start with the first one. As I noted earlier in this chapter, Broadbent points out that metaphors have limits in effectively conveying information because our understandings of metaphors are shaped by experience and by culture. Many metaphors rely on an act of imagination. If I say that a given wine feels like jumping out of an airplane, I may be able to approximate the meaning by imagining what that is like, perhaps by way of a series of other analogies. However, if I do not know what an airplane is, then this metaphor fails completely. To illustrate the second problem a bit more in terms of wine writing, I am going to draw upon an admittedly loaded example by choosing a note from one of the wine world's most loquacious reviewers (so much so that you can find parodies of his notes online) and also a note from his favorite Châteauneuf-du-Pape from the lauded 2010 vintage, namely the Domaine de St.-Préfert Charles Giraud. Here's James Molesworth's review:

> Massive yet remarkably graceful at the same time, with layer upon layer of fig, plum sauce and linzer torte flavors studded with espresso, graphite and black tea. Petrichor, shiso leaf and smoldering tobacco notes fill in on the broad and very muscular yet refined finish. This has terrific weight and loads of grip, yet it's effortless to drink thanks to the seamless mouthfeel. A stunning combination of power and grace. Best from 2015 through 2035. 665 cases made.

You might first observe that Molesworth draws upon the same kind of testosterone-heavy language associated with Parker. He does not call this wine "well-endowed," but he, like Parker, does pay that compliment to many other wines. You might also observe his array of descriptors that could easily escape the knowledge of most readers. While it turns out I have experienced petrichor, I will admit that I had to look it up. I have seen a linzer torte, but I have not eaten one. I know what shiso is, and I am sure that I have tasted it, but I would need to look up what it tastes like. I may not be Molesworth's ideal reader (who is?), but I do have a lot of experience with a wide array of foods, and I still hesitate to tell you what this wine tastes like based on his descriptions. Because of that, as a reader, I am more likely to rely on the score, which much less ambiguously signals his approval. As included here and in almost all the tasting notes I have quoted, there is also such an array of descriptions that it is truly hard to believe that the average person could catalogue them all. You can almost hear Jack from *Sideways* say, "Yeah, definitely espresso but not the pencil."

Lastly, I would return to the problem of descriptors that simply do not convey information most people associate with food. Let me pick on Molesworth one last time. In a blog post from December 3, 2014, on the *Wine Spectator* online site, Molesworth concludes his preview of the 2013 wines by Michel Chapoutier. In this passage, he uses a descriptor I have run across from him elsewhere:

> The 2013 Crozes-Hermitage Les Varonniers has a gorgeous violet aroma that gives way to ganache, tar and warm paving stone notes, while the core of blackberry and plum paste waits in reserve. There's lots of bass here, but it has the tension and drive to stretch out fully after cellaring.

The phrase that particularly befuddles me is "warm paving stone notes." From how this is written, I cannot fully tell if that is a taste or smell descriptor, though perhaps it's best, as winemaker Elizabeth Vianna suggested to me, to see all descriptors as on a continuum since our taste and smell intersect so much. In any case, like most people, I have encountered paving stones, but I don't know what they smell like (they can be made from different stones or even concrete, after all), and I certainly don't know what they taste like (although the same could go for tar, I have come to associate a certain taste in these wines with what he calls tar, but I could be totally wrong). While it is possible that "warm paving stone notes" conveys something clear to some readers, I think that the general point stands that wine descriptors of this type do a lot more to muddle the meanings conveyed by these notes than to clarify them. In essence, these problems lead a reader to interpret what is already an interpretation.

One possible explanation for the tendency to mix these various factors comes from Dr Jamie Goode's book, *I Taste Red*, which uses a review of scientific studies to explain how exactly people physically taste wine. During that process, Goode makes the case that wine tasting is essentially driven by synesthesia, that "there is a good deal of binding together of different inputs from different sensory modalities." He elaborates by saying, "What we refer to as the 'taste' of wine is actually a multimodal experience with significant input from the modalities of taste, smell, touch, and vision."[44] He goes on, for instance, to suggest the ways in which our sight or what we see in a wine has a powerful effect on other expectations of what we will smell and taste. In short, then, one explanation for the kind of tasting note James Molesworth and many other writers compose is that it simply attempts to capture the very real, synesthetic experience the wine taster has. However, even if we grant Goode's explanation, it does not follow that parsing the interpretation of such an experience—that is, interpreting the interpreting—is any more likely to allow a reader to home in on or fix meaning.

★   ★   ★   ★

My wife and I joke that 95 percent of all winemakers would likely tell me three things: (1) that they do as little as possible to make their wine (see the later chapters on art and ecology), (2) that they seek to express the land, and (3) that they seek to make wines of balance. Of all the descriptions and words used to describe wine, no other has been more recently a vexed subject—and that even includes "natural"—than *balance*. If we stick with nouns, we quickly find that the *Oxford English Dictionary* (*OED*) provides at least six definitions of the word. The most obviously relevant one is: "A situation in which different elements are equal or in the correct proportions." However, I would also have us take note of three others: one that applies to human health, "Mental or emotional stability"; one that applies specifically to art, "Harmony of design and proportion"; and lastly, one that suggests a kind of odd contradiction, "A predominating amount; a preponderance." The first definition I cited and the one that applies to art resemble one another, though the latter includes a kind of aesthetic complement in the word *harmony*, which Kramer wishes to substitute for *balance* as a wine descriptor. The human definition suggests the way in which we might think of balance as being a part of a larger set of principles and priorities other than just describing an object or artwork. The last meaning, however, suggests that definitions of balance also suggest a majority, a summation of *imbalance* within our larger understanding of the word.

It strikes me that the artistic definition, which probably dates back to the ancient Greeks and their development of aesthetics, explains how one of the greatest compliments any reviewer or taster can pay a wine would be to call it balanced. In this, the evaluator suggests that harmony, to borrow from both the *OED* and Kramer, has been achieved and also that wine can be thought of as a pleasing aesthetic object. Many psychological studies have suggested that humans tend to find proportionality attractive—people with apparently "balanced" faces typically get more praise for beauty in clinical studies, for instance—so it should come as no surprise that wine critics would praise wines that they like as balanced and that winemakers would seek to produce wines in balance. As we shall see in chapter 4, balance is also a key feature in some ecological positions. Whatever meaning we might focus on, we rarely find folks aligning themselves with imbalance: what I most wish to achieve in the next year is to focus exclusively on work and ignore my family; what I most desire in wine is high alcohol and little of everything else! I would like to explore this particularly vexed word because it speaks to many of the problems associated with translation and interpreting, both for wine and elsewhere, and it also points to some of the complexities between interpretation and larger fundamental views of how to best describe the world, metaphysics, that I introduced in the previous chapter and to which I will keep returning.

So how did a word so common and so seemingly banal come to be so complicated? Well, it more or less starts with the creation of In Pursuit of Balance, a loose association of American winemakers founded in 2011 (and disbanded in 2016) and mostly associated with its founders, Rajat Parr and Jasmine Hirsch. A good place to begin tracing the issue would be with the initial manifesto the group produced in anticipation of its first gathering (and tasting). The manifesto, which Parr credits to Hirsch, first attempts a definition, just as I began this section with one:

Balance is the foundation of all fine wine. Loosely speaking, a wine is in balance when its diverse components—fruit, acidity, structure and alcohol—
coexist in a manner such that should any one aspect overwhelm or be
diminished, then the fundamental nature of the wine would be changed.

Here, I would say, we remain in the banal in that I cannot imagine that any
winemaker reading these words out of context would have any issue with this
notion. After some rather poetic remarks on pinot noir—and the desire to express
the land—we begin to see where the tension arrived: "The purpose of this event is
to bring together like-minded growers, winemakers, sommeliers, retailers, journalists and consumers who believe in the potential of California to produce profound and balanced pinot noirs. This isn't a rebellion, but rather a gathering of
believers." I will return to this idea again, but the notion of "believers" implies that
others are nonbelievers, and here we begin to see how this group began to actively
stir the pot. In short, balance is now a matter of faith. I will add two of the four
bulleted points of conversation from the manifesto:

- Growing healthy fruit and maintaining natural acidity to achieve optimum
  ripeness without being overripe. What is ripeness and what is its relation to
  balance?
- A question of intention: Can balance in wine be achieved through corrections
  in the winery or is it the result of a natural process informed by carefully
  considered intention at every step of the way?

The first one I've cited speaks to one of the main areas of vexation, the notion of
ripeness, which if it is connected to brix, the measuring of sugar content in the grapes,
usually becomes important in determining when to pick the grapes. One way of
measuring ripeness is that it has achieved [fill in the blank] brix; however, brix also
predicts what percentage of alcohol the wine will have, as fermentation converts the
sugar to alcohol. If the brix is too high, fermentation will become difficult, which may
in turn require some interceding in the winemaking process to finish the wine. As
these debates about balance expanded in the wine world, they often got associated
with the wine's percentage of alcohol; if the alcohol by volume registered too high, it
made for an imbalance. The second bullet point raises the complexity of a number of
other issues this study undertakes: winemaker intention and intervention.

This matter of intention can also be used to divide winemakers, though they all
claim to prize balance. As Steve Matthiasson told me,

> Everyone thinks they're making balanced wine, but is balanced wine your
> goal, is it a side-effect, you know? Generally, I think the people that don't
> agree with it are less focused on balance every step of the way. They're more
> like, 'It tastes really good'—they're focused on it tasting really good, and then,
> by the way, it's balanced, see, it's balanced. But their destination isn't balance.
> Destination might be power, might be deliciousness, might be suppleness.

If both the supposedly balanced focus and the winemaker focused on, say, suppleness both do arrive at balance, you could also see that some winemakers might have issues about their intentions being questioned. This, of course, also recalls the long-standing debate in the literary world about whether an author's intentions matter and how you can know them. Wherever you stand, this manifesto is where the debate, conversation, and/or controversy began in earnest (though it arrived after the formation of IPOB).

Why should this create such tension? Paradoxically, part of the reason is that IPOB divided the wine world by way of a principle seemingly everyone shared. It also, as I mentioned above, asserted that it was a gathering of "believers," which suggested that there were others who did not share the faith. As Elizabeth Vianna said to me, trying to choose her words carefully, during a visit at her winery:

> I struggle with their ... well, I struggle with their, with the name of their thing. Because I think most winemakers are in the pursuit of balance. Most good winemakers are trying to make wines that are balanced. So it alienates the whole world, right? It's like, nobody else has ever thought about balance before.

Another winemaker who makes wines on the other end of the stylistic spectrum from most of the IPOB producers, Josh Widaman, says succinctly: "The only thing that I don't like about In Pursuit of Balance is that by saying that you're saying that everybody else isn't." As Josh's assessment suggests, many of the winemakers who felt excluded by IPOB, particularly on a value they all reputedly shared, clearly resented IPOB.

No winemaker that I met more fully exemplified this than Michael Browne, then of his eponymous winery, Kosta Browne. In Jon Bonné's *New California Wine*, he essentially aligned Kosta Browne with wines that show "irrational exuberance" and are suited for "novices." In short, they aligned with the antagonists of his narrative—"Big Flavor"—and many winemakers who fit the model IPOB strove for served as the protagonists of this story. When Michael began showing me around the impressively large, clean, and shiny new location for Kosta Browne in Sebastopol, he took me on a detour through his lab, where his winemaker and another assistant were tasting barrel samples. I suspect Michael wanted me to see a plaque, which leaned against the wall with the words "In Pursuit of Balance" emblazoned upon it. Pointing at it, Michael said, "We got our plaques from In Pursuit of Balance because we wanted to take [the idea of balance] back." While Michael remains fairly open minded—he and other winemakers who share a similar style often say something like "to each his own, and if you can sell your wine, good for you"—it is also clear that being a part of a narrative in which you and your work get cast as the antagonist can make you defensive or at least put in a position where you must reassert your values.

When I traveled to Lompoc, about an hour outside of Santa Barbara, to meet with Rajat Parr in what has come to be known as the Wine Ghetto, I had a

FIGURE 2.2 In Pursuit of Balance plaque in the laboratories of Kosta Browne

chance to ask Parr directly about the origins of IPOB and his view on what it was about. Prior to my visit, I had read Bruce Schoenfeld's *New York Times* article on the movement, titled "Wrath of Grapes," a title that ironically evokes a deadly sin associated with being *out* of balance. The article, while covering a lot of ground, draws the focus on Parr and Parker in particular. (Who is the protagonist and who the antagonist in Schoenfeld's telling is not entirely clear.) Schoenfeld had summed up the controversy as in some way exemplified by the name of Parr's organization:

> The name itself is polemical. It seems to imply that those outside its ranks don't mind if a single attribute of their wines (sweet fruit, perhaps, or alcohol, or the flavors that result from prolonged aging in oak barrels) dominates the rest.[45]

In fact, Parker has taken it that way, accusing the group of snobbery and labeling them the "anti-flavor elite," a name some wine consumers who support Parr have taken on for themselves in another version of taking it back or in a semi-ironic statement of unity. By asserting this label, Parker got the chance to reclaim his old advocacy for the common person with which he began his career, after having come to embody the wine establishment he had originally challenged. Parker also had other very critical remarks for Parr and his group, and Schoenfeld, despite at one point comparing Parr to a "teddy bear," had led me to expect that, in Parr, I would face an aggressive figure who, in Schoenfeld's phrase, "proselytizes" for his views. Parr's own book, *Secrets of the Sommelier*, was not exactly coy in stating its point of view either.

However, the figure I met seemed closer to possessing a kind of Buddha-like calm than the temperament of a fire-and-brimstone preacher. He talks quietly and gently, and many of his friends describe him as lovable. When I mentioned some of Parker's critiques or those of *Wine Spectator*, Parr simply asserted that he has positive feelings about both and is generally reluctant to escalate any of the name-calling. He seemed surprised, too, about some of the ways he had been described in that article. While Parr is not without contradiction—he at once spoke of the importance of difference in wines rather than a hierarchy and then praised his Bentrock chardonnay as a favorite later in the same conversation—his view of the entire controversy seemed a good deal different than I had been led to believe. The backstory he narrated of how IPOB came about suggests a series of accidents that began with a casual conversation with Jasmine Hirsch. Nevertheless, it also becomes clear that things like the manifesto do derive from strongly held beliefs.

Much of the controversy about the use of the word *balance*, as Schoenfeld has asserted, has to do with how balance has seemingly been used to focus on a particular aspect of a wine as creating imbalance, and the factor that is identified most frequently is alcohol. Standing on the sloping hillsides of the Rorick Vineyard in Calaveras County, I asked the man who tends the surrounding vines why alcohol. Why has, for so many people, alcohol become the measure of balance? Isn't it just one factor? Matthew Rorick—tall and iconoclastic with a look that can convey Elvis, Joe Strummer, and Wolverine all at once—responds quickly:

> I would say the reason that people focus on it so much is that it's the one factor that's actually listed on the wine label. So it's the one thing that everybody sees when you bring a bottle out. But they're all tied together. Everything—you know, alcohol, acid, pH, flavors, aromas—they're all tied together and all depend on when you pick … . So, you could talk about any of them, and probably should talk about all of them if you want to talk about balance. But alcohol, yeah, that is the one thing that we are required to put on labels, so it becomes an easy thing to say.

That focus on alcohol, on really the only ingredient required to be listed on a bottle of wine in the United States, troubles many people. Justin Smith, the winemaker and owner of Saxum, makes what most drinkers would call big wines, often tipping over 15 percent alcohol by volume, according to the labels. Parker loves Saxum wines and calls Smith a superstar, a label that seems foreign to the self-deprecating Smith when you meet him. He's good-humored, quiet, and consistently even-tempered. When I mention IPOB to him, he characteristically softens his disagreement by introducing his views with the caveat, "I've got no personal beef with them." However, he does think their understanding of balance, or at least how that view has come to be popularized, is flawed. As Smith says,

In Pursuit of Balance, that's a funny name because it's implying that you have to have this lightness to have balance, when the whole thing with balance is, you've got as much [on] one side as the other side, and if you've got something big on one side and you put something big on the other side, it's balanced. Their whole thing is, "Oh, we like these lighter, more elegant wines," and that's great—I do too—but I don't think that dictates balance.

He adds a further example to make his point about isolating alcohol as the key factor, for that

is like saying that someone that's—a girl that's 145 pounds is fat. No, just because you've got this one number doesn't mean everything else has to stem from it. I think you can totally have a wine over fourteen and half that's balanced, just like you can have a person that weighs over 145 pounds that's not overweight.

Not surprisingly, Michael Browne agrees, even echoing Justin's own analogy:

Well, I'm not going to pick my fruit 22 brix [in order to achieve low-alcohol wines]. That's fucking green, man. You know what I mean? … Typically, those wines are anorexic to me. But you go the opposite direction, you're too big, too huge, too fat, but that's not cool either. It's this nice, beautiful, slender woman. Wow, in proportion. Some are bigger than others; that's okay, it comes from the beginning of what it came from. So we're not out to make a 13 percent wine, that's just too simple.

For Browne, many other factors as Rorick also mentioned—that are less visible to consumers—shape the consumer experience of a wine:

in my opinion, people that say, "Hey, the wine's gotta be below 13 percent to be in balance," I think that's bullshit. I've had 13 percent alcohol wines that taste totally alcoholic, and they suck. Fifteen's getting high, right? But there's a certain range, yeah, cool, it's not hot, it's luscious, delicious, it's cool, the pH is cool and dialed in. And I think pH is much more of a critical factor than alcohol percentage, you know. And nobody talks about that because it's not on the label, but that to me is much more important than alcohol, but they have to be in balance.

★   ★   ★   ★

A 2011 wine forum titled World of Pinot Noir became, for a short time, the epicenter of the wine culture wars centered on balance and alcohol. At a panel meant to reflect the range of producers and points of view on pinot noir, Rajat Parr once again found himself at the center of controversy. The panel's moderator,

Eric Asimov, wrote his account of what happened in an article for *The New York Times* titled "A Gadfly in the Pinot Noir." The panel featured Adam Lee, wine-maker and then owner of Siduri, and Michael Browne to represent the richer side of pinot noir, as well as a few California pinot noir pioneers, Jim Clendenen of Au Bon Climat, Adam Tolmach of Ojai, Josh Jensen of Calera, and Parr, from the Central Coast of California to represent a more Burgundian orientation on the grape. From all accounts, the conversation was lively, convivial, and informative. Over lunch, Asimov underscored to me that this was not a tasting event. That is, this was not panelists leading an audience through their wines, though the wine-makers did have wines there for guests to taste. By this time, Parr had already been the center of controversy for the policy he had enacted at the restaurant he had developed with Michael Mina called RN74, named after a road in Burgundy. For wines made with the grapes of Burgundy, particularly pinot noir and chardonnay, Parr had let it be known that he would not put any wine on the list if it had over 14 percent alcohol. In his article, Asimov quoted Parr as saying that he made that choice because it is with wines 14 percent or under that he finds the "most balance and pleasure." The "gadfly" of Asimov's article is the Patton Oswalt look-alike, Adam Lee. Here's how Asimov describes the moment:

> Soon, everybody on the panel had spoken. I was wrapping things up when Mr. Lee grabbed the microphone. The two pinot noirs he had poured earlier were a 2008 Cargasacchi Vineyard from the Santa Rita Hills at 13.6 percent alcohol and a 2009 Keefer Ranch from the Green Valley at 15.2 percent. Now, he wanted to let everybody know that Mr. Parr had just offered to buy some of the Cargasacchi.

Then, Lee delivered the punchline:

> Before I came here I personally took all of the bottles of these two wines, steamed off the labels and re-glued them on the other bottles. The wine that Raj just asked to buy was not the Cargasacchi; it was the Keefer Ranch pinot that is 15.2 percent alcohol.

As Asimov recounts, the "stunt" was immediately used to point out the supposed hypocrisy of the IPOB crowd and the faultiness of its patriarch. In fact, when I interviewed Michael Browne some five years later, he told me this same story, and his narration points to the takeaway of the non-IPOB group:

> [Parr] tastes these wines, and he was like, "Oh yeah, I want this wine on our list. Can I get some of this wine?" Because it was luscious and delicious, and 13.5, how'd you do that? And then at the end of things—he switched the labels. So the wine that Raj Parr really loved was like 15.2. So [Lee] was making a point, and it was very awkward, very awkward. And it was a pretty big deal; people were kind of freaked out by it. But that's Adam Lee. He's

like, "This is bullshit. You liked the wine. Who cares what the alcohol is? You liked it, and you wanted to buy that wine." ... Raj Parr's really cool. His wines are very anorexic, in my opinion, and there's some people that like them; they're a little bit tight for me. But he's going for a different style, and that's cool, and some people like them.

So, for Michael Browne, the event both points to the fact that everyone can enjoy a wine because of its pleasures, whatever the alcohol, and that the problem with the wines of folks like Parr is not that they emphasize the differences in their approach but alienate the consumer who wants pleasure.

For his part, Parr insisted to me that while others became angered by the stunt or felt vindicated by it, he felt it was largely beside the point:

I was just sitting there, and I asked Adam, you know, this wine is nice, I would buy it for the restaurant. Trying to be nice to him, right? And then he reveals that this wine is 14.7 or whatever, it's like—then the press took that... . Eric was pissed off. I was not offended. I was like, whatever, you know, I'm not a super taster [for] the alcohol, not going to be judge what the alcohol— Adam's plug was that nobody can tell alcohol, and I wasn't even thinking about that. But then the press spun it out of control; it became "this guy tricked everyone."

From there, Parr says, the story

just took off, and there were a bunch of bloggers and writers and everyone commenting, and there was—that's when it really got [overblown] and me and Adam, we were like, whatever. We still talk to each other, Michael Browne. I hang out; it didn't change our relationship, but it just became much more heated because I said that and then that happened.

In contrast to Browne in particular but also the press to which Parr refers, Asimov concluded,

In the end, the stunt was counterproductive. Up to that point, the panelists had surprised me by their live-and-let-live attitude. Each had insisted that they would never presume to dictate to others what sorts of wines to make. Yet strikingly, each seemed to feel threatened by any criticism of the style of wines they preferred.

While Parr does see that it was a "cheap stunt," it has not produced enemies nor does he take the consequences of it all that seriously. He says people try to challenge him with blind tastes of wines every day, and he cannot possibly get them all right. In any case, whether the event actually proved anything, the stunt did provide a central moment in these culture wars to which both sides could point.

Asimov also draws a conclusion that really does line up with my experience of talking about these issues with winemakers on both sides. They do tend to emphasize a live-and-let-live attitude, as Michael Browne emphasized many times; however, they staunchly defend what they do and sometimes at the expense of the wines in styles that differ from their own.

★   ★   ★   ★

Parr would no doubt agree with various aspects of the critiques about how people discuss balance offered by Justin Smith and Michael Browne, particularly the idea that achieving balance in a wine certainly does have more to it than just the alcohol level. Undeniably, though, Parr does favor wines, particularly Burgundian wines, that come in under 14 percent ABV, for he does view achieving balance with that level of alcohol in a pinot noir as fairly impossible. What strikes me as one of the important factors in this particular debate is that it complicates the relationship between maker and interpreter in some key ways. While I have introduced this controversy and its positions as particularly one that exists among the believer and nonbelievers, if you will, as Parker's resentment of IPOB suggests, the real controversy might be said to be among a group of winemakers and a group of critics.

Part of the problem is the chicken and egg question; that is, what came first: Parker's favorite producers and wines or Parker's taste? Certainly, as Schoenfeld and many other writers like Alice Feiring have claimed, the fact that Parker has rewarded wines made in a certain style, including a high level of ripeness and alcohol, with high scores has had an effect on the spread and popularization of that style. Schoenfeld summarizes the trend as one of reinforcement and escalation:

> If ripe wines are considered good, many California producers reasoned, those made from grapes brought to the brink of desiccation, to the peak of ripeness (or even a bit beyond), should taste even better. That logical leap has created a new American vernacular for wine, a dense, opaque fruitiness well suited to a nation of Pepsi drinkers. More sweet fruit, more of the glycerol that makes wine feel thicker in the mouth, more alcohol.

How, then, does IPOB become a challenge to interpreters, for instance, critics like Parker and the folks at *Wine Spectator*? They do so by essentially challenging the very grounds of how they interpret. Consider that what those critics favor—that they interpret in a wine as something to be celebrated—IPOB suggests is not only not worthy of praise but might actually be considered a flaw.[46]

In a tellingly titled article written about the end of IPOB, "An Unexpected Twist in CA's Wine Culture Wars," for the online magazine, *Punch*, Jon Bonné reflected on how the critical establishment felt about being challenged, noting, "Defenders of the riper, higher-alcohol wines that once largely defined the state derived a certain satisfaction from savaging the group and its supporters."[47] Writing for *Wine Spectator*'s Mixed Case blog, Mitch Frank claims, "Partisans claim that folks on the other side are not making wine they believe in, they're just making wine that will appeal to fruit bomb-loving critics/acidity-loving hipster somms."[48] In short, both sides in this debate accuse the other of making wines and supporting a certain style as a means to make money.

Frank's view is that this simply is an unfair "cudgel" used on both sides, but one cannot deny that by challenging the critical establishment, IPOB also attempted to carve out a space in the market since Parker and *Wine Spectator* seem to have such power to influence the market. *Wine Spectator* has repeatedly written about IPOB with a certain degree of skepticism. In one article leadingly titled "Tilting at Balance," James Molesworth claims, "Burgundy is the only benchmark for great wine? It can come off as elitist, which is exactly what can make wine no fun."[49] While he says he does not begrudge IPOB for what they do, while simultaneously implying their movement is quixotic, he reinforces the view that ideas are not the driving force: "But let's be honest here: IPOB is less genuine movement and rather more clever marketing—the group's ultimate purpose is to sell wine."[50] Bonné concedes that of course it was marketing: "But it was also a movement, in the way that any reactionary form of music—from grunge to punk to gangster rap—exists in both commercial and aesthetic spheres."[51]

Bonné's contextualization of the struggles of IPOB as part of the culture wars of wine reminds me of how prominent that phrase has been in the world of literary studies. While the literary culture wars had a lot to do with the canon of great books rather than arguably any particular style of writing, it did create an ongoing dialogue about what texts should be studied and how those texts should be interpreted. The canon, after all, had long been thought of by some as having been judged to be great. The many challenges to that notion also sought to redefine the grounds for that judgment. By taking on the question of how wines should be evaluated as well as made, IPOB's push certainly had echoes of a vast array of developing interpretive communities in literary studies that placed an emphasis on race, class, and gender. In literary studies, those critical communities seemed to be rather unambiguously political and derived from strong views of how the world should be and the hopes that literary critical views could change and also help change the world. When Bonné aligns IPOB with something like punk, he suggests that IPOB has more to say about the world than just how wine should be made and judged.

During my conversation with Parr, I, too, began to suspect that when Parr spoke of balance, it seemed to be as much from the philosophical perspective on balance as from the aesthetic sense. When I proposed that it was, Parr asserted, "It's a 100 percent philosophical; it's all philosophy." This brings us back to my suspicion and the question I raised at the start of the previous chapter of whether an examination of these points of view on interpretation in both literature and wine could also suggest an understanding of how to describe the world. It strikes me that while Bonné was onto something when he said that fighting for a piece of the market certainly can be seen as a goal of IPOB, we also ought to realize that, for

Parr, all of these pieces—winemaking, wine judgment, and simply living one's life—should be about pursuing balance.

★   ★   ★   ★

When I had met up with Parr in Lompoc in the fall of 2015, after touring his Domaine de la Côte vineyards and tasting some of his wines, we retired to the back of his facility and spoke at length about IPOB, as well as *The New York Times* article that had seemingly only fanned the controversies. At one point in the conversation, after recounting the history of IPOB, he confessed that if he could get out of the organization, he would. About a year later, he had managed it. In fact, he and Jasmine Hirsch had agreed to close its metaphorical doors.

A few months after the news of IPOB's end had spread, I had a chance to catch up with Parr in New York City. We met at the bar of one of Danny Meyer's Italian restaurants. As always, he appeared relaxed even as he had carved out this lunchtime conversation between hosting a tasting and moving on to a distributor seminar that would feature his wines. It was during this conversation that I asked him to reflect on the World of Pinot incident. When he talks about any controversy he has found himself in, he is wont to declare that he cannot understand how this happens so often because, "you know, even things I say, I don't take all these things that seriously." Of course, Parr has something of the pixie in him; most of these comments have a hint of a chuckle in the delivery. As I pointed out to him, when you say in a manifesto that this will be a gathering of "believers," didn't he think that someone might take offense? He just laughed.

As some of the articles I mentioned above suggest, cynics have accused IPOB of being a marketing tool. Others have doubted exactly what IPOB accomplished. Had it, for instance, redefined what balance is? Just a month prior to this conversation with Parr, I had met with Dan Petroski, who formerly made the wine for

FIGURE 2.3 Raj Parr

the Napa label Larkmead but is now solely with his own label, Massican. A native New Yorker who once worked in publishing and holds an MBA, Petroski has one of the more unusual backgrounds you will encounter in the California wine scene. We met on the kind of rainy day in California where roads close, mudslides are feared, and showing up at a winery marks the visitor as a bit crazed. The rain had chilled the air, and Petroski and I sat in the luxurious, glass-enclosed tasting area of the historic Larkmead winery. Although ownership has changed hands several times, Larkmead's origins go back to the nineteenth century. However, while it was once a testing ground for all sorts of grapes, including some of Petroski's beloved Italian varieties, it is now primarily planted to cabernet sauvignon, like most of the valley. At that time, between his day job at Larkmead and his private label, Dan straddled two sides of these culture wars, though I don't know that Larkmead quite fits what Jon Bonné called Big Flavor.

It doesn't take long for the red-haired and-bearded Petroski to reveal his inner New Yorker. He speaks eloquently, quickly, sprinkled with bursts of colorful obscenity. Like legendary New York Yankee Reggie Jackson, Petroski likes to stir the drink. When our conversation turned to the culture wars, he focused initially on the role of Jon Bonné, whose controversial columns in the *San Francisco Chronicle* and eventually in his book *New California Wine* set the stage for the California culture wars in many ways with its pioneers or outliers combatting the corporate, sometimes faceless forces of Big Flavor. Reflecting on Bonné's departure, Petroski feels a "constant voice for California wine" has been lost. He continued,

> He had self-imposed motivation, he was writing a book about California wine, so he wanted it to be part of the conversation. Well, that conversation when Jon left was part of, I think, the reason why the tension subsided, because he created the tension. He got on the soapbox and he screamed to the heavens, and it was like East Coast–West Coast rap battles, he was always talking about—it was back and forth, who's going to yell at Parker's, Parker cronies, who's going to yell at the California cronies. It was just this weird frickin' thing that was going on, it was politicized, it was tension—and the conversation has stopped. And I agree, we're not a threat. Massican's not a threat to Larkmead.

Laughing, he concluded, "I am large; I contain multitudes." After reflecting on what Dan sees as the decline of the "conversation" around California wines since Jon's departure he also points to another loss, IPOB, and explains why he thinks it stopped: "In Pursuit of Balance decides it's, you know, closed-up shop. Why did they close up shop? They worked their asses off, for what? There was no economic benefit."

In some ways, Dan's theory of the failure of IPOB and also Bonné's role has to do with a theory of social media he encountered. In short, he feels that IPOB and New California Wine made stars of Parr, Hirsch, and Bonné, and by becoming stars, they lost some of their power:

If you're an advertiser, so the superstar actors and actresses who tweet or do whatever, the influence there versus you can get ten micro-influencers who will have a better impact than that one top-notch macro-influencer because the way social media works and the speed of social media, you actually lose a lot viewership in that sense, and you actually lose a lot of impact, and you'll pay more for it as a celebrity or a star. I think what happened with Raj and Jasmine and Jon, they became like—they went from micro-influencers to macro-influencers without knowing it at the time, or us knowing how to define that, and I think they lost a lot of their impact.

When I brought up some of these critiques to Parr when we got together in New York, he argued that IPOB, while not personally benefiting him (he insisted he never even comped expenses for it) had a greater impact than Petroski would suggest. Though Parr will often say something, as I have suggested, with the echo of a chuckle in his voice—a cue that at the least he has a sense of humor about whatever he's saying—he will also flip around and say that he does believe in his views. He believes that it's not enough to hold a philosophical position; you have to act in accord with it: "You gotta go all the way down the line." I tried to steer our conversation to two points I felt had been left hanging: one from our previous conversation and one from earlier in this current one. During my first conversation with Parr, as we explored the concept of balance, I had burst out with the question of whether the issue of balance had more to do with personal beliefs or wine. At that time, he had said philosophy, but our conversation had then veered into an entirely different direction, and I never got him to explain further.

While we sat over some Italian food and an old bottle of Sangiovese, Parr returned to that point. He recalled, "I've admittedly spent many years of my life in a very unbalanced way, and I'm not saying my life is balanced right now," but he implied in the hesitation that balance is the goal now. For wine, from his point of view, he immediately started in an unusual direction for people in the trade in the States: "I went straight to Burgundy. I never went through California wine or Bordeaux or anything else." He continued trying to sort how these two elements, the personal and the wine, came about for him: "I'm not sure if my life [is where the interest in balance started]" and whether "the word was taken out of my existence to the wine, or the other way around. But I'm always, I'm always—you know the Sandhi bottles all have a little Matisse quote on the back of the bottle, you know." The full quote from Matisse to which Parr referred is as follows: "What I dream of is an art in balance, of purity and serenity devoid of troubling or depressing subject matter—a soothing, calming influence, on the mind, rather like a good armchair, which provides relaxation from physical fatigue." Parr then drew making wine, tasting wine, and his sense of balance together by comparing them to what he strives for in cooking:

> When I make wine I think the same thing: what gives you sweet, sour, salty, bitter, bitter being a very essential part of the wine, but that direct comes from

the soil, you don't get bitterness—unless if you over-extract you could, but in a normal way. So then the same idea from life to tasting.

For Parr, a clear continuum exists in how he strives to live his life, what he wants to eat and drink, and the kinds of wines he wants to make.

As to the end of IPOB, if he has regrets about it closing its metaphorical doors, they were not evident over lunch. However, he also has pride in what he did and pushes back against Petroski's claim that it didn't really have an impact. At first, Parr suggested that IPOB began for "a selfish reason to taste other people's wine and discuss how we can achieve freshness in the wine; that was the whole idea." And he demurs at the idea that he wanted to start any kind of movement. However, Parr argues that IPOB had tangible effects on people's careers. He used the example of his friend, the late Jim Clendenon, who sat on the panel at World of Pinot:

He's been making the same wines since 1982. He hasn't changed his style. And he was in a little slump ... . But IPOB comes around, [his business] skyrockets. Everything is selling, his exports are bigger, he sells a lot of wine in Japan, he's a hero in Japan, he has a fan club in Japan. Literally, they printed a business card, Jim Clendenen Fan Club. He has business in England, in Germany, all just because of this conversation.

Parr continues, then, with another example:

I'm not sure you know that—so in Norway it's a state monopoly like in Sweden or Canada. They always buy wine by tender, so they put a tender out: we are looking for blah blah blah wine, this kind of wine. The pinot noir tender two years ago said you have to be in IPOB.

Parr concluded that "the halo effect went everywhere."

★   ★   ★   ★

Thus, it strikes me that there is a remarkable analog between these debates, which leads to some larger conclusions we might draw about interpretation itself. The title of my first chapter deceives because not only am I not against interpretation, I am not against tasting (I could barely function in my job or in my leisure without them). And it seems to me that these all do describe a metaphysics. Let's return here to that particular question about whether types of interpretation imply particular worldviews. First, we might expand our initial discussion of what is meant by that term. An excellent place to go is Stephen Mumford's *Metaphysics: A Very Short Introduction*. For Mumford, metaphysics is "trying to understand the fundamental nature of reality."[52] He distinguishes this attempt from science by saying that the philosophical undertaking is "very general and abstract."[53] For our discussions, Mumford helpfully adds, "Metaphysics seeks to organize and systematize all these specific truths [what can be discovered about the nature of reality] that science discovers and to describe their natural features" and the kinds of questions philosophers ask help in "getting into the issues of properties in general and particulars in general."[54] It might be that, at best, our current use resembles how Mumford defines Immanuel Kant's take: "One way [to understand Kant's view of metaphysics] is [to] see his metaphysics as a description of the structure of our thinking about the world, rather than being about the world itself."[55] Theories of interpretation, then—while sometimes applied specifically to a given object, literature, film, art, and so on—can be said to be based in a metaphysics because how to interpret is often linked with how we should best think about something in order to understand it. It strikes me that the debates about how to taste and evaluate wine and how to interpret literature get so passionate and fiery (tasting notes are "pernicious"!) because underlying this haggling are ideas about how we should *understand* this world, how we ought to *think* about it, and often how we ought to *live* in it.

This is not to say, however, that any of these ideas lead to consistency. Just because I think that the fundamental nature of the world is *A* does not mean that all my thinking about the world will be consistent with *A*. This problem of consistency undermines a lot of the arguments about interpretation or at the least complicates them. To begin with a theory of interpretation and then to apply it because you think that this theory is always the most accurate way to interpret, to understand, and so on may be best considered useful in the abstract but maddeningly unreliable in practice. While humans rarely manage to consistently apply their operating theory to their practice, other human beings tend to become infinitely frustrated with this failure.

We see this problem all the time in how people respond to rulings by the United States Supreme Court. The Supreme Court rulings regarding same-sex marriage and the surrounding coverage offer a case in point. Consider this recap of the late Justice Scalia's objections by Mark Joseph Stern at the online magazine *Slate*:

> In a predictably raging dissent, Justice Antonin Scalia accuses the majority of writing "the mystical aphorisms of the fortune cookie," and howls that its "opinion is couched in a style that is as pretentious as its content is egotistic." The opinion's "showy profundities," he writes, "are often profoundly incoherent." He also calls the ruling a "threat to American democracy."[56]

Although I am tempted to recap some of the discussions of tasting notes as I look over this language, I will hold off to continue with the point. None of this outrage surprised people exactly since Scalia has been consistently opposed to same-sex marriage. It was the inconsistencies in Scalia's rulings that seemed to particularly gall commentators like Jon Stewart. As Stern pointed out in a separate article on *Slate*, Scalia's logic for opposing the same-sex marriage ruling of the Court stands in opposition to his views of a case regarding national health care:

> Justice Antonin Scalia's dissent is equally hypocritical, especially in light of his *King v. Burwell* dissent just yesterday. Scalia calls the decision a "judge-empowering" "Putsch" based on "hubris," a "naked judicial claim to legislative—indeed, super-

legislative power." These complaints, arriving exactly one day after Scalia hoped to cripple a major act of Congress through a strained, implausible reading of one phrase in a sub-sub-subsection, rings quite hollow.

Stewart's litany of Scalia's contradictions is even more extensive, but I think this will suffice.

Now, of course, these are all highly charged political issues and of the kind that rankles folks from the start. However, even fewer political examples would show that people want to see others remain consistent in applying their theory to their practice—to be, if you will, guided by their metaphysics. I am sympathetic, however, to the fact that people may in fact develop a theory from practice and that, well, we can only invent theory sometimes in the aftermath of practice. Perhaps the view that most accepts the problems of this gap in theory and practice would be pragmatism. In Louis Menand's wonderful intellectual history of American pragmatism, *The Metaphysical Club,* he outlines how pragmatism understands how humans make decisions. Menand begins with a statement he concedes is "banal": "People reach decisions, most of the time, by thinking."[57] What Menand says interferes with or complicates "principles" is always "circumstances," the factors that make sorting out what your principles exactly say to do in a given moment so difficult. As Menand remarks after giving a hypothetical example of decision-making, "In the end, you will do what you believe is 'right', but 'rightness' will be, in effect, the compliment you give to the outcome of your deliberations."[58] In other words, our sense of having followed principle properly only results out of the end: "When we think ... we do not simply consult principles, or reasons, or sentiments, or tastes; for prior to thinking, all things are indeterminate. Thinking is what makes them real." He derives this conclusion in part from the example of deciding what to order in a restaurant: "Deciding to order the lobster helps us to determine that we have a taste for lobster."[59] In essence, Scalia's explanations for his decisions all come after he has reached his decision.

Is the same true for literary interpretation, for wine tasting? Perhaps we might think of the fact that to some extent we can only arrive at our metaphysics, our theories of interpretation, how best to interpret, how best to taste, evaluate, to write about wine, after we have done so. That it is, in Menand's phrase, simply the compliment we give to ourselves as part of explaining how we have arrived at our judgment. It forms, at least, one way of dealing with the seeming contradictions that can interfere with the application of worldviews, of principles, or even of supposed tastes. ("How can you like this merlot? You don't even like merlot!" Or, "I like this wine; therefore it must be balanced because I only like wines that are balanced.")

In fact, if one buys the argument that Mailloux offers, that there can be no secure foundation for any form of interpretation but only the constant need to persuade others of the best means in an ongoing contingency, then you are no doubt also lining up with larger notions of antifoundationalism such as those offered by philosophers like Richard Rorty. We cannot really get around interpretation or perhaps even tasting—or the arguments that go along with them. It strikes me that both Broadbent and Sontag take paradoxical positions since only through interpretation can they determine what interpretation or what tasting should take place and which should be verboten. In some ways, we can find ourselves back in the dilemma of needing Rhyme and Reason to square and reconcile the interpretive vulnerabilities that lie behind and through the bold declarations of numbers and words. I am inclined to draw no lines with permanent marker.

Notes

1 Anthony Gottlieb, *The Dream of Reason: A History of Western Philosophy from the Greeks to the Renaissance* (New York: W.W. Norton & Company, 2016), 28, 29.
2 Ellen McCoy, *Emperor of Wine: The Rise of Robert M. Parker, Jr., and the Reign of American Taste* (New York: Ecco, 2005), 63.
3 Hugh Johnson, *A Life Uncorked* (Oakland: University of California Press, 2006), 40.
4 Matt Kramer, *True Taste: The Seven Essential Wine Words* (Kennebunkport: Cider Mill Press, 2015), 19.
5 James Laube, "Grading the 100-Point Scale," *James Laube's Wine Flights, Wine Spectator*, online blog (November 11, 2013).
6 Ibid.
7 Hugh Johnson, *A Life Uncorked* (Oakland: University of California Press, 2006), 41.
8 Eric Asimov, *How to Love Wine: A Memoir and a Manifesto* (New York: William Morrow, 2012), 166.
9 Hugh Johnson, *A Life Uncorked* (Oakland: University of California Press, 2006), 42–43.
10 Eric Asimov, *How to Love Wine: A Memoir and a Manifesto* (New York: William Morrow, 2012), 167.
11 Hugh Johnson, *A Life Uncorked* (Oakland: University of California Press, 2006), 41.
12 The website Wine Berserkers has a similar thread mocking the word choices of reviewers, titled "Critic Bingo." It has over 450 entries in the thread at the time of this writing.
13 Michael Broadbent, *Michael Broadbent's Wine Tasting* (London: Mitchell Beazley, 2003), 92–93.
14 Ibid., 93.
15 Matt Kramer, *True Taste: The Seven Essential Wine Words* (Kennebunkport: Cider Mill Press, 2015), 61.
16 Ibid., 23.
17 Ibid., 18.
18 Ibid., 20.
19 Ibid., 23.
20 Ellen McCoy, *Emperor of Wine: The Rise of Robert M. Parker, Jr., and the Reign of American Taste* (New York: Ecco, 2005), 268.
21 Ibid., 269.
22 Maynard Amerine and Edward B. Roessler, *Wines: Their Sensory Evaluation* (New York: W.H. Freeman & Company, 1976), 197.
23 Ibid.
24 Thomas Mclaighlin, "Figurative Language," in *Critical Terms for Literary Study*, ed. Frank Lentricchia and Thomas McLaughlin, 2nd ed. (Chicago: University of Chicago Press, 1995), 82.
25 Matt Kramer, *True Taste: The Seven Essential Wine Words* (Kennebunkport: Cider Mill Press, 2015), 20.
26 Ellen McCoy, *Emperor of Wine: The Rise of Robert M. Parker, Jr., and the Reign of American Taste* (New York: Ecco, 2005), 271.

27 Ibid.
28 Ibid.
29 Eric Asimov, *How to Love Wine: A Memoir and a Manifesto* (New York: William Morrow, 2012), 84.
30 Ibid., 85.
31 Matt Kramer, *True Taste: The Seven Essential Wine Words* (Kennebunkport: Cider Mill Press, 2015), 29.
32 Ibid., 74.
33 Ibid., 75.
34 Ibid.
35 Ibid.
36 Ibid.
37 M.H. Abrams, *A Glossary of Literary Terms*, 11th ed. (Boston: Cengage Learning, 2014), 70.
38 Adrienne Lehrer, "Can Wines be Brawny?: Reflections on Wine Vocabulary," in *Questions of Taste: The Philosophy of Wine*, ed. Barry C. Smith (Oxford: Oxford University Press, 2007), 128.
39 Ibid.
40 In response to similar issues they perceive in terms of the value-laden nature of the humanistic practice of close reading, Franco Morretti and Matthew L. Jockers have pushed for something Moretti calls "distant reading" and Jockers's "macroanalysis" that essentially draws upon attempting to read literature in large quantities at once by studying things like the frequency of certain words and syntactical patterns in Victorian novels.
41 Ibid.
42 M.H. Abrams, *A Glossary of Literary Terms*, 11th ed. (Boston: Cengage Learning, 2014), 72.
43 Adrienne Lehrer, "Can Wines be Brawny?: Reflections on Wine Vocabulary," in *Questions of Taste: The Philosophy of Wine*, ed. Barry C. Smith (Oxford: Oxford University Press, 2007), 134.
44 Jamie Goode, *I Taste Red: The Science of Tasting Wine* (Oakland: University of California Press, 2016), 14.
45 Bruce Schoenfeld, "Wrath of Grapes," *New York Times Magazine* (May 28, 2015).
46 Bruce Schoenfeld, "Wrath of Grapes," *New York Times Magazine* (May 28, 2015). www.nytimes.com/2015/05/31/magazine/the-wrath-of-grapes.html.
47 Jon Bonné, "An Unexpected Twist in CA's Wine Culture Wars," *Punch* (May 24, 2016).
48 Mitch Frank, "Wine Doesn't Feel Wrath," *Mixed Case: Opinion and Advice* (online blog), *Wine Spectator*.
49 James Molesworth, "Tilting at Balance," *Stirring the Lees with James Molesworth* (online blog), *Wine Spectator* (February 24, 2015).
50 Ibid.
51 Jon Bonné, "An Unexpected Twist in CA's Wine Culture Wars," *Punch* (24 May 2016).
52 Stephen Mumford, *Metaphysics: A Very Short Introduction* (Oxford: Oxford University Press, 2012), 99.
53 Ibid.
54 Ibid.
55 Ibid., 101.
56 Mark Joseph Stern, "Supreme Court 2015: The Conservative Justices' Gay Marriage Dissents Are Petty and Hypocritical," *Slate* (June 26, 2015).
57 Louis Menand, *The Metaphysical Club: A Story of Ideas in America* (New York: Farrar, Strauss & Giroux, 2002), 352.
58 Ibid.
59 Ibid.

References

Abrams, M.H. *A Glossary of Literary Terms*. 11th ed. Boston: Cengage Learning, 2014.

Amerine, Maynard and Edward B. Roessler. *Wines: Their Sensory Evaluation*. New York: W. H. Freeman & Company, 1976.

Asimov, Eric. *How to Love Wine: A Memoir and a Manifesto*. New York: William Morrow, 2012.

Bonné, Jon. "An Unexpected Twist in CA's Wine Culture Wars," *Punch*, 24 May, 2016. https://punchdrink.com/articles/what-the-end-of-ipob-means-for-ca-wine-culture-wars/

Broadbent, Michael. *Michael Broadbent's Wine Tasting*. London: Mitchell Beazley, 2003.

Frank, Mitch. "Wine Doesn't Feel Wrath." Mixed Case: Opinion and Advice. Online blog. *Wine Spectator*, June 12, 2015. www.winespectator.com/articles/wine-doesnt-feel-wrath-51742.

Goode, Jamie. *I Taste Red: The Science of Tasting Wine*. Oakland: University of California Press, 2016.

Gottlieb, Anthony. *The Dream of Reason: A History of Western Philosophy from the Greeks to the Renaissance*. New York: W.W. Norton & Company, 2016.

Johnson, Hugh. *A Life Uncorked*. Oakland: University of California Press, 2006.

Kramer, Matt. *True Taste: The Seven Essential Wine Words*. Kennebunkport: Cider Mill Press, 2015.

Laube, James. "Grading the 100-Point Scale." James Laube's Wine Flights. Online blog. *Wine Spectator*, November 11, 2013. www.winespectator.com/articles/grading-the-100-point-scale-49214.

Lehrer, Adrienne. "Can Wines be Brawny?: Reflections on Wine Vocabulary." In *Questions of Taste: The Philosophy of Wine*, edited by Barry C. Smith. Oxford: Oxford University Press, 2007.

McCoy, Ellen. *Emperor of Wine: The Rise of Robert M. Parker, Jr., and the Reign of American Taste*. New York: Ecco, 2005.

Mclaighlin, Thomas. "Figurative Language." In *Critical Terms for Literary Study*, edited by Frank Lentricchia and Thomas McLaughlin. 2nd ed. Chicago: University of Chicago Press, 1995.

Menand, Louis. *The Metaphysical Club: A Story of Ideas in America*. New York: Farrar, Strauss & Giroux, 2002.

Molesworth, James. "Tilting at Balance." Stirring the Lees with James Molesworth. Online blog. *Wine Spectator*, February 24, 2015. www.winespectator.com/articles/tilting-at-balance-51250.

Mumford, Stephen. *Metaphysics: A Very Short Introduction*. Oxford: Oxford University Press, 2012.

Schoenfeld, Bruce. "Wrath of Grapes." *New York Times Magazine*, May 28, 2015. www.nytimes.com/2015/05/31/magazine/the-wrath-of-grapes.html.

Stern, Mark Joseph. "Supreme Court 2015: The Conservative Justices' Gay Marriage Dissents Are Petty and Hypocritical." *Slate*, June 26, 2015. https://slate.com/news-and-politics/2015/06/supreme-court-2015-the-conservative-justices-gay-marriage-dissents-are-petty-and-hypocritical.html.

3

DEATH OF THE WINEMAKER

Are Winemakers Artists?

Standing in profile across from Evelyn Mulray, the enormous white bandage on his nose visible to the camera, Jake Gittes explains that he has not had a day like this since his time working for the district attorney in Chinatown, in the film of the same name. "Doing what?" Evelyn asks. "As little as possible." At the end of the film, Gittes will repeat the line after Evelyn has been shot through the eye trying to save her daughter from her incestuous father. It is one of the bleakest final scenes ever filmed. Chinatown, in the film, represents a place where comprehension of events always seems out of reach. The best you can do, then, is not to act because you cannot do the right thing when you do not really understand what the best thing is. Gittes fails, in part, because he has twice—once in the past and again in the present of the film—tried to do something and tragedy ensued. The film's underlying philosophical stance veers then from the existentialism typical of *noir* to a kind of weary, almost unbearable nihilism where actions not only do not have meaning but can only further worsen the world.

This probably seems like a strange place to continue our discussion about wine and art, but the phrase "Do as little as possible" has been echoing in my head for the last several years. It started during casual visits to wineries where either the winemaker or the tasting coordinator would inform my group that the wine we held in our glass had been manipulated as little as possible, that the wine had been made in the hopes of translating the vineyard site with as little interference as possible. They foreswore such techniques as reverse osmosis, which removed alcohol from the wine, adding acid or sugar, or in any way intensifying color through the addition of the concentrate Mega Purple. At first, I shrugged and nodded at these claims in the same way I would when told whether the winemaker had preferred the chardonnay to undergo malolactic fermentation or just how much new oak this wine had encountered. However, as I kept hearing the phrase, it started to ring in my ear as almost a kind of political stance or a

DOI: 10.4324/9781003399810-4

philosophy, and it seemed to imply that there were others out there—though I would never meet them—who did more than a little to the wine. *Do as little as possible*, I would think to myself.

★   ★   ★   ★

The more time I have spent with winemakers, the more I have come to realize that this phrase is both remarkably straightforward—it means for the winemaker to do the bare requisite needed to transform grapes into wine-—and also, in its place in the discourse around wine, far richer and loaded with implication than its more obvious meaning. Like seemingly all language, the phrase is quite open to inter- pretation; simply put, what one winemaker might take as "doing as little as possi- ble" might be far more than the next winemaker would venture to do. As Steve Matthiasson suggested to me as we sat in his backyard, everyone draws their own lines. *Little*, then, is a relative term in this construction. In essence, that little depends largely on an interpretation in concert with a view that they seek to construct of themselves. To those outside the wine world, doing as little as possible can invoke a kind of magisterial ride where the grapes, almost as in a minimalist magic show, become wine, as the winemaker does little more than press the juice out of the grapes and move them from one vessel to the next. This may be con- sidered one version of what winemaker Abe Schoener calls the sentimental or pastoral myth of winemaking. Clark Smith, in his controversial treatise *Postmodern Winemaking*, suggests that this impression of grapes mystically transforming derives from the fact that the "winemaker will often be less than frank about the treat- ments his wine has undergone."[1] Smith considers winemaking a form of cooking, and thus, winemaking using technology should be viewed more like it is in the culinary world, where technological innovation—like *sous vide* machines—are not looked at with the same level of suspicion. In the wine world, Smith claims, technological innovations have not been largely publicized, so "wines got way better" but "by magic, folks are left to suppose."[2] Smith sees wine critics who are suspicious of these new technologies as creating a controversy over "manipulation" that should not exist. Clearly Smith is critical of a view that sees winemaking in terms of feeling rather than reason. However, ironically, in disputes I will cover in later chapters, Smith seems to support the opposite position. Some of this con- troversy has to do with the current debates in the wine world surrounding what has come to be called "natural wines." In fact, Smith has often been targeted by Alice Feiring, a wine writer and champion of "natural wines," as a symbol of "spoofulated wines," Feiring's term for manipulated wines. My focus in this chap- ter, however, will be more on the implications for "manipulation" in terms of how winemakers interpret what they do and what they produce. I will take up the question of natural wines in the following chapter. For now, my focus will be on how this phrase interacts with questions of the degree to which winemaking aspires to artistry, for, in short, not all winemakers would see this talk of doing as little as possible in quite the same light as Clark Smith.

★   ★   ★   ★

I had made the drive north from Napa up the Silverado trail, passing the divided verdant rows of trellised grapes that run up short of the sloping edge of the valley wall, and turned right through the stucco and iron gates of Chimney Rock before pulling up in front of the famous Cape Dutch buildings of the estate now owned by the Terlato group. A few minutes later, I stood in front of the vineyards with Elizabeth Vianna, the Brazilian-American winemaker, who began explaining to me that at Chimney Rock, they "try to do as little as possible." However, when pushed a little bit on the subject, Elizabeth realized that while they try to do as little as possible, there is in fact quite a lot that they actually do—in the vineyard, after harvest, while in barrel, in making selections, and in blending. I would venture to say, though, that nothing Elizabeth described that happens in the making of her wine would be particularly unusual for any other winemaker. So the question becomes, then, why is this the default phrase? Why call all of this important work *little*? Why, if not calling the methods minimal, do winemakers invoke another description that means more or less the same thing, noninterventionist? Why, for winemakers, does seeming to do very little in making the thing upon which your occupational identity is based become both a matter of form and of pride? After all, a winemaker makes wine, a thought as mundane and tautological as saying that a wine tastes grapey. Was repeating this claim hiding the truth as Clark Smith suggests, or helping to perpetuate a myth as Abe Schoener seems to imply? I cannot imagine, for instance, even the most libertarian of presidents, despite their allegiance to free markets or small government, standing before the American people and proudly saying, "I try to do as little as possible in running the United States government."

Wine very rarely makes itself except under the guidance of a winemaker. The very word *make* evokes a series of other questions that also trouble the winemaking world. Consider that the ancient Greek word *poetes*, which means maker or to create, forms the etymology of the word *poet*. Although not all makers of things get described as artists—a term I am using broadly to encompass all producers of creative arts, such as poets, writers, painters, sculptors, and musicians—all artists do make or create art. While not a terribly profound thought, laying claim to that notion of creating seems essential to thinking about oneself as an artist. Consider James Joyce's Stephen Daedelus's famous proclamation at the end of *A Portrait of the Artist as a Young Man*: "I go to encounter for the millionth time the reality of experience and to forge in the smithy of my soul the uncreated conscience of my race."[3] Joyce's protagonist here and elsewhere sees that artist next to God, as a creator, as a maker of things, ideas, and art. However, Stephen also explicitly ties the imagery, invoking his mythical namesake, to other kinds of making not always elevated by the culture to the status of art with the phrase "to forge in the smithy."

What has become clear to me over the last few years is that winemakers, particularly the winemakers I met who make relatively small amounts of wine, within relatively small-scale operations, would be much more comfortable comparing themselves to blacksmiths using substances brought forth from the earth than to someone like Joyce. These winemakers do not totally dismiss the idea that there are artists in their ranks, but they tend to deny, with some variation, that they themselves are artists. To be a winemaker who is an artist is, in the winemaker's world, generally a bad thing.[4] I vividly remember winemaker and viticulturist Steve Matthiasson joyfully cavorting around his front yard, late into the evening, laughing and calling to me that he'd be sure to avoid those artist wines! Matthiasson may have thought the matter a bit overdramatic, but most winemakers I've met do reject Clark Smith's assertion that "all wines"—with no exceptions— "become distinctive through artifice."[5] Usually, winemakers express this view almost instinctively, like Elizabeth did, especially when I first meet them.

Let me explain by way of a few examples. In the pristine, metallic, and shiny space that hosts the operations for Michael Browne's former wine projects, Kosta Browne and Cirq, Michael and I stood with his newly promoted winemaker, Nico Cueva, as Michael spoke volubly, and by necessity loudly, about what he and his team strive to do at Kosta Browne.[6] Speaking forcefully over both the ventilation system and the seemingly endless hits of Michael Jackson being played over the loudspeakers, Michael began making a series of analogies to music. I took this as an invitation to ask about a more direct comparison and raise the notions of creativity and being an artist. Michael stopped talking, stepped back, and looked at me directly to emphatically deny that he was an artist.

> Yeah, and the way I look at it, and there's a lot of people making wine out there that think they are artists: I'm in control of this, and I'm going to make it mine, you know? Well, you kind of rip the soul out of it, in my opinion. And that's fine; people do what they're going to do.

Although Nico claimed that a winemaker had to deal with something like 40,000 variables, navigating those could be seen as a mixture of science and instinct formed from experience but not an artistic sensibility. Artist winemakers, Michael went on to suggest, were folks that heavily put their mark on whatever wine they made: "Work the wines too much, or control it too much, or they want to make it theirs, right." In short, those artistic winemakers intervened.

I grew to feel that if I were to raise the question of artistry, I should try to do so by way of the backdoor. Instead of raising the question of whether a winemaker's work compared to an artist—and I grew to realize that, for some reason, the word *artist* always evoked someone like Kandinsky or Rothko, folks associated with abstraction—I would instead ask whether winemaking involved creativity or allowed them to express themselves.

★   ★   ★   ★

Justin Smith laughs easily. He stands roughly a hair under six feet tall, he's thin, and on the day we met, he had a knit cap pulled down tight on his head, guarding

FIGURE 3.1 Justin Smith in his caves, near his new fermentation eggs

against what passed for a chilly morning in notoriously warm Paso Robles. We had left the back end of Saxum's newly blasted caves and found ourselves next to a custom-made fermentation egg forged, he told me, from the very rock that had been removed to form the caves.

He loves music, like many of the winemakers I have met, and I used that as a gateway. He chuckled at the comparison to making music, but when asked about whether winemaking involved being creative, he immediately said yes. However, Justin has a cautionary tale about the time that he pushed things too far, when he thought, *Well, let's see just how ripe I can get my grapes before I pick them.* That year, Justin ran into problems. He'd gone too far, and when he intervened to try to save his wine, using all the creativity at his disposal, that's when he really screwed it up. "Do as little as possible."

A similar sort of story seems to hang over Ted Lemon. In some ways, it is hard to find two people more different, and wines more different, than Ted and Michael Browne. Yet, both dismissed the idea that they were artists in ways that evoked Jake Gittes, for each of them felt that what winemakers lack—and what they found themselves reminded of over and over even in a genial growing region like California—is control (though ironically, Jake's main antagonist in *Chinatown* seeks to control the environment by manipulating the water supply). No, for both men, control belongs to nature. To act as if you were in control was to court tragedy. As another winemaker, Morgan Twain-Peterson, suggested to me, even if a winemaker might guess right or see the weather has changed, he will still probably struggle to get his crew together and get his grapes picked. The best you can do is adapt, improvise, and react quickly.

★   ★   ★   ★

Ted and I sat in a small, bare room, in what might pass for a kitchen in a warehouse, both leaning toward each other over a brown table. He wore a dark brown knitted sweater with elbow patches, a kind of perfect representation for Ted, who could declare himself a farmer one moment and then ease, professorially, into a discussion of shifts in scientific paradigms the next. Early in Ted's life, before he famously became the first American to run a Burgundy estate, the esteemed Domaine Roulot, he had taken some time off to write the Great American Novel. He spent that year, he sheepishly confesses, *not* completing the Great American Novel. For Ted, however, that attempt had been instructive. Ted's father, a writer and editor, had been angered by Ted's plan not because he wanted to be a writer but because his father felt that Ted simply did not yet know how to do it. He had not learned his craft. He would not make a similar mistake as a vigneron.

Craft, it will turn out, has a big role to play in understanding how winemakers think about what they do, but instead of following up on that, I asked Ted about whether he saw much relationship between those writerly aspirations and his future career in winemaking. He seemed resistant to make the connection, so I brought up something he had said years ago: "Less is better; listen to the vintage and the vineyard. Don't be afraid to take radical steps, but make sure you know when they are required and when to do nothing." When asked if this winemaking philosophy had altered much over the years, Ted said, no, it really had not. Ted's philosophy underscores his overriding desire to be invisible to the drinker of his wines. Asked if winemaking involved creativity, he hesitated because the answer is not straightforward. "I think if you start thinking you're artistic, you're not going to make wines of place, because suddenly you're elevating yourself above the place the fruit came from." The issue for Ted might also be seen in terms of ego, for if you're making art, "It's becoming you and not the place." This same idea hangs behind Michael Browne's assertions on the subject. Lemon spoke of a time when he, like Justin Smith, also had to "take radical steps." A few years back, forest fires had a very strong impact on the grapes grown in Anderson County, leaving the wine possibly overwhelmed by acrid smoke flavors. Ted began to describe some of the extreme measures he had to take to try reduce that smokiness and save that wine. Excited, I said, "Well that certainly demonstrated creativity!" Then, patiently, explaining his ideas to an overly enthusiastic student, Ted said plainly, "I don't want to have to be creative." In fact, being creative, taking "radical steps," is about the last thing Ted ever wants to do, but Ted, echoing Michael exactly, said there are years where Mother Nature lets you know quite clearly that she is in charge, and then you just have to do the best you can. This lesson also resembles the one that Justin learned when he thought he could pick grapes at such an extreme level of ripeness.

★   ★   ★   ★

The hesitation I found in winemakers as seemingly different as Michael Browne and Ted Lemon to see themselves as creative artists, as the authors of their wine, has led me to think of two seemingly radical theories of the role of author in the history of literature and literary criticism. Although these two theories seem quite similar, they tend to get associated with two very different philosophical positions on human agency, one clearly aligned with a culture of feeling and the other a bit more so with reason. The first is derived from the English Romantic poets, such as Coleridge, Wordsworth, and Shelley. One of the twentieth century's great critics of Romanticism, M.H. Abrams makes the case that starting with Coleridge, the Romantic poets used the figure of the Aeolian lyre or harp as a "persistent analogue of the poetic mind, the figurative mediator between outer motion and inner emotion."[7] Those harps, a kind of sophisticated, ancient wind charm, become a way of understanding how nature—in the form here of wind, which Abrams reminds us permeates much Romantic poetry—flows through the harp, a stand-in for the poet, producing music. This way of thinking about artistic creation both humbles the artist—she becomes simply a conduit for nature's inspirational force— and elevates the artist, for only a select few can act as these instruments of nature and can thus produce beautiful music, grand art.

When winemakers tell me that their goal is for the land to speak through the wines, to achieve a kind of transparency of place, they can thus sound a lot like Romantic poets, or American figures like Walt Whitman who saw the land as his poetic source, or Aldo Leopold in works like "Thinking Like a Mountain." On the one hand, there is something remarkably humbling in this rhetoric, for it is not then about the ego of the winemaker; what they seek is not so much to express themselves, but to aid in the land expressing itself, to become a conduit or perhaps an amplifier of nature's voice like all those metaphoric winds of Romanticism. However, it also speaks to the question of how winemakers can become great and still make wines that are not about them; they become the great transmitters of the land, or to use two linked phrases that winemakers have employed, the interpreters or the translators of the land.

Winemakers can get pretty emotional talking about the land, but for the most part, they tend to be more pragmatists than Romanticists. Clark Smith has argued that this Romantic conception of "Naturalness in wine is an illusion born of much study and struggle."[8] In other words, winemakers "ought to be proud of what they do instead of pretending to do nothing."[9]

Others simply seem skeptical of the illusion itself. The winemaker and owner of Forlorn Hope, Matthew Rorick, not only makes wine but has, in the past, made guitars. Like many winemakers I've met, Matthew also has a strong connection to music, and indeed he plays. As we talked through the notion of whether he felt a kinship between playing guitar and making wine, his face tightened for a moment before answering. Matthew told me afterward regarding many of his answers to my questions, although he "was sometimes sarcastic and had a bit of fun with some of [his] responses, [he] did speak from the heart." The answer he gave me to this question fits this ironic sheltering of the "heartfelt." His way of describing the creation of music at its highest actually spoke to a kind of Romantic ideal, since for him it meant losing self-consciousness, of the ego dropping out, as the music, often played with others, seemed to be almost spontaneously created—the poet becoming the instrument of the imagination. In winemaking, however, he never reached that kind of creative fugue state; he always had to pay attention to what he did, always be aware of the details—perhaps a version of what Smith calls "a very intensive sort of doing nothing"[10]—but, as Matthew told me on another occasion, winemaking is very process oriented. In contrast, when Matthew imagines this Romantic ideal of wine transforming by way of a mystical or natural process, he conjures a vision of the winemaker as artist akin to a sort of Jesus figure:

> Maybe there are winemakers out there who are just like that, when they come into harvest, and they're just floating off the ground with their arms out like a Jesus figure and they're just pointing at things like, "Press that! Barrel that down!" and then they wake up two months later, like, 'Was it good? Did harvest go well?' Like, "Yeah, man, you were awesome!" "I was just in the flow, man. I mean, I saw grapes, I saw people, but I didn't really know what was going on, I was just like, yeeeaah!"

Simply by gesture, these imaginary winemakers transform the bounty of the land into something that might end up at your dinner table. This mocking depiction of a romanticized winemaking would seem to be in at least part due to the failure to acknowledge the rational steps that proper wine making requires.

Many years ago, Matthew shared a workspace with another winemaker, Abe Schoener. Matthew briefly moved away from oenology to pursue a graduate degree in anthropology from the University of Chicago, and Abe has a doctorate in philosophy and in fact taught for many years at his alma mater, St. John's College, before taking a sabbatical to wine country from which he never returned. Abe sees two distinct ways

FIGURE 3.2 Matthew Rorick among his barrels

that ideas out of Romanticism seem either to cloud or be at work in the way wine-makers and observers of winemakers—whether writers, critics, or simply wine enthusiasts—think of winemaking. While reflecting on the general public's perception of vineyards, Abe declares, "There's absolutely what I would call a sentimental worship of the vineyard." Abe goes on to explain that "the people who worship the vineyards have no understanding of them, and that's why I call the worship of the vineyards sentimental," for

> when I say sentimental, the other word I have in mind at the same time is pastoral. […] None of this discourse is aimed at people who live in the country. It's aimed at people who live in the city. It's pastoral. All of it is pastoral.

I will explore Abe's ideas about the pastoral, which intersect with Michael Pollan's concept of the "supermarket pastoral," at greater length in the next chapter, but here it's worth considering that, for Abe, this emphasis on the winemaker as "translating" the vineyard is a kind of sentimentalizing and really narrative building, that in many ways echoes Clark Smith's critique that there is a mystification at work. Abe suggests that this is particularly aimed at consumers of wine who have become distanced from farming, living lives where food products appear neatly packaged for consumption, but who now seek a greater authenticity in their relation to food—and wine. Thus, it is a failure to properly interpret the winemaking process but it also points to what Mailloux describes is central to interpretation in that we find winemakers interpreting for two audiences—themselves and consumers.

Matthew's irony-laced skepticism and Abe's critique lead us back to the second theory I would like to entertain. Our contemporary understanding of the author or poet as a creator, a powerful figure of imagination, owes a lot to the Romantic poets for whom the poetic point of view so closely resembled the poet himself. Roland Barthes, a French writer, participated in two distinct movements that pushed back against those conceptions of what authors do. His essay, "The Death of the Author," is often seen as part of Barthes' transition from his structuralist phase—which was an approach that sought a very scientist, objective, and rationale analysis of culture—towards a more post-structuralist position, seen largely through the essay's critique of what Derrida called the "transcendental signifier"—here, the author. The author, in a now traditional conception, Barthes argued, placed a limit on a given text's meaning, for "the explanation of a work is always sought in the man or woman who produced it."[11] For Barthes, this explanation, which sees something like literature as the "voice of a single person, the author 'confiding' in us," fails to accurately describe the way culture works. Though folks like the Romantic poets may have cultivated this notion of the author, it is really an illusion—an illusion of control.

Putting aside some of the structuralist linguistics that Barthes draws upon to make his argument to replace the author with a figure he calls the "modern scriptor," we can turn to the key alteration Barthes makes to our conceptions of how art is produced, as it has the most resonance for our discussion of winemaking.

Barthes asserts that the "text [poetry, art, novels, etc.] is a tissue of quotations drawn from the innumerable centers of culture."[12] In other words, writers do not invent or create unique, wholly original art; instead, what they do is connect elements of the culture together into a form that can be understood within the context of that culture. An example might help make the case simpler. Consider Shakespeare, who wrote many plays but almost always drew upon either stories already alive in his culture, myths, or narrative histories of his own culture. Nevertheless, he made those plays sites in which his own culture could recognize itself and see issues related to contemporary politics, social questions, and the arts. Because Barthes favored dramatic rhetoric, including calling his essay "The Death of the Author," people can feel threatened by his claims. Many of my students over the years have read this argument as suggesting writers lack originality, that they are simply byways through which parts of the culture get relayed in different combinations back to the members of that very same culture. While for Barthes the writer is never akin to a supreme maker—he is in fact arguing against the notion of the author on that level too—his views do not suggest that the "modern scriptor" cannot be skilled. Again, we can consider Shakespeare, whom the critic Stephen Greenblatt identifies as an exemplar of someone who "improvised" within his culture. Shakespeare makes clear that not all "scriptors" are created equally: some find ways to be inventive and creative as they take pieces of the culture into unusual, unexpected, or simply powerful combinations.

This second model of the writer, then, might be said to resemble the way in which many winemakers interpret their work. They acknowledge their lack of control and accept that they are not the starting point for the creation of great wine, for that starts outside themselves in the land. Although no one, with the possible exception of a court reporter or stenographer, is likely to embrace a title like modern scriptor, the idea of a figure who takes something else—cultivating grapes from a very specific parcel of land, let's say—and recombines it with other natural elements such as native yeasts and wood in the form of barrels, and helps shepherd these elements of the land to become wine most certainly has appeal to winemakers' sense of what they do. These are the winemakers for whom the term *terroir* is an ideal. Winemakers who would instead see themselves as authors can never be said to embrace the notion of *terroir*, for what they produce always reflects themselves rather than the land. Therefore, following Barthes' logic, those winemakers make all their wine "mean" one thing; it is a path that returns back to them rather than a proliferating invitation to the land, its history, its particularity, and the culture that helped produce that wine in that place. This artist conception strikes me as antithetical to Romanticism since it argues against concerns with individual interiority.

★   ★   ★   ★

While these theories of the artist that see the artist as catalyst, interpreter, or translator rather than a source may help explain what it is winemakers do or believe they do, it does not necessarily follow that winemakers are artists and that what they produce is art. This problem became pronounced to me during a visit to California's Central Coast.

Rajat Parr carries himself with a certain ease and confidence, which extends to his driving. As I sat in the back of his black BMW with its cracked windshield, another passenger complimented him on the way he treats his sports car like a pickup truck. The car whipped around the curves in the valley near Lompoc, and I closed my eyes in the back and hoped this was not how I was going to die. Later, still alive, I would gratefully look out from his Domaine de La Cote vineyards, including a parcel named Bloom's Field after the main character in James Joyce's *Ulysses*, and see a wonderful panorama of gorgeous vineyard sites down below.

It made sense that the first thing Rajat would want for us to do would be to get out to the vineyards. When I raised the question to him later of whether wine-making involved creativity, he was having none of it. Wine, for Rajat, is "an expression of where it's from, and [...] that's the most important. It's not necessarily about creating anything." When I asked him if there was no "art" to wine-making, he simply confided, "There's no art to winemaking. There's an art to wine growing, but making the wine is the easy part." For Rajat, whose aspirational models derive from Europe, part of the problem lies in language itself, for in Europe, the two acts of grape growing and winemaking get united in terms like the French *vigneron*, whereas in English, we lack such a phrase. If there was no art to winemaking, I wondered, how is it that he had claimed in *Secrets of the Sommelier* that great winemakers make great wine every vintage? Rajat would only point back to the vineyard, that perhaps there the vigneron needed to be creative as a caretaker of the land and the fruit, but his insistence that the operations for creating wine be always simple and the same would mean that the wines would always be different, reflecting place and weather—the great variable from vintage to vintage. If Rajat is right, that there is no art to winemaking, then, it follows, wine cannot be art.

★   ★   ★   ★

Not everyone, however, agrees with Rajat. Recently, sitting with friends at a restaurant in New York City's East Village, a young, bearded sommelier pivoted around our table, carafe in hand, pouring and talking. As if he had been peeking into my notebook, the enthusiast launched into a monologue on the nature of wine and the brunello in his hand. Wine is definitely art, he declared, adding that he considered this wine "agile" before disappearing back into the dining room. Although he may have been an overly dramatic sommelier getting a touch rapturous about the wine he'd encouraged me to order, he's not alone in holding this position. Every winemaker I spoke to and most wine writers seemed, at best, skeptical of the notion, but the writer W. Blake Gray asserts rather directly, "I believe wine can be art. I think this is obvious. Wine can be a product of creativity; it can be made to express a feeling, and to have its drinker feel something. It can be a means of communicating an idea." In his memoir, *Harvests of Joy*, Robert Mondavi repeatedly asserts that he considers wine to be art.[13] Mondavi recalls an early epiphany when he recognized that, in contrast to contemporary winemaking in California, "the great European chateaus were treating wine as high art."[14] Later, he decided that in order to achieve his goals, "I was going to work like a fanatic... . But great artists are always fanatics."[15] Toward the conclusion of his memoir, he reiterates something of a mantra: "Making good wine is a skill; making fine wine is an art."[16] So while it may not be fashionable for winemakers to make such bold claims or to have artistic pretension, Mondavi asserts that his entire ambition lay in aspiring to create wine comparable to "high art."

Even winemakers who do see themselves as artists or wine as art can seemingly become quite conflicted in trying to express that idea. For example, during a conversation with the former winemaker of Lewis Cellars, now of Pine Ridge, Josh Widaman, we found ourselves on the subject of art, beginning with Josh trying to explain the process by which they make wine at Lewis. Although Josh does employ scientific tools in measuring ripeness, he says a lot of the key decisions come down to questions like "What did those seeds taste like?" or "How exactly did I find them crunching under my teeth? What was the texture of the skins?" Trying to determine blends with the Lewis family is not done with "calculators," so, he said, "Yeah, it is art." He also draws this conclusion partially as a means of explaining his own commitment to himself, for "I couldn't go to the extent that I go if it was just a job where I was processing a food product." And yet, this does not let Widaman easily conclude that if there is an art to what he does and he is producing an art form, that he himself is an artist. He names a range of folks he considers artists including Michelangelo, Raphael, and Robert DeNiro, before asserting,

> Those are all artists, those are all people I consider artists, those are all people that I have a high esteem for what they do. And so, I feel—I don't feel comfortable saying, "Oh yes, I am those people." But I do feel that wine is art. And so, if you're a winemaker, and wine is art and you're being creative, then you must be an artist, but I don't feel—but I'm not doing it just so I can be an artist, and I don't have that kind of awe for myself. But I do have it for other people like Justin Smith and Raj Parr, you know, Robert Mondavi.

Josh was one of the few folks I spoke with who saw naming a winemaker an artist as a compliment, but like almost all of those winemakers, he found it difficult to embrace that label, a label some of his examples, like Rajat Parr, would likewise reject. A clue can be found in his phrase, "I don't have that kind of awe for myself," which reminds me of an argument that Eric Asimov makes in his book *How to Love Wine*, that great winemakers must be "humble," something that becomes evident in my earlier discussions of Ted Lemon and Michael Browne and their emphasis on the limits of control.

Asimov himself takes up the issue of whether wine is art, and his discussion becomes a somewhat tangled affair. He asserts first firmly, "Wine itself is not an art," but then in the same sentence modifies that to, "at least not in the same way as music or paintings."[17] For him, part of the problem has to do with the inability to hold or review it since "it is consumed" and "an experience can never be duplicated precisely."[18] Regarding the comparison of wine to art in performance, he says it does not hold up since performances can be recorded. Wine also fails his litmus test because "it cannot offer new and different ways to understand life and the human condition."[19] Nevertheless, I sensed some real hesitation in Asimov's view, as he concedes that "wine does have the capacity to move us" and that wine "has something to tell us, about where it came from, both geologically and culturally, and about the people who shepherded the transformation of grapes to wine and that year in history."[20] As I read Asimov's discussion, I sensed some of my own struggles with this question, particularly in the way Asimov wrestled with objections and concessions. Over a lunch in NYC on one of the hottest days of the summer, I brought my sense that he had some conflicted feelings on the issue up to him. Eric is in his mid-fifties, has gray in his hair, wears rounded glasses, and possesses a vibrant curiosity and enthusiasm for wine along with an easygoing charm. He listened patiently to my theories, sipping at a Corsican red he had accidently ordered. As I wrapped up my presentation, I told him that during the very last interview I had conducted, I finally found a winemaker who embraced being thought of as an artist—and not only that, but she was someone he admired very much.

In fact, the declaration had come as quite a surprise to me. It happened about three days after I had dined with Steve and Jill Klein Matthiasson when, over grilled fish and several of Steve's wines, I told them about my investigations into this question of winemakers and art. At the time, I had become convinced that no winemaker would ever tell me that he or she were an artist. That the most anyone would ever confess is that, yes, there were some artists out there—like Josh Widaman had said—but that is not me. So, a few days later, I found myself in the winery of Cathy Corison, who started making wine two years before the Judgment of Paris, the famed triumph of California wine over French wine in a blind tasting, during the early 1970s. As seemingly all wine writers note of the essentially first full-time woman winemaker in California, Cathy is quite petite and quite energetic and forceful in her opinions. After visiting her Kronos vineyard and a brief tour of her small winery, we sat in a spacious, uncluttered room above the winery that had a large open window overlooking her vineyard. The room, spare and resembling the top floor of a well-appointed barn, held just one table, a few chairs, wine glasses, and a bottle of her 2013 Napa cabernet, which we sipped while we talked and laughed. Cathy's wines fell out of fashion at the height of what Jon Bonné has called "Big Flavor" and what Alice Feiring and others called the "Parkerization" of wine—that is, the shift to high-alcohol, ripe wines that saw heavy doses of new oak. I asked her about how bad things got and whether she had seriously entertained changing her style as many winemakers had done. She repeated something she has said before, that "a house has to stand for something." When I mentioned that she had asserted that there is almost something moral about that, she chuckled and then declared, "There is!" As we tried to make sense of how the choice to make her cabernet in a style she felt it should be made in could be seen as a moral or ethical duty, it became clear that it had to do with her conception of herself as an artist. That what would be betrayed, besides in her mind the grapes and the vineyard, would be her own artistic vision to which she felt she had a moral obligation to be true.

Eric Asimov digested this story for a bit and then offered up another theory to consider, one that divided this question between the Old World and the New. Maybe, he suggested, one had to be something of an artist in the New World because one could not draw upon culture and history to guide what you should do. His theory echoed a story Steve Matthiasson shared on Levi Dalton's wine podcast about the time an esteemed winemaker from Burgundy came to his home and tasted his white wine, which Steve blends from multiple grapes and vineyard sources. The French winemaker remained quiet for a time, making Steve anxious that he did not like his wines, but then when he spoke he said, "You get to do something that I do not get to do. I can only 'reveal' with my wines; you get to 'create'." Revealing, then, is what the Old World winemaker does, following the lead of generations before, whereas the New World winemaker, not so bound, can create anew. It seems the French winemaker was a bit envious.

Winemakers might be said to be crafting their own narratives by way of interpreting what they do. In his essay, "Narrative," J. Hillis Miller rather coyly introduces the metaphysical dispute at the core of the function of narrative—here emphasizing fiction—by sharing the very terms that the French winemaker used in his conversation with Steve Matthiasson: "With fictions we investigate, perhaps invent, the meaning of human life."[21] That conditional clause implies a great deal, and he goes on to say that "To say 'reveal' presupposes that the world has one kind or another of preexisting order and the business of fiction is one way or another to represent that order." He then goes on to complicate this view by noting that "To say 'create', on the other hand, presupposes that the world may not be ordered in itself."[22] It may certainly be possible to replace "fictions" with "wine" and think about how seeing one's wine in relation to the land via either revealing or creating implies two very different metaphysical positions. The fact that so many winemakers I met had reverence for old world winemakers may also suggest why so many of them tended to align themselves with "revealing."

★   ★   ★   ★

In conversations with other winemakers after my meeting with Cathy, those who knew her were a little surprised that she would be the rare winemaker who would be willing to see her work as aligned with other artists. However, when the conversation about artistry came up over the course of my many visits out to California, I would always get asked at some point, "Have you spoken to Abe yet?" By the time I finally did talk to Abe Schoener, I felt like I already knew him. I had met with many winemakers and writers who told many tales about both Abe as a figure and the importance of his role in what Jon Bonné has called The New California.

Hearing and reading about Abe is not quite the same as meeting him. Abe and I finally met at a bar on the Lower East Side in Manhattan. I had tried to secure us a relatively quiet table, but when Abe sauntered in, signature scarf wrapped around his neck and a pack over his shoulder, he asked if we could sit at the bar itself and ordered himself a martini. When we began to talk, I immediately recognized the academic in Abe as he asked me nearly as many questions as I asked him, first an intellectual feeling out and then an engaging give-and-take. Perhaps more than any other winemaker I met, Abe had a willingness to consider both his winemaking as artistry and wine itself as art. Abe distinguishes between the great mass of wines—those he calls "serviceable"—and those that aspire to art, which returns us to the problem of distinctions between types from chapter 1. Those wines that do resemble an art object are capable themselves of long life:

> The serviceable wines have no capacity to induce anything like the experience of the sublime, or to make you, even in an unreflective way consider materiality and eternality at the same time. And so for me, that's the value of really beautiful wines that have the capacity to age and that one experiences at a certain point in their lifetime, that at the same time, they make you think of eternality and materiality and its transitory nature, and for me those things are tied to tragedy and also to something like the notion of doom.

Like the wines that Michael Broadbent suggests require monastic attention, these wines have the power to make us become moved and reflective. The invocation of the sublime, a recurrent concern of the Romantics, again speaks to the tangle of art and nature, for what the Romantics often sought to capture in their poems was the sublime effect of the overpowering "awe-ful" sights of nature, like Mont Blanc. The poem becomes a translator of that sublime. Thus, Abe seems to come at the notion of wine as art here from the position of a culture of feeling, though like Clark Smith, his allegiances are not consistent. Clark Smith also leans toward the artistic view of wine, calling it "liquid music" and saying that the "soulful wine" he aspires to make matches the same "inherent quality of an artistic product."[23] A few years prior to Gray's article to which I referred earlier, but well after the publication of Mondavi's memoir, wine writer and critic Alder Yarrow posted a Twitter conversation among three wine writers who, in general, seemed much more skeptical of the notion that wine was art. While the three writers seem to largely agree in their doubts, they still cannot agree on what art is. Yarrow first argues that "wine becomes part of our bodies, it is food. Art is always outside us," but then Bruce Schoenfeld responds, "But 99% of wines are just something to drink. No greater ambition is sought. All art is ambitious"—which suddenly forces Yarrow to hesitate.

This small moment in the maelstrom of social media, though, touches on a rather large question that underlies the basic questions of this chapter and the book itself. In other words, while we can certainly explore the logic of whether winemakers (or vignerons) and critics see wine and winemaking as either being art or something else, we cannot really avoid a question debated for much longer than whether wine is art, namely, what is art itself? Cynthia Freeland's wonderful introduction, *But Is It Art?*, provides not so much an answer but answers, for this is a question humanity has been trying to settle for at least as far back as the ancient Greeks. Gray's position focuses heavily on defining art by way of communicating meaning, ideas, or emotion, which then would align art with many of the aspirations of the winemakers that I have met, that their wine would be a link to a place, would invoke not just a sensual pleasure but an intellectual one, where the drinker grew to know the place, to get tied to the culture of an area. However, we don't need to dwell on this too long before we see the parameters of that definition crumble as, deliciousness aside, one could say a Twitter post might do many of those same things. But, while not all Twitter posts are art, could some be?

In many ways, the problem might lie in deliciousness. When I asked Duncan Meyers and Nathan Roberts of Arnot-Roberts what they hoped their ideal drinker would get from their wines, they confounded my expectations regarding *terroir*, history, and culture by saying, "Well, first, that it's delicious!" Similarly, Yarrow's recorded conversation places a lot of emphasis on wine as food, as something consumed rather than something that stands apart, and these notions go back to the earlier debates surrounding aesthetics, particularly how to define beauty. Probably, as Freeland describes, the most important argument in this discussion came from Immanuel Kant, who "warned that enjoyment of beauty was distinct from other sorts of pleasure."[24] Tellingly for us, Freeland employs the example of fruit to illustrate Kant's position: "If a ripe strawberry in my garden has a ruby colour, texture, and odour that is so delightful that I pop it into my mouth, then the judgment of beauty has been contaminated."[25] In order to appreciate something as truly beautiful, as a hallmark of art, "our response has to be disinterested—independent of its purpose and the pleasurable sensations it brings about."[26] So, at least one problem with considering wine as art, from Kant's point of view, is that you can never look at wine disinterestedly; in fact, most of the hallmarks of its beauty would be inextricably tied to the pleasures it can provide us.

Not surprisingly, Abe Schoener's perspective complicates this view. In explaining his own view, he invokes that of Robert Parker:

> What I think is really special about Parker is he put hedonism at the center. And the only difference between me and Parker is we disagree on what are the sources of pleasure. But not that it should be at the center. So when I say, judge [a wine] on its ability to conjure up the tragic, I don't mean that in opposition to pleasure, that's specific—as Aristotle points out, that is a specific form of pleasure. Parker has a different pleasure in mind. But we both agree that in the long run it's about pleasure.

Nevertheless, it is that notion that wine is tied to pleasure, that we can expect it to bring us pleasure, that has, following Kant, complicated the extent to which it can be considered beautiful in a way that resembles art.

However, the question does not end there—not even for Kant, for as Freeland later explains, Kant went on to argue that the gardens of Versailles conformed to his notions of beauty because they did not emphasize the growing of food and they allowed for the "free play of imagination," a much broader, more abstract conception of art.[27] In his attempts to specific beauty, Kant seems to directly anticipate academic attempts to limit the vocabulary to describe wine, as I discussed in the previous chapter. In this wiggle room regarding beauty, we might then start to consider if Mondavi's "fine wine" starts approaching the Versailles notion of a garden. Kant, of course, has had far from the final word on the question of how to define art and, in fact, much contemporary art, such as Andy Warhol's famed *Brillo Boxes*, have essentially forced art theorists to continue to reevaluate their sense of what art is. The art philosopher Arthur Danto has said that seeing Warhol's *Brillo Boxes* altered his entire way of thinking, and eventually, he developed an argument that, according to Freeland, "anything can be a work of art, given the right situation and theory," for "a work of art is an object that embodies a meaning." Like Barthes's notion of the scriptor, which ends up putting a lot of emphasis on the reader to construct meaning, Danto argues, "Nothing is an artwork without an interpretation that constitutes it as such,"[28] a proposition that might be said to boil down to art being in the eye of the beholder. Alas! Danto's conception of art, however, with its emphasis on art being defined by interpretation seems almost an inversion of Sontag's view of interpretation's relation to art.

I don't want to leave this discussion with the sense that Danto had the final say. His proposition, like Warhol's work that inspired it, was and is subject to further dispute and critique. What tracing the long history of the debate of what should constitute the beautiful and art itself shows us is that our answer can be culturally dependent, that it has shifted greatly over time—often as a means of explaining or, as Danto would have it, theorizing, the changing nature of what artists produce—and that definitions have usually become more and more expansive. Freeland herself settles close to a definition provided by the anthropologist Richard Anderson, who claims art to be "culturally significant meaning, skillfully encoded in an affecting, sensuous medium."[29] Such a definition strives for flexibility, one that puts aside some of the objections to wine's status as art offered in that Twitter dialogue, such as the fact that we consume wine, that not all winemakers are ambitious, or that wine does not stand apart from ourselves. While Danto seems to come at art via reason, Anderson might be said to attempt a marriage of reason and feeling in his broader approach.

However, while we can find a theory of art that has room for wine, it does not follow that we necessarily need to view wine as art, and our imagined theory does not answer the question as to why so many of the winemakers that I have encountered, unlike Robert Mondavi, typically see themselves not as artists but as craftsman. When pressed on questions of whether there are analogs to artistic creation in the process of making wine, among the most common defenses is, inevitably, that what winemakers do is a craft. This division between artist and craftsman or art and the artisanal does not leave behind the disputes about art but instead brings us right back to it, for it seems to me that one of the main ways we divide craft work from art has to do with Kant's objections to seeing strawberries as beautiful. Kant thus casts a long shadow. He tends to describe the problem in terms of desire, but we might also rename the problem as one of function. Kant's disinterestedness speaks to the notion that beauty, in whatever medium, has no practical purpose; we benefit only in its trigger of our inner mind, but not in any kind of utilitarian way. The problems with these kinds of divisions, though, have to do with the fact that (a) like most other problems of definition in the world, they rely on interpretive work (Versailles in, for example; your vegetable garden out), and (b) this has become something of an either/or battle rather than a sliding scale.

★ ★ ★ ★

Every morning when I set up two handmade, well-designed, and aesthetically striking coffee mugs next to our drip pot, I am reminded of this divide. I turned to the maker of those mugs while working my way through this problem of whether winemakers were actually more craftsman or more artist. Scott Cooper of St. Earth Pottery calls himself a studio potter, and his milieu, more broadly, would be called ceramics. When we met over coffee, I was surprised to learn that within the world of ceramics there are major disputes about whether to emphasize functionality— that is, to make things like mugs and plates that people can use every day—or to emphasize making aesthetic objects, that in Scott's terms tell stories, convey messages, and emotions, that begin with intellectual intent. In short, either to make things that

FIGURE 3.3 A coffee mug made by Scott Cooper

people can use or to make things that "mean" something. As the plates and mugs crammed into my cabinets attest, Scott's emphasis has largely been on functionality, and his immediate way of presenting his own work is in opposition to what he considers academic ceramics (though he says most potters start out in academia), which has largely forsaken functionality and, in his mind, overly deemphasized craft.

When I began explaining how winemaking and winemakers might be said to resemble what he did, he immediately turned the conversation to scale. He had a point. He works entirely alone. Even if he wanted to, he's incapable of making large-scale productions of any one piece. He literally does not have space in his kiln, so his work will never line the shelves of your local store. On the other hand, he worries about things like whether a handle will both function properly and be tactilely pleasing. I told him about Matthew Rorick, who essentially said that he never wanted Forlorn Hope to get so big that he needed another full-time employee, and Scott immediately identified. And we should not then miss the point that Scott made me see that the scale of a given winery's enterprise certainly matters in how much it reflects any single individual's vision. Nevertheless, most people writing about wine tend to view winemaking in a manner similar to how the French viewed filmmaking: that the director, like the winemaker, was the *auteur*, the provider of vision so that all the folks involved simply become part of making that vision. The winemaker could also be said to resemble someone like Warhol or Jeff Koons, whose name appears on work he may not have literally made with his own hands. It is probably not a coincidence, though, that many of the filmmakers that the French New Wave critics celebrated, like Howard Hawks, insisted they were merely craftsmen—not artists, or that Warhol famously worked in The Factory.

It turns out the ceramics' debates are quite heated affairs. My conversation with Scott drew me back to part of the problem in this question of art versus craft, namely, those involved in the debate tend to put too much emphasis on taking extreme positions and not seeing that most potters might simply be seen on a broad spectrum. After all, consider Scott's own work. Yes, he makes plates and cups that I literally *use* every day—and that's exactly what he wants me to do with them— but those pots and plates are extremely distinct. They fit, as Scott told me, within the aesthetic history of ceramics, but they borrow from that tradition and extend it. At Scott's last sale, for the first time, he also included the work of other potters, but there was no mistaking Scott's work. A set of his mugs revealed recurring patterns of lightly daubed tan circles that might appear once on a given mug or, on another mug, alternate between pale vertical bands with recurrent small black dots. He has a style, and his work is beautiful. Sorry, Kant! So while Scott sees himself on the functional, crafts side of the ceramics divide, it becomes clear that his work probably stands a lot closer to the purely aesthetic folks than he would initially have you believe.

Nevertheless, I find myself returning to the question of why Scott and the many winemakers I met immediately back away from the artist label. Part of the issue for Scott and potters of his ilk have to do with taking pride in owning their emphasis on functionality within an academic context that has shifted strongly in favor of aesthetic objects without function. For the most part, the academic influence in wine circles is there—a tension created in part by the influence of the University of California, Davis on viticulture—but it cannot as easily explain a desire to be seen as a craftsman. Abe Schoener, though, provides some very clear rationales for how the craft of winemaking can seem to be quite separate from art. Abe came to winemaking late in his life; he arrived in California after already establishing himself as an academic, so he recalls that when starting, there simply is no way to intellectualize his new occupation:

> At the beginning and for the first several years, seven to ten years, I did not see what I was doing as artistic in any way; there was just no question. I would say my point of reference was something like being a lab technician, in any case, clearly a technician, not a—you know, you work for somebody brilliant like Maxwell or somebody like that, Maxwell needs to run a lot of experiments, you need people in the lab that are competent. I feel like that's my job. Even if I'm the one who's thinking of the experiments, I still have the responsibility of being the competent lab technician, fundamentally, that's my job.

In this description, Abe also calls to mind the issues of scale of operations (e.g., Are you alone in a lab, or is one of the assistants trying to make someone else's experiments work?), but also how does that change when you are the one dictating the work. Abe also emphasizes the physicality of winemaking:

> And it was really hard for me. I didn't come in with the physical skills, I didn't know how to run equipment, it was really difficult. But what was in the front of my mind, there was no question, it was never fucking artistry, it was like, move the wine from here to there, and put a minimum amount on the floor.

These descriptions really do echo around the wine world. I recall when Matthew Rorick told me over dinner how much importance simply cleaning barrels properly held in the winemaking process. I remember another winemaker, Chris Brockway, thinking that considering himself as an artist would be a kind of barrier put up between what he thought he was doing and the actual, mechanical work he needed, and he joked then about all the mopping his job entailed.

However, most of these views perhaps derive from what Abe might call a sentimentalizing of the actual work, in a physical sense, involved in most art. Even someone like Andy Warhol, whom Danto defines artistically in terms of ideas, also emphasized the notion of physical labor in the very conception of The Factory and in stressing the mechanical labor of assembling his *Brillo Boxes*. Therefore, for me, craft seems almost like a fallback or a defense against being considered an artist. Michael Browne, physically moving back a step from me as I posed the question of art, insisted that no, the work he did had to do with craft. Yet perversely, in my ears, the word *craft* did not move winemakers away from art but toward it, because in the context of the arts in academics, such as my university's creative writing program, the term *craft* appears all the time. Visiting writers present craft talks. Our writers wanted courses that put an emphasis on students reading for the craft, rather than the meaning, of the story, for meaning was the purview of literary critics, not writers.

Craft, in terms of creative writing and other arts, can be seen as a solution to the nagging question of whether you can teach someone to be an artist, to use the term broadly here. By promoting craft, academic creative writing attempted to make it a more academic subject and move it away from a view of the artist embedded in a culture of feeling towards a culture of reason (in a kind of reversal of how Romanticism tended to push back against neoclassical academies, as detailed by Blanning). Mark McGurl's history of academic creative writing, *The Program Era*, traces the crucial role craft played in balancing other key features of creative writing programs, self-expression, and creativity. His definition of craft should help clarify this issue a bit more. "Craft—also called technique," McGurl observes, "adds the elements of acquired skill and mental effort to the [creative] process and is strongly associated with professional pride and the lessons or 'lore' of literary tradition."[30] Frequently, McGurl modifies *craft* with the word *impersonal*, and that seems crucial to our discussions here. Although creative writers likely have little trouble, at least in their private moments, of seeing what they do as producing art, within the more public spaces of, say, a creative writing class, there is a hesitance to see writing as simply about the self. In fact, McGurl argues that "impersonality" is a Modernist "value,"[31] despite the fact that Modernists like Joyce, Faulkner, and Woolf all developed highly personal, unusual writing styles.

When winemakers, then, fall back on seeing themselves as craftsmen, they do seek on some level to de-emphasize the role of the self or ego. As we have seen in my comparisons of winemakers to either the ideals of Romantic poets or Roland Barthes's modern scriptors, the emphasis or inspiration resides outside the self whether the conception is based more in reason or feeling. For winemakers, inspiration lies in the land, in particular, but also in the culture. However, craft itself does not arguably lead to an erasure of the self or to making the hand of the winemaker truly invisible. This argument is made rather potently by Elaine Chukan Brown in her essay, "Personality in Winemaking." Brown concludes that "how a person approaches his or her craft is an expression of his or her personality. In this way, an individual's personality is integral to the creation of their product."[32] While craft, as a set of impersonal techniques used in the creation of something—a novel, a painting, or a bottle of wine—seems to suggest elements unreflective of self-expression, they become integrally tied to self-expression when understood in the way that Brown describes. In fact, they might be thought of, in their deployment, as evidence of the maker. As Chukan Brown observes, personality "determines the ways he or she manages the skills, tools, and choices needed in the craft of winemaking, and how he or she channels the craft in relation to its context."[33] While winemakers may wish to frame the choice as to be an artist or to be a craftsman, those identities do not separate as neatly as they might hope.

Nathan Roberts, more so than his partner, Duncan Meyers, tends to chew on a question for a bit, wading into a response gently. When I asked him and Duncan whether they felt they were expressing themselves through the wine they made, Nathan hesitantly said that yes, "your voice does come through a lot." He knew to fully embrace that possibility might be to be accused of being an artist, of making it be about himself and Duncan, but he also conceded that yes, winemaking can be an outlet for self-expression. As Nathan said, "You can do as little as possible, but our wines taste different than someone else's who thinks they're doing hands-off wine making." Whenever I got any winemaker to concede, even a little bit, that they felt this way, I felt, ever the contrarian, that I had won some kind of hard-fought battle.

In *Chinatown*, one way of seeing Gittes's repetition of "do as little as possible"—indeed much of the movie itself—is that it is a defense against hubris. Although in the film that response to humanity's sense of prideful mastery has a rather dark bent, the winemaker's similar unwillingness to claim control can be seen as part of a healthy antidote to what many have perceived as an embrace of the technology that allows grapes to be changed dramatically by human hands. Nevertheless, it also reflects a process of both interpretation—both of their own work and their sense of their relation to the land—and narrative building as they tell the story of the winemaking process. To emphasize that the wine reflects the land, that it can be a gateway to culture, and that, yes, it tastes delicious might not prevent it from being art and the winemaker akin to certain conceptions of the artist, but it may be healthier for winemakers to feel that way.

Notes

1 Clark Smith, *Postmodern Winemaking: Rethinking the Modern Science of an Ancient Craft* (Oakland: University of California Press, 2013), 1.
2 Ibid., 240.
3 James Joyce and Chester Anderson, *A Portrait of the Artist as a Young Man: Text, Criticism and Notes* (Harmondsworth: Penguin Books, 1977), 253.
4 It may be that in some ways the work in the smithy puts an emphasis on more stereotypically masculine behavior, whereas the description *artist*—to the ear of some Americans—can seem effete. However, there are clear complications to this division, and one could argue that a figure like Jackson Pollack with his aggressive, active mode of painting tried to reclaim a more masculine mode for art.
5 Clark Smith, *Postmodern Winemaking; Rethinking the Modern Science of an Ancient Craft* (Oakland, University of California Press, 2013), 245.
6 Since the time of that interview, Michael Browne and Dan Kosta no longer manage their namesake winery, and Nico Cueva is the winemaker for Kosta Browne. Browne continues to make the wines of his own label, Chev.
7 M.H. Abrams, *The Mirror and the Lamp: Romantic Theory and the Critical Tradition* (New York: Norton, 1958), 26.
8 Clark Smith, *Postmodern Winemaking; Rethinking the Modern Science of an Ancient Craft* (Oakland: University of California Press, 2013), 7.
9 Ibid.
10 Ibid., 7.
11 Roland Barthes and David H. Richter, "The Death of the Author," transl. Stephen Heath, in *Falling into Theory: Conflicting Views on Reading Literature* (Boston: Bedford/St. Martin's, 2000), 254.
12 Ibid., 256.

13 I am grateful to Jon Bonné's *The New California Wine* for drawing my attention to Robert Mondavi's viewpoint.

14 Robert Mondavi, *Harvests of Joy: How the Good Life Became Great Business* (Boston: Houghton Mifflin Harcourt, 1999), 6.

15 Ibid., 53.

16 Ibid, 347.

17 Eric Asimov, *How to Love Wine: A Memoir and Manifesto* (New York: HarperCollins, 2012), 224.

18 Ibid.

19 Ibid.

20 Ibid., 225.

21 J. Hillis Miller, "Narrative," *Critical Terms for Literary Study*, ed. Frank Lentricchia and Thomas McLaughlin, 2nd ed. (Chicago: University of Chicago Press, 1995), 69.

22 Ibid.

23 Clark Smith, *Postmodern Winemaking; Rethinking the Modern Science of an Ancient Craft* (Oakland: University of California Press, 2013), 301.

24 Cynthia Freeland, *But Is It Art?* (Oxford: Oxford University Press, 2001), 12.

25 Ibid., 12.

26 Ibid., 14.

27 Ibid., 47.

28 Ibid., 57.

29 Ibid., 88.

30 Mark McGurl, *The Program Era: Postwar Fiction and the Rise of Creative Writing* (Cambridge: Harvard University Press, 2009), 23.

31 Ibid.

32 Elaine Chukan Brown, "Personality in Winemaking," *The World of Fine Wine*, no. 49 (September, 2015).

33 Ibid.

References

Abrams, M. H. *The Mirror and the Lamp: Romantic Theory and the Critical Tradition*. New York: W.W. Norton, 1958.

Asimov, Eric. *How to Love Wine: A Memoir and a Manifesto*. New York: William Morrow, 2012.

Barthes, Roland. "The Death of the Author," translated by Stephen Heath. In *Falling into Theory: Conflicting Views on Reading Literature*, edited by David H. Richter. Boston: Bedford/St. Martin's, 2000.

Chukan Brown, Elaine, "Personality in Winemaking." *The World of Fine Wine*, no. 49 (September 2015).

Freeland, Cynthia, *But Is It Art?* Oxford: Oxford University Press, 2001.

Joyce, James and Chester Anderson, *A Portrait of the Artist as a Young Man: Text, Criticism and Notes*. Harmondsworth: Penguin Books, 1977.

McGurl, Mark, *The Program Era: Postwar Fiction and the Rise of Creative Writing*. Cambridge, MA: Harvard University Press, 2009.

Miller, James Hillis, "Narrative." In *Critical Terms for Literary Study*, edited by Frank Lentricchia and Thomas McLaughlin. 2nd ed. Chicago: University of Chicago Press, 1995.

Mondavi, Robert, *Harvests of Joy: How the Good Life Became Great Business*. Boston: Houghton Mifflin Harcourt, 1998.

Smith, Clark, *Postmodern Winemaking; Rethinking the Modern Science of an Ancient Craft*. Oakland: University of California Press, 2013.

4

ON THE SUPERMARKET PASTORAL
AND NATURAL WINE

When Highway 29 in Napa becomes the St. Helena Highway, running along the west side of Napa Valley, a driver will pass seemingly one winery after another. This is Napa Valley as Disneyland for adults. Some tasting rooms stand connected to working wineries, often on vineyard parcels. Others have squeezed tasting rooms into the available land adjacent to the highways and estates. Interspersed, the driver will see the occasional restaurant, shop, or luxury lodging. You will see few signs of the homes where the employees of these businesses live.

However, south of here, as one comes into Napa proper, where Highway 29 resembles a highway rather than a one-lane road, vineyards and wineries appear less frequently and the landscape looks much more overtly suburban and includes the home of Steve and Jill Matthiasson. In John Bonné's *The New California Wine*, he describes being at a barbecue hosted by the couple. The crowd includes various avatars of the new, Morgan Twain-Peterson and Tegan Passelaqua among others, and Bonné notes that the Matthiassons are the rare upstarts lucky enough to own vineyard land in Napa itself.[1] I was on the way to their home early on a spring morning myself. I turned off of Highway 29, made a few quick turns and found myself on what looked like a suburban street that could have been about anywhere in the United States. My directions instructed me to make a left between two houses—like the split between stations where Harry Potter picks up the Hogwarts Express—and that I should proceed cautiously. The driveway took me between two nondescript houses onto a path that runs quite literally behind the neighborhood homes facing the street. It felt almost as if I had made a sharp turn onto a movie set. Then, after a few hundred feet the driveway opened up onto an old, elegant and white-painted farmhouse, very different from those on the street. To the left, I could see farm equipment, some vines, and one of the most elaborate—and successful—home vegetable gardens. Behind the garden and the house I could see some of the Matthiasson's own vineyards stretching out across the horizon.

DOI: 10.4324/9781003399810-5

FIGURE 4.1 Matthiasson garden and home vineyard

There's something uncannily remarkable about this scene. Perhaps it is the juxtaposition between the suburban homogeny and the lush green of the vineyard, the garden bursting with life. Mircea Eliade, in his famous structuralist analysis of religions, *The Sacred and the Profane,* notes that for what he calls "religious man," humanity prior to the industrial revolution, the sacred was often marked by such breaks in homogeny (and the profane could be defined by its undifferentiated sameness).[2] Eliade would say that, despite our individual commitments to religion, we live in a profane world, but that we hunger for some of the same things as "religious" man. Perhaps my reaction to the site of the Matthiasson home echoed that hunger for a break in the homogeneity.

In fact, I was far from the first writer to be affected upon seeing the Matthiassons' home, garden, and vineyards. Not only had I followed Jon Bonné's footsteps, I had also followed those of Eric Asimov. In *How to Love Wine,* Asimov describes his visit. Like me, he notes that "plenty of people work in those wineries [further north], and they have to live somewhere." With perhaps greater precision, he notes the "tidy streets" that can be found "North of [the town of] Napa" and remarks that following the driveway I have described "another agricultural world opens up behind those neat houses, including a rambling old house with a tumbledown barn and a small vineyard, all invisible from the street."[3] Asimov's description resembles the concise, elegant prose of a veteran newspaper reporter more than mine, but thus far our impressions seem similar. However, Asimov celebrates the space by invoking its relation to the old world, calling the Matthiasson home "a kind of modern-day ode to the sort of community subsistence farming that defined how generations of Europeans lived their lives." He also notes that the Matthiassons "raise and kill their own animals for meat."

What is it about this place that makes me at least the third writer—I'm sure there are more—to rhapsodize about it? Jill and Steve truly are warm, welcoming, and generous. On the day that I interviewed Steve for much of the morning, they invited me to come back to join a professional tasting of their wine and then, finding me without plans, invited me to dinner. I walked the garden with Jill and Steve as they gathered shishito peppers and zucchini to go with our fish, and I felt myself impressed with the fecundity of their garden. While it's possible that my impressions of their home, then, are colored by subsequent experiences with the owners, I am fairly certain that the impressions I have recorded here do reflect my initial reactions. Both Asimov and myself are native New Yorkers (Bonné lives there now!) who at least for a time pursued literary studies. Steve and Jill observed more than once that I reminded them of Asimov, but I sense that my response to seeing their home transcended any resemblance I might have to the *New York Times* wine critic.

All of these responses to the Matthiasson home speak perhaps to the ways in which most of our lives in modern America are, as Asimov suggests, quite separate from the agricultural sources of our food. Perhaps I should not dismiss the fact that Asimov and I have both lived large stretches of our lives in urban environments, and perhaps this does make us both more likely to idealize the kind of local economy that the Matthiassons participate in, but I am also struck by how its beauty affected me. In his introduction to *The Countryside Ideal*, Michael Bunce notes that it has been a commonplace that our culture has a "growing nostalgia for the countryside and an ambivalence towards the city."[4] However, rather than seeing this dichotomy as reductive, Bunce argues that it "may reflect fundamental human values and psychological needs which can be traced to a basic human desire for harmony with land and nature, for a sense of community and place and for simplicity of lifestyle."[5] Seeking such "community and simplicity," winemaker Martha Stoumen's first experience making wine occurred while working at what she described as a largely self-contained farm in Italy. The owners assigned Martha to the vineyard and she became immediately charmed. After all, she said, the vineyards were "romantic." When I caught up with her much later in her career, I asked if she still found vineyards romantic. She suggested that while she still loved being out in the vineyards, the more time she spent there the more that glow faded.

So, did I enter into what Eliade called a sacred space? I'm not sure that this accurately describes my experience, though undeniably both its contrast with the adjacent suburban homogeny and much of my own lived experience jolted me. However, what I think happened to me might be best described by Michael Pollan's notion of the "supermarket pastoral." In fact, I may have been living the dream of the supermarket pastoral as I drove up that driveway.

★　　★　　★　　★

In his important book, *The Omnivore's Dilemma*, Michael Pollan introduces the concept of the "supermarket pastoral" in a chapter entitled "Big Organic" via a discussion of the high-end supermarket chain, Whole Foods. The chapter begins with Pollan referring to the "literary experience" of Whole Foods, by which he means the way in which Whole Foods encourages us to choose among items labeled with "evocative prose" and ultimately suggests that the "literary critic" might just be the best consumer for the store.[6]

As a literary critic, I don't often get noted for my utility in real world situations, but I get Pollan's point. This chapter and the next will be focusing primarily on several interlocking trends in the wine world, natural wines, as well as biodynamic and organic farming—or more generally the contrast between a variety of alternative or sustainable farming practices and more conventional—often chemical-based—farming techniques. Like Pollan's analysis of the way Whole Foods compels consumers to interpret and engage in narratives, all of these practices and concepts require both engagements in narratives and interpretation. While consumers may believe in these associated environmental causes, their experience of these products—whether at Whole Foods or in purchasing wine—is guided by the narratives being actively constructed around and through their encounters with these products. Pollan's own analysis culminates in the introduction of the supermarket pastoral.

As Pollan notes, "the story on offer in Whole Foods is a pastoral narrative in which farm animals live much as they did in the books we read as children, and our fruits and vegetables grow in well-composted soils on small farms."[7] When we reach into the cold case and grab a milk container labeled organic, Pollan argues that

> label conjures up a rich narrative, even if it is consumers who fills in most of the details, supplying the hero (American Family Farmer), the villain (Agribusinessman), and the literary genre, which I've come to think of as Supermarket Pastoral.[8]

You will recall that winemaker, Abe Schoener, had decried what he called the "sentimentalizing of the vineyard" and I would suggest that Pollan's and Schoener's ideas go hand in hand. We might adjust the hero—small-scale wine producer (Donkey and Goat's Jared Brandt might call this hero the artisan winemaker) or vineyard owner (or leaser), and the villains are the wine world's equivalent of the agribusinessmen or what Bonné called the corporate avatars of Big Flavor—but the story remains similar. The fact that more and more large-scale corporate entities are buying up labels, including many named after the families and individuals who created them, helps underscore this point. In this wine-related narrative, the villains march truckloads of megapurple to dump in giant wine tanks, bring chemical trucks full of Roundup into the vineyards, or in the case of say Alice Feiring's nightmares, take grapes from prized vineyards, heavily sulfur them and cram them into tiny new French oak barrels.

To return to my earlier question, then: why was I at least third in line to have an ecstatic experience as I drove down the Matthiasson driveway? It could be that the Matthiasson home, so close to the suburban world of Whole Foods, seems to confirm that "supermarket pastoral" is not just a new literary genre or a myth I unconsciously let myself believe in every time I drive to the northside of Indianapolis to shop, but that it's real and just behind the facades of suburbia. Pollan says, "Supermarket Pastoral is a most seductive literary genre, beguiling enough to survive in the face of many discomfiting facts." Why? Because, according to Pollan, "it gratifies our deepest longings, not merely for safe food, but for a connection to the earth and to the handful of domesticated features we've long depended on."[9]

Consider how Asimov invoked these very ideals when he described the Matthiasson homestead. Pollan goes on to quote a Whole Foods spokesperson who says that their shoppers are "engaging in authentic experiences" and conjures a "return to a utopian past with the positive aspects of modernity intact."[10] How does Pollan analyze this claim? By invoking a forerunner of what we now called ecocriticism, the literary critic Leo Marx. Pollan says that Whole Foods—and here we can substitute these many narrative invocations of the Matthiasson homestead—"offers what Marx terms 'a landscape of reconciliation' between the realms of nature and culture, a place where, as the marketing consultant put it, 'people will come together through organic foods to get back to the origin of things'."[11] If anything, when winemakers and critics talk about wine, they foreground this connection even more. It's in the clichés embedded into winemaking discourse: the best wines are made in the vineyard; I want this wine to tell the story of the vineyard; wine should express a sense of place.

These issues also draw moral and ethical questions to the center of the wine world. Can you make the world a better place while growing grapes for wines? Can your farming or winemaking practices stand as a city on a hill or a model farm, inspiring others to follow your path? In this way, beginning with Pollan's book makes perfect sense because these issues in the wine world are an extension to similar movements across agriculture and within the culinary world (farm to table, anyone?). In addition, there is a clear link in the growing popularity of ecocriticism in literary studies. One of the central questions, then, of this chapter is how can some of the central metaphors that form both subject and content of much ecocriticism help us understand these nature-centered debates and movements in the wine world.

If you live outside graduate programs and departments of literary studies, you might be surprised by ecology-centered approaches thriving in a variety of humanistic fields, particularly literary studies. After all, ecology belongs to the sciences, and according to the two cultures theory of C.P. Snow, knowledge has been siloed into either the humanities or the sciences.[12] Thus, these appear as radically different positions from which to view the world. They speak to the key ideas behind many of our discussions: the split between a metaphysical sense that we should comprehend the world through how it makes us feel or through how we can rationally strive to understand it—through study, experiment, building knowledge brick by brick. Humanities and sciences should be spaces where the evidence simply does not overlap. And the fact is that they don't always, even in certain ecological movements that inform some approaches of ecocriticism. Some ecocritics, like some nature-focused wine folks, actually tend to eschew or oppose modern science. Others say that it's crucial that ecocritics learn the science that their graduate work has elided. Then, yet another group argues that what plays as ecology among ecocritics is a reductive, simplified version of a scientific field that ecocritics seek for objective certainty—a kind of false veneer of reason—whereas the real field is still riddled with doubts and open questions. In short, not all ecocritics see the relationship between literature and ecology the same way, but they share a desire to see connections between them.

What many of this school of literary critics and many winemakers also share, it strikes me, is a desire to see their work as having a tangible effect on the world around them. By its nature, ecocriticism invokes interdisciplinarity. In his book, *Marketplace of Ideas*, Louis Menand concludes his chapter on interdisciplinarity by trying to consider what has driven its rise in the academy. What has driven academics to leave the security of their silos to bridge to others? Menand's answer is that interdisciplinarity is an attempt for academics to get a say, to get in the game, that academics

> want to feel we are in a real fight, a fight not with each other and our schools, which is the fight the outsiders seem to be encouraging us to have, but with the forces that make and remake the world that most human beings live in.[13]

This is one way to do so. Many other literary approaches have engaged in real world issues—gender bias, racial bias, economic inequality—but those approaches draw more fully on the kinds of cultural analytic work thought to be the domain of the humanities. Ecocriticism, in contrast, often can be seen more aligned to approaches sometimes grouped under the awkwardly labeled category, antihumanist. One key factor that many of the approaches grouped under this umbrella share is a focus on "decentering" the human subject.

This "decentering" of the human subject might strike you as an unusual move for folks housed in humanities departments. Let's consider its implications in further depth. To discuss this approach to literature, I will lean heavily on Greg Garrard's excellent overview entitled *Ecocriticism*. It is, however, important to note that Garrard's main task is to synthesize the pioneering and innovative work of a number of critics rather than developing his own particular approach. Garrard suggests that the "widest" definition of what ecocritics take as their subjects would in fact be "the study of the relationship of the human and non-human, throughout human cultural history and entailing critical analysis of the term 'human' itself."[14] Garrard underscores a core issue of ecocriticism: namely, how folks from the humanities can help to solve scientific problems centered in the environment such as pollution. However, to make the case for the utility of ecocritics, Garrard refers to Rachel Carson's *Silent Spring*, often cited as the start of the modern environmental movement. According to Garrard, the "great achievement of [Carson's] book was to turn a (scientific) problem in ecology into a widely perceived ecological problem that was then contested politically, legally and in the media and popular culture." For those very reasons, then, "ecocriticism cannot contribute much to debates about problems in ecology, but it can help to define, explore and even resolve ecological problems in a larger sense."[15] In other words, when environmentalists make claims about ecological problems in the public sphere, the problem shifts from purely scientific to cultural, and thus engages in culture by way of rhetoric—acts of persuasion and the invocation of figurative language—and often uses narrative to give shape to both these problems. Once that occurs, literary critics can help us interpret those gestures in much the way Pollan claims they can help make sense of the verbal landscape of your local natural market. In this chapter, then, I will not seek to argue whether winemakers should, for instance, avoid sulfur in winemaking, but I will consider the nature of the arguments surrounding this and related debates.

★   ★   ★   ★

One of the reasons that Pollan cites Leo Marx in his discussion of the supermarket pastoral is that Marx's most notable foray into ecocriticism focused on the role of the pastoral in American literature. Two classic literary genres, the pastoral and the georgic—and the prismatic tropes they provide—might be thought of as providing the lenses by which many critics and winemakers think of the relationship between the vineyard and their work. Introducing his own discussion of the pastoral, Garrard claims that "no other trope is so deeply entrenched in Western culture, or so deeply problematic for environmentalism."[16] Terry Gifford, according to Garrard, offers a helpful troika of versions that we can consider here: there is the genre that dates back to Ancient Greece and Rome from folks like Theocritus and Virgil, a broader notion of any kind of literature that "describes the county with an explicit or implicit contrast to the urban," and an "idealization of rural that obscures the realities of hardship."[17] In *The Environmental Imagination*, Lawrence Buell sums up the contradictions concisely: the pastoral "may direct us toward the realm of physical nature, or it may abstract us from it."[18] In essence, it can push us to focus on feeling or reason. Therefore, it strikes me that the overt rhetoric of most winemakers regarding the land—that it is a priority, that the land should make the wine and not the winemaker—might be embedded not only in the question of being an artist but also in the implicit contrast between the countryside—the vineyards themselves—and the urban in the form of the industrial winemaking facility (the more the winemaking operation resembles a factory in its reliance on machinery, in its scale, and even for some like Alice Feiring, its cleanliness, the more it seems to invoke the modern industrial complex, which stands in contrast to the more pastoral landscape of the vineyard).

I realize that in much pejorative discussion of the city it is viewed as dirty, but Feiring's version is to see dirt as a sign of the traditional ways, the ways of the winemaker who worked small, on his own land. For her, the implication seems to be that the cleaner and more machine-filled the space, the more the modern urban world has come to overwhelm this more "natural" winemaking. In her book, *The Battle for Wine and Love*, Feiring finds herself at a reclusive Rhone producer whose wine she has loved and Feiring "focused on noting the utter mess of the winery (always a good sign to me; nothing worse than a winery as clean as laboratory)."[19] The very notion that the vineyard somehow makes the wines by making the grapes and that we should trust nature to do this has echoes of one of the dominant features of the pastoral, the pathetic fallacy. As Garrard notes, the "pastoral often suggests that nature responds to human emotions," and this occurs because "it wrongly locates feelings (*pathos*) in, say, mountains or trees" or perhaps vineyards.[20] This fallacy opens the way for the more negative invocation of the pastoral and the one implied in Schoener's "sentimentalizing of the vineyard." However, Lawrence Buell argues forcefully that "the ideological valence of pastoral writing cannot be determined without putting the text in a contextual frame."[21] By this claim, he wishes to complicate the tendency he sees in literary study to either read from a "sympathetic" or "skeptical" position rather than seeing invocations of the pastoral within a specific cultural and historical framework.[22] For example, he cites how the much criticized "dream of the simple life" evoked by the pastoral takes on a very different meaning in the context of Fredrick Douglass' writing from the perspective of how that life has been denied to African-Americans and here specifically, the enslaved.[23] Similarly, Buell shows how Carson's *Silent Spring* invokes the "simple life" in a text that "helped inspire contemporary radical environmentalism."[24] Thus, we need to be cautious not to oversimplify how the pastoral functions in our culture at any given time, and pay careful attention to the context of its use.

Garrard goes on to note the centrality of Romanticism in the modern popularization of the pastoral, and I wish to return to it shortly as I believe Romanticism and its origins in its dialogue with the Enlightenment become the central framework for many of the ongoing debates about best farming practices and the term natural. However, before we explore those debates further, we might also consider the related but competing trope and literary genre, the georgic. Virgil played a key role in the development of both, the pastoral in the *Eclogues* and the georgic in the poems of the same name. In *American Georgics*, Matthew Sweet underscores a key distinction between them: "Where in the *Eclogues* Virgil understands the natural world primarily as a site of leisure, in the *Georgics* he understands it as primarily as a site of labor."[25] As Sweet and Garrard observe, there is a long history of critiquing the pastoral for its mystification of agriculture. Sweet summarizes Raymond Williams' famous critique thusly: "in pastoral, nature as an object of beauty or site of bounty is screened off from human activities of creating and maintaining that beauty or producing that bounty."[26] Yet, the Georgic has, at least to some extent, more fully engaged the notion of labor, though in the form of Jefferson's gentleman farmer it is still clearly capable of mystifying the primary source of labor even as it celebrates human manipulation of nature. Sweet explains that in the early decades of the American republic, "the literature of agricultural improvement developed a discourse of rural virtue that linked economic-environmental intensification to national stability."[27] Although as Sweet remarks, the pastoral has emerged as the more dominant trope in terms of how Americans view the environment—whether it be idealized in contrast to the urban, a way of critiquing reductive views of nature, or as an idealized site of leisure—there is also no doubt that other visions of the vigneron, the ideal of the winemaker who grows his own grapes, who can directly connect the vineyard to the winemaking process seemingly by his or herself, draws also on the ideals of the georgic, for as Sweet claims, the georgic seeks to answer "what is the relationship between humankind and the rest of nature? What ought it to be?"[28] And these answers must recognize that human labor is a necessary part of that relationship.

★   ★   ★   ★

It may be that, when wealthy individuals come to Napa, buy up a vineyard site, build what looks like a chateau from Bordeaux, hire a consulting winemaker, and make a cabernet that sells north of 200 dollars, this individual is imagining some version of Jefferson's gentleman farmer. More and more, the wineries of those gentlemen farmers dominate the landscape up and down the Silverado Trail, the St. Helena Highway, Pritchard Hill and the four mountains that frame the valley. Of course, while the traditional georgic speaks to labor in a way that the pastoral may not have, from Jefferson on down, the American version frequently participated in the kind of mystifying that hides the actual labor in the vineyard and the cellar. Certainly, the Matthiassons speak to the kind of georgic ideal that Sweet hopes to revive and celebrate: there, they are living on and working the land, and as Steve told me during my first visit, they were in the process of hiring a full-time crew so as to also more fully acknowledge and support those who also work the Matthiasson land.

Yet, as Garrard suggests, the dominant trope for imagining—or even critiquing—our relation to the land remains the pastoral, a conception that entered the popular imagination via the long influence of the Romantic pastoral. Of the Romantics, the figure most associated with the pastoral remains William Wordsworth. However, as Garrard argues, "Wordsworth is, on the whole, far more interested in the relationship of non-human nature to the human mind than he is nature in and of itself."[29] If we look for a moment at one of Wordsworth's most famous poems, "I Wandered Lonely as a Cloud," we can see one of the ways in which the Romantics and Wordsworth in particular saw their relationship to the natural world. The poem begins with the title and that first line puts an immediate emphasis on the poet. The simile of that line also engages with a typical pastoral move, namely the pathetic fallacy, a trope where human emotions, like loneliness, are found in non-human nature or reflect the emotions of humans. As critics have also noted, the scene is a mystification of an actual experience, but one that did not feature a solitary William, but also his sister, Dorothy. However, it is the last stanza of the poem that really speaks to Garrard's point:

For oft, when on my couch I lie
In vacant or in pensive mood,
They flash upon that inward eye
Which is the bliss of solitude;
And then my heart with pleasure fills,
And dances with the daffodils.

The poem moves from the solitary wanderings of the poet in nature back to his human dwelling, and the real import of nature gets revealed in its ability to trigger the imagination. While the Romantics typically celebrated nature and the emotions it could bring, its focus often had to do with what nature could do for us rather than the kind of decentering that many contemporary ecocritics would endorse, where nature is something to be supported independent of its relation to humanity.

In many ways this gets at the heart of the problematic relationship between vineyards, winemaking, and an ecological mission. Vineyards, like any other kind of farm, largely exist to benefit humans. Unlike many other kinds of farms, the human population cannot be said to *need* grapes for wine. Today, wine is quite clearly a luxury, a want rather than a need, something that adds to our everyday pleasure but is not a matter of life and death for anyone ... even if there are days where it feels like it is! We may in fact be using the products of these vineyards in ways that remind us of Wordsworth, for many use wines as not just a beverage, but, as I have already frequently argued, to make meaning, as a source for the human imagination, a site of beauty, and perhaps following Schoener, a cause of the sublime.

★   ★   ★   ★

The rise of Romanticism in its "dialectic" relationship with the Enlightenment can also provide us a way of understanding some of the conflicts about how to both farm vineyards and make wines that have dominated the wine world for much of the last decade or more. As I mentioned earlier, in his concise history of the period, *The Romantic Revolution*, Tim Blanning suggests we can comprehend culture shifts through the broad prism of a "running dialectic between a culture of feeling and a culture of reason."[30] If Blanning is right and the divide between Romanticism's recurrent emphasis on feeling and emotion in opposition to the Enlightenment's emphasis on reason is part of a long-running cultural pattern, then we can then extrapolate that the elements that mark the disagreement may also help us understand our current moment. For Blanning, the start of Romanticism can be located in France with Jean-Jacques Rousseau, who argued that the "civilizing process was leading not to liberation but to enslavement"; therefore, Rousseau claims, "our minds have been corrupted in proportion as the arts and sciences have improved."[31] This sets the pattern for Rousseau, who largely invented the noble savage, a figure who is truly happy thanks in part due to escaping civilizing education.

FIGURE 4.2 Abe Schoener

While it has sometimes been the case that Romanticism's relationship to science has been oversimplified into a formula where it is simply anti-science, that clearly is not the case. Richard Holmes' magnificent book, *The Age of Wonder*, makes explicit how the Romantics like Coleridge and Keats became fascinated by elements of science, and he describes several important figures of Romantic science like Humphrey Davy and William Herschel.[32] However, folks like Coleridge opposed very fundamental elements of the Enlightenment and created a blueprint for how many in the wine community have pushed back against conventional farming that derives in part from that form of scientific reasoning. For Coleridge, the Enlightenment employed the wrong methods for understanding nature. As Blanning explains, Coleridge disagreed with the view of John Locke that the mind was a "lazy-Looker-on" that was shaped by external stimuli. For Coleridge, "deep Thinking is attainable only by a man of deep Feeling."[33] The fault of the "Experientalists" is the failure to acknowledge "the testimony of their own senses."[34] As we shall see in chapter 5, this need to rely on your own individual senses becomes crucial in many of the anti-science approaches currently in vogue in the wine world.

In addition to Locke, Sir Isaac Newton particularly drew the ire of the Romantics. Based on Newton's discoveries, according to Blanning,

it was now clear that the only true form of knowledge was scientific knowledge, that is to say knowledge established by a combination of empiricism and mathematics, that is the scientific method, and whatever could not be verified in this way was not knowledge at all.[35]

That which cannot be empirically and conclusively proven by repeated experiment cannot rise above hypothesis. However, in opposition to this seeming triumph of the Enlightenment project's champion, reason, ran a counterclaim in which "the fundamental charge that the scientific method could explain everything but understand nothing was advanced in many different ways."[36] One of the main "charges" against the rationalists was that they focused on the very small, but could not appreciate or understand the big picture. As Coleridge wrote to his friend Thomas Poole, those who "were rationally educated [... .] were marked by a microscopic acuteness, but when they looked at greater things, all became blank and they saw nothing."[37]

As we look back at these critiques, we can see emerging patterns. The followers of reason can master the small, they can presume to know, but the kind of knowledge they possess is inadequate to the task of a broader, humanistic under-standing that can be provided through the arts, individual genius, human emotion, and faith that extends beyond the scientifically provable. Contesting what can be proven via laboratory work, the descendants of the culture of feeling argue that humans must understand the world holistically—as many approaches to ecology stress—and must trust their own observations and intuitions. We may live in a world often described as postmodern, but, for Blanning, postmodernism comes from a direct line that can be traced to Romanticism, for "all postmodernisms have in common a rejection of grand narrative, teleology, and rationalism. They squarely belong to the culture of feeling in a line that stretches back to fin de siecle and romanticism."[38] In this way, we can see our world as once more entangled in many of the kinds of arguments about how best to understand the nature of reality and what it means to be human that affected the turn into the nineteenth century.

★   ★   ★   ★

This emphasis on feeling comes to the fore when people discuss one of the hottest if most controversial recent trends in wine, namely the rise of what has come to be called "natural wine." In some ways, natural wine is the other side of the coin of the winemaker as artist question that we focused on in the previous chapter. Proponents of natural wine claim to do as little as possible and frequently suggest this is the proper way to make wine. In the article, "Wine Doesn't Make Itself" from *Punch*'s March 14, 2018 edition, Zachary Sussman, however, places the issues squarely into the tropes of nature we have discussed: "As far as myths go, the 'shepherd vigneron' is a persuasive one, feeding into an increasingly popular pastoral fetish." Sussman seeks to deflate this myth and, in doing so, rehearses some of the more common critiques of natural winemaking, noting, for instance, that "one of the tragic consequences of this overly democratic 'the wine makes itself' mentality is how frequently it serves as an excuse for sloppy and uninformed winemaking."[39]

These kinds of critiques surface in almost all discussions of natural wine. In an article for *New York Magazine* that came out soon after Sussman's, Maureen O'Connor leads with Pascaline Lepeltier, an influential sommelier and natural wine proponent and close associate of Alice Feiring, suggesting the positives of natural wines that feature "dirty, sweaty smell[s]" or simply the aroma of "horse shit."[40] Like Sussman, O' Connor cites John Bonné's complaining that "there's a lot of fucked up natural wine out there." In an article for *The Guardian*, published literally between the articles by Sussman and O'Connor, Stephan Buryani also rehearses the problems: "To its many detractors, it is a form of luddism, a sort of viticultural anti-vax movement that lauds the cidery, vinegary faults that science has spent the past century painstakingly eradicating." He goes on to cite a British critic noting one natural wine that had "an acrid, grim burst of acid that makes you want to cry."[41] Even the television show, *Succession*, has gotten into the act, mocking both biodynamics and natural wine in the third season episode, "What It Takes." As Tom Wamsbgans (Matthew Macfaydn) and his wife, Shiv Roy (Sarah Snook) sample and puzzle over a bottle of their own German Spätburgunder, Tom notes that "has quite a funk to it" and ultimately concludes that "it's quite agricultural."

In the United States, the most outspoken proponent of natural wine from the wine writing community has been Alice Feiring. Most of her books take up the case of natural wine, often opposing it to the "spoofulated" wines she associates with Robert Parker (who is repeatedly cited as calling natural wine a "scam" in piece after piece!) or simply the larger modern wine industry that has spread throughout the globe, which she sees as both industrial and homogenizing. In her book, *Naked Wine*, her primary focus is natural wines in Europe and the challenges of making natural wine in California, where Feiring herself makes her first wine as a part of the narrative.[42] Elaine Chukan Brown's article, "In Defense of Natural Wine," summarizes the point that Feiring tries to make by noting that in France, where local governments "demand particular farming practices," "the natural wine movement arises from the very real need to protect against what proponents see as legally enforced ecological damage."[43] Both Chukan Brown and Feiring point out how difficult it can be for California winemakers to control both the viticulture and the winemaking, something that repeatedly arises in discussions of all facets of American wine, and thus how elusive the dream of being a vigneron is.

Therefore, Chukan Brown contends that it may be easiest to put the emphasis on winemaking when we talk about natural wine. For as she notes, someone who buys organically farmed grapes can still manipulate the wine in ways that the natural wine movement abhors. Feiring defines her basic conception of natural wine as "based on nothing added and nothing taken away."[44] She responds to the critique posed by Sussman that folks like Feiring "were seduced *only* by romantic notions of wine. Somehow critics felt we were seduced by concept, not taste."[45] Feiring believes that some resistance comes from "winemakers who could be threatened by change in the winemaking paradigm,"[46], though, ironically, the winemaking that she endorses is often linked to not a future paradigm, but a return to a previous one. Like many of the winemakers I spoke with, however, Feiring doesn't disagree that humans play a pivotal role in making wine, but "how far human intervention goes is what is debated."[47]

Although Feiring often offers these reasonable caveats—in a later section of her book, she concedes that there's a difference between say the treatment of animals in factory farms and natural wine—and attempts to distinguish her commitment to natural wines from romanticism, there remains a tremendous amount of evidence that Romanticism—as in an allegiance to feeling and emotion—does strongly influence her promotion of natural wine. Let's consider a few examples. First, there's a tendency to apply the pathetic fallacy to natural wine. For instance, borrowing the term "naked wine" from a French winemaker, Jules Chauvet, Feiring says, "there is something exposed, vulnerable, but true" about such wines.[48] In describing the effects of natural wine, such as those produced by Marcel Lapierre, Feiring notes that "one sip of the natural stuff often changes your attitude toward the wine forever and often fills your life with (forgive me for saying it) meaning."[49] In a later scene in the book, Feiring, while listening to a Tom Waits song, "burst into tears." "A wine can have the same effect on me that Waits does," Feiring explains. "The reaction goes beyond science. A technical wine cannot provoke me in this way. There's an emotional truth in natural wine that I can't ignore."[50] Collected together, these assertions clearly suggest that the crucial relationship between an individual and natural wine should be emotional. That, in fact, natural wine can be seen as both a product of a kind of anti-science aesthetic—though this may misstate the degree of technical skill required—and a trigger for experiences that transcend reason. Later in the same trip where she cried, Feiring participated in a tasting of a French natural wine organization hosted by Nicolas Joly where "everything was judged on an emotional level."[51]

The wines from California failed miserably at this tasting. They lack "music" or "a voice" or a "sense of place." For a while it seems hopeless that Feiring will find California winemakers who can match these emotional standards, but she eventually does. However, in my experience, many of the winemakers from California that Feiring associates with natural wine are either less evangelical or more conflicted—either about the label or their own approach. When I met with Chris Brockway in his Broc Cellars winery in Berkeley, he only half-jokingly said that he started making wine this way because "I couldn't afford to buy yeast and barrels." When I asked about his motives for making wine this way, he confessed that "I know what I'm doing but I don't know what I'm doing in a more philosophical sense." One of the winemakers that Feiring champions, Gideon Beinstock, suggested to me that if natural wine does provide meaning it's entirely constructed:

We as humans define these things with other words and attribute to them all kinds of other values that they have for us, from our perspective. But does the fact that they have these meanings from our perspective truly give them that meaning in themselves, on their own? Take humans out of the picture. The natural wine that happens in nature, which is very short-lived, but it does occur. Would you attribute to it any cultural [significance]? The culture only is attached to our human existence, not to the wine actually.

In short, what meaning natural wine might possess derives from extrinsic elements.

★   ★   ★   ★

Of all the winemakers I have met, only Abe Schoener came with more advanced notice than Hardy Wallace. Some had suggested to me that Hardy was a bit more showman than great winemaker. Yet, when I met Hardy, cherubic face, oversized designer glasses, slightly wild hair, I pretty quickly found someone quite different from what I expected. Hardy can certainly sell his wine. His tasting notes can be among the most exuberant and over the top you can find. His labels are eye-catching—both from his original Dirty and Rowdy wines and now for his Extra-dimensional Wine Co. Yeah!—and he can talk in a kind of crowd-pleasing banter. Nevertheless, the man I met at the Cruise winemaking facility in Petaluma could also be serious and earnest. He may have had an atypical path, but it's also clear that he has created a loyal fanbase for single-vineyard mourvedre in the United States, a pretty unusual wine for Americans, and he does not make any of his wines in the fashion of big, ripe, heavily oaked wines.

He is also a winemaker who gets frequently grouped in with the natural wine movement (he has a brief cameo in Feiring's book, mostly as a partygoer). We retreated into a room with a long table where we sipped at some of his Dirty and Rowdy Antle vineyard mourvedre and talked. As our conversation moved into questions about natural wine and the environment, it became clear that Hardy aspires to minimize the environmental impact of his winery:

FIGURE 4.3 Hardy Wallace

this is a conscious decision, this is the lightest domestically made glass we can find that is not what we call eco-glass. So the eco-glass is made out of recycled materials: [unfortunately], the eco-glass has a much higher breakage rate through the bottling line. So, this is about 440 grams, the eco-glass is about 375, but this is a very conscious way to make the footprint as light as possible.

He is concerned to

shorten the footprint from production to bottling, and even in the Familiars [of his previous winery], you notice the corks, we use those Nomacorcs, so those are hundred percent plant-based, recyclable, carbon neutral, breathable, compostable. And knowing that is going to be a wine that is going to be consumed within four or five years, it's more environmentally friendly than a screw top. The labels on most of them are recycled coffee bags.

When I asked about natural wines, he remarked that

it's a term I used to love—and actually, deep down inside I think I still love it. What I don't love about it is how people react to the term. They've taken something that I think really started as something really positive and they've turned it into something so negative. And for me, natural wine is something really simple: it's organic or biodynamic or "do nothing" farming at the core, and it's nothing added, nothing removed, and zero or minimal sulfur.

The question, though, is how did the term, natural, become something negative? The recurring theme is that the wines are flawed or that it's almost a con where flawed damaged wines are being marketed as exceptional. Underlying some of this is a generational split. Natural wines, at least in terms of their rising popularity, often get directly tied to young, disparagingly labeled, "hipster" sommeliers who proselytize for these wines or make them the focus of natural wine bars.

However, it's also clear that part of the problem lies in the very name. Here, we return to a semantics problem akin to that of the In Pursuit of Balance controversy. Though natural wine does not have the equivalent group to IPOB, we still find a variety of its proponents offering documents akin to manifestos. For instance, on his website for La Clarine Farm, Hank Beckmeyer declares,

this philosophy [of do nothing farming] can very easily be carried into the wine cellar. Once one can accept what the season has given in the vines, it is no great leap towards a minimalist approach to fermentation. You realize that fermentations will happen of their own accord and carry on with their own tempo, that there is no need to augment or to "help out". Surprises do occur, most of them very pleasant. Sure, weirdness does pop up, but more often than not, "problems" resolve themselves over time, adding to the richness of the wine. My role is to maintain a healthy environment and allow these resolutions the space in which to work (time).

Here's a piece of Tracy Brandt's "manifesto" for Donkey and Goat:

> That is one of the problems we have with inoculations. Winemakers choose cultured yeast for various attributes that include performance and aromatic profile. But the lab yeast need huge amounts of food. So the regimen becomes, kill the microbial life with SO2 & Lysozyme, add super yeast, add vitamins and nitrogen (DAP or diammonium phosphate being very popular) to feed these hungry microbes. Then hope the yeast doesn't put off any off aromas like H2S because of the imbalance in their diet. If they do, add Copper. Then rack and filter and add more SO2… it never stops. And don't get me started on the great irony of adding vast amounts of DAP to the vat to feed yeast. Guess which yeast also LOVES DAP and for that matter any additive rich in thiamin. Read the ingredients on most wine additives and you'll see thiamin at the front. That would be brettanomyces, the dark angel.

While I am not sure that either of these examples rises to the level of "believers" and "non-believers" of the IPOB manifesto, it is also easy to see why winemakers who do use commercial yeasts or who filter, use reverse-osmosis, or employ some other intervention might take offense at the tone of natural winemakers. After all, implied in these documents, no matter how many caveats of, I just do what's right for me, is that there is a proper way and an improper way to make wine. When that way gets labeled as "natural," a whole host of negative implications comes with the inverse—artificial, manipulated, inorganic, and most obviously, "unnatural." Beckmeyer suggests that some of this controversy has been blown out of proportion:

> I think a lot of that is—especially that criticism that comes from the more traditional part of the industry, is just magnifying a problem. It's like picking one thing: that I had natural wine once, and it was volatile, so all natural wines are volatile. You know, it's just kind of, it's an over-simplification. It's just amplifying something that isn't really as big a problem. And, I also think that there's no reason why natural wines can't be perfectly delicious and satisfy everybody's technical palates, you know? I can certainly understand why somebody may not like that style, maybe they don't like cloudy white wines or they have a problem with that—that's fine, don't drink it.

It may be that Beckmeyer is right—that the notion of flawed bottles does get magnified in this dispute—but there's also some sense that the very language used to identify this genre of winemaking has led to some of this controversy.

I would argue, then, that we can think of part of the issue that natural wine has become part of another polarizing narrative construct in the wine world, but also that like IPOB, natural wine may actually seek to challenge the grounds for evaluation and interpretation in a way that threatens those outside that community. The narrative of natural wine resembles the allegiances of the pastoral as Sussman suggests. Since natural wines are, to pardon the tautology, supposed to be as close to nature in its ideal form as wine can be, natural wines then partake of the supermarket pastoral in that the consumer gets a connection to the natural world by theoretically purchasing this wine. In doing so, the consumer seems to reject the artifice of modernity. Thus, part of what is being sold is how natural wines can make us feel. At one point Buranyi implies that wine seems to *always* bespeak the natural: "Wine's own iconography, right down to the labels, suggests a placid world of rolling green hills, village harvests and vintners shuffling down to the cellar to check in on the mysterious process of fermentation." However, he quickly gives voice to the objections of natural wine advocates regarding the amount of pesticides and fertilizers regularly employed in the wine industry (he notes that in France alone, despite being only 3 percent of the land dedicated to agriculture, the industry uses "20% of total pesticides").[52] Therefore, natural wines may in some ways be thought of as attempting to either reinstitute this natural iconography that invokes the pastoral or make it authentic. Perhaps the issue derives from the fact that most wine producers attempt to appeal to the desire for the pastoral to some degree, but the natural winemakers, with their insistence on seeing their wines as more truly natural, appear to then exclude other wine. This pattern also, however, returns natural wines to one of the basic problems, namely what counts as natural wine.

Feiring finds herself struggling with this repeatedly in part because a number of the winemakers she highlights fall short of the ideal in one way or another. Some use sulfur more than others, some use some form of intervention that others would not do, or, in say America, some have little to no control over the growing of the grapes. In Feiring's personal winemaking narrative, someone picks the grapes for her and she struggles to recover from this break in the natural continuum of plant to wine. Later, Feiring talks with a young woman who went to France to make wine who complains, "this whole natural movement is kind of a cult thing. So you're like me. You do your best; you make your wine with nothing, and you add sulfur, and you get booted out of the club."[53] O'Connor quotes Lepeltier suggesting that it's not just what you do, but what you look like: "if you are not, like, tattooed, bearded, dirty wine, you are not 'natural enough'."[54]

This story, then, needs not only heroes and villains but also insiders and outsiders. For some, like one of Napa's most sought-after consulting winemakers, Celia Welch, this raises a particular kind of skepticism: "unfortunately these 'I can sell my product in Whole Foods' approaches, I have found, often are more involved with marketing than they are with actually taking care of the earth." Others who think they are making wines in a natural way find themselves excluded for other reasons. When I spoke with Tegan Passelaqua about this, he noted that he has received the critique that his wines are in fact "too clean." The question of deception, however, also links to the need to be able to fasten these folks into a narrative. Tegan grew exasperated recalling that there's this Cali-fermentation tasting at Terroir, and all my friends poured, and they were supposed to be from organically farmed grapes with no more than 55 parts of sulfur, and 90 percent of my friends, they don't farm their vineyards organically. And they're pouring there, and I'm like, it's a total fucking fraud. They're just not certified. And I'm like, bullshit!

To make his point, Tegan highlights the way someone can become a kind of ideal figure in the natural wine movement. He presents the example of a pretty well-known winemaker. That winemaker is

a farmer and makes wine, he's mister natural wine organic—and you know, he filters his wines, he inoculates, he acidulates, and I don't have a problem with any of these, but, I mean, there are supporters of [this winemaker] that if you mention that or correct them, they will argue with you until they're blue in the face that you're wrong, and how dare you say this about [this winemaker]. it's not taking anything away [from that winemaker] but you're unfortunately misinformed.

The implication seems to be that for this person to fit as a hero of natural wine, it's best to not know the reality. Even in Feiring's accounts, we see this in a variety of ways. She focuses in more than one book on Eric Texier, an iconoclastic winemaker in the Rhone who also served as a teacher and mentor for Jared and Tracy Brandt from Donkey and Goat. At one point, Texier confesses that "I'm industrial for some and hard-core [natural] for others." Tegan's analysis of the way the natural movement requires simplification to tell its story gets echoed by Texier's resigned comment that "more and more, the world has no tolerance for gray but needs one to be extreme."

It's worth remembering Garrard's definition of the pastoral developed from critic Terry Gifford wherein the pastoral also suggests "an idealisation of the rural life that obscures the realities of labour and hardship."[55] For instance, consider the situation of Hardy Wallace. When I spoke with him initially he told me that one time

the VA got way out of control and we could've reverse osmosis and de-VAed the wines, and it's like, those wines ended up going down the drain, because it's like, well, we could do that, but then what am I going to do with it? It's not going to be a Dirty and Rowdy wine, it's not something that I want to [sell]. Yeah, I can clean it up, but it's not enough to bulk off to a bulk wine broker that's then going to sell it, and we're not going to sell it as is.

He explained that one of the problems of natural wine—one that has led to so many of its critiques—are the folks that would put out such a wine. However, a while after that initial conversation, I was back in California at the same time that an article by Esther Mobley about Hardy appeared in the *SF Chronicle*. It recounts the challenges that Hardy faced during the 2017 vintage when he experienced an extremely painful and debilitating infection that made him blind in one eye and unable to work. His brother-in-law, driving down from Oregon to help, died in a car accident. Because he could not get to his grapes, located in a variety of locations, he could not release his single-vineyard wines and admittedly had to use things like reverse-osmosis in order to produce a wine, his newly named Unfamiliar Red, that he could sell. The same night I read the article I met up with Hardy at the Cadet Wine Bar in Napa. Over a bottle of Aligoté, Hardy explained just how dire things were— not just with his health, but his business. He was really close to losing it all and so had to resort to the interventionist techniques he had forsworn. He let people know what he did, but his experiences help illustrate the ways in which real labor and hardship complicate not just the individual's philosophy but also the grander narrative and mythology that sometimes develops around natural wine and viticulture.

As I mentioned previously, the other major element of the natural wine movement has been the kind of cultural challenge it has made to the established wine world. Like the IPOB challenge relating to what they viewed as wines made for Robert Parker, proponents of natural wine may be challenging the grounds for evaluating wine. Earlier we saw how Feiring and some of the French appear to emphasize emotional response over all else. One of the surprising critics of these reevaluations has been Jon Bonné. When Bonné worked for the *SF Chronicle* and wrote the *New California Wine* he championed any and all winemakers who fought Big Flavor. However, in interviews, he seems to view natural wines as a bridge too far. In O'Connor's article, for instance, Bonné proclaims that natural wines are "being curated for the correct virtue points; they're not being curated for quality." He goes on to say, "what used to be considered a fuck-up is now considered character." O'Connor's conversation with Bonné also touches on the notion that what he calls "modern natural" fails because "the sole purpose is to be gluggable." With generally low alcohol, natural wines are easy to drink, and to drink fast and in quantity. Bonné then refers to the very same comparison he used in his IPOB retrospective to compare it to punk. "When do you learn how to play your instrument and become Johnny Rotten?", he asks. Besides the fact that it's unclear that Rotten ever learned to play an instrument—his memoir details Malcolm McClaren preventing Rotten from continuing his guitar-lessons with Chrissy Hynde because he didn't want him to learn how to play—Bonne's analogy does highlight his view that natural wines are making technical know-how seem elitist or artificial.

Ironically, however, O'Connor goes on to argue that natural wines themselves are a form of snobbery. She notes the related French term, "glou glou," a "wine designed to be gulped, not sipped." Paradoxically, "glou glou is a maddening form of luxury, one that simultaneously rejects and performs elitism. Glou glou rejects the near past in favor of a modernized version of the old past." Buranyi doesn't necessarily endorse this direction but does see natural wines as part of larger alteration in taste, for this new type of wine fitted perfectly with a wider revolution of taste, as vague terms such as "natural" and "artisanal" become bywords for sophistication, and consumers found themselves wanting to dine at farm-to-table restaurants and furnish their homes with reclaimed wood and industrial fittings.

Although someone like Bonné is overtly critical of what he sees as this change in what matters in a wine, he hits at why it remains so polarizing. Even as I wrote this, a poster on the American wine chat site, Wine Berserkers re-posted Buranyi's article, clearly having just discovered it, and the polarized debates about natural wine return.

I have perhaps artificially attempted to separate these notions of taste and narrative from one another. It's clear that convincing people to alter their methods of evaluating and refurnishing what they value in wine—and perhaps in most things—requires a new way of seeing and thinking, and that new way requires narrative to both explain the past and chart a way forward. Yet, as Texier and Passalaqua both noted, these stories tend to work best when they simplify the world they describe. In Timothy Morton's book, *Ecology without Nature*, he accuses most ecocriticism of some of the same flaws, saying the approach relies "more [on] ideas of nature, which set people's hearts beating and stop the thinking process."[56] Morton's approach finds some echoes in the views of another critic, Dana Phillips, whose *The Truth of Ecology* also seeks to challenge what he perceives as either mystifying or oversimplifying tendencies among ecocritics. He particularly challenges the work of Lawrence Buell, one of the foremost ecocritics. Buell, Phillips contends, "seems to want there to be a relationship between trees in literature and trees in the world closer than a relationship of mere semblance would be, whether that semblance would be descriptive, iconic, or metaphorical and symbolic."[57] The underlying issue Phillips raises is that ecocritics who rely on literature seem to be making the case of the importance of connecting to nature via that literature rather than simply going outside and exploring the natural world. Of course, the same problem lies with the supermarket pastoral and natural wines. "Devoting our time and energy to the perusal of environmental literature," Phillips suggests, "would seem to be a roundabout way for us to secure a bond with the earth: it is as if we should spend our time pouring over the personal ads, instead of striking up a conversation with the lonely heart next door."[58] Perhaps as with ecocriticism, what all this discourse concerning natural allows most of us is to feel as if we are connecting with nature, but without actually having to shed the comforts of industrialized society to do so. The power of the term natural, then, depends on the consumer's interpretation of that term, just as we saw the term balance. In order to encourage the sought-after interpretation, then, that term is presented through narratives that suggest why "natural" is desirable and significant. The fact that few can agree on the criteria for what makes a wine "natural" highlights the constructed nature of the term, whose understanding relies on rhetoric and interpretation—and perhaps an appeal to a culture of feeling—to have meaning and value.

Notes

1 Jon Bonné, *The New California Wine: A Guide to the Producers and Wines Behind a Revolution in Taste* (Berkeley: Ten Speed Press, 2013).
2 Mircea Eliade, *The Sacred and The Profane: The Nature of Religion*, trans. Willard R. Trask (New York: Harcourt, 1959).
3 Eric Asimov, *How to Love Wine: A Memoir and Manifesto* (New York: William Morrow, 2012), 242.
4 Michael Bunce, *The Countryside Ideal: Anglo-American Images of Landscape* (London: Routledge, 1994), 1.
5 Ibid., 2.
6 Michael Pollan, *The Omnivore's Dilemma: A Natural History of Four Meals* (New York: Penguin, 2006), 134–136.
7 Ibid., 137.
8 Ibid.
9 Ibid.
10 Ibid.
11 Ibid., 138.
12 C.P. Snow, *The Two Cultures and the Scientific Revolution* (New York: Cambridge University Press, 1961).
13 Louis Menand, *The Marketplace of Ideas: Reform and Resistance in the American University* (New York: W.W. Norton & Company, 2010), 125.
14 Greg Garrard, *Ecocriticism* (London: Routledge, 2012), 5.
15 Ibid., 6.
16 Ibid., 37.
17 Ibid., 37–38.
18 Lawrence Buell, *The Environmental Imagination: Thoreau, Nature Writing, and the Formation of American Culture* (Cambridge, MA: Harvard University Press, 1995), 31.
19 Alice Feiring, *The Battle for Wine and Love, or How I Saved the World From Parkerization* (Boston: Mariner Books, 2008), 84.
20 Garrard, *Ecocriticism*, 40.
21 Buell, *The Environmental Imagination*, 49.
22 Ibid., 33–36.
23 Ibid., 42.
24 Ibid., 44.
25 Timothy Sweet, *American Georgics: Economy and Environment in Early American Literature* (Philadelphia: University of Pennsylvania Press, 2002), 2.
26 Ibid., 4.
27 Ibid., 8.
28 Ibid., 5.
29 Garrard, *Ecocriticism*, 47.
30 Tim Blanning, *The Romantic Revolution* (New York: Modern Library Chronicles, 2010), xvi.
31 Ibid., 7–8.
32 Richard Holmes, *The Age of Wonder: How the Romantic Generation Discovered the Beauty and Terror of Science* (New York: Vintage Books, 2008).
33 Blanning, *The Romantic Revolution*, 20.
34 Ibid., 21.
35 Ibid., 16–17.
36 Ibid., 17.
37 Qtd in Blanning, 19.
38 Blanning, *The Romantic Revolution*, 182.
39 Zachary Sussman, "Wine Doesn't Make Itself," *Punch*, March 14, 2018.
40 Maureen O'Connor, "Sommeliers Are Obsessed with Natural Wines. But Do They Actually Taste Good?" "Grub Street," *New York Magazine*, July 23, 2018.

41 Buryani, Stephen, "Has Wine Gone Bad?" *The Guardian*, May 15, 2018.
42 Alice Feiring, *Naked Wine: Letting Grapes Do What Comes Naturally* (Cambridge: Da Capo Press, 2011).
43 Elaine Chukan Brown, "In Defense of Natural Wine," *Hawk Wakawaka Wine Reviews*, November 19, 2014.
44 Feiring, *Naked Wine*, 28.
45 Ibid., 28–29, emphasis hers.
46 Feiring, *Naked Wine*, 29.
47 Ibid., 30.
48 Ibid., 36.
49 Ibid., 41.
50 Ibid., 71.
51 Ibid., 77.
52 Buryani, "Has Wine Gone Bad?"
53 Feiring, *Naked Wine*, 113.
54 O'Connor, "Sommeliers Are Obsessed With Natural Wine."
55 Garrard, *Ecocriticism*, 54.
56 Timothy Morton, *Ecology Without Nature: Rethinking Environmental Aesthetics* (Cambridge: Harvard University Press, 2007), 7.
57 Dana Phillips *The Truth of Ecology: Nature, Culture, and Literature in America* (Oxford: Oxford University Press, 2003), 6.
58 Ibid., 7.

References

Asimov, Eric. *How to Love Wine: A Memoir and a Manifesto*. New York: William Morrow, 2012.
Blanning, Tim. *The Romantic Revolution: A History*. New York: Modern Library, 2012.
Bonné, Jon. *The New California Wine: A Guide to the Producers and Wines Behind a Revolution in Taste*. Berkeley: Ten Speed Press, 2013.
Buell, Lawrence. *The Environmental Imagination: Thoreau, Nature Writing, and the Formation of American Culture*. Cambridge: Belknap, 1995.
Bunce, Michael. *The Countryside Ideal: Anglo-American Images of Landscape*. London: Routledge, 1994.
Buryani, Stephen. "Has Wine Gone Bad?" *The Guardian*, May 15, 2018. www.theguardian.com/news/2018/may/15/has-wine-gone-bad-organic-biodynamic-natural-wine.
Chukan Brown, Elaine. "In Defense of Natural Wine." *Hawk Wakawaka Wine Reviews*, November 19, 2014. https://wakawakawinereviews.com/2014/11/19/in-defense-of-natural-wine/.
Eliade, Mircea. *The Sacred and the Profane: The Nature of Religion*, translated by William Ropes Trask. New York: Harcourt, 1959.
Feiring, Alice. *The Battle for Wine and Love: Or How I Saved the World from Parkerization*. Boston: Mariner, 2008.
Feiring, Alice. *Naked Wine: Letting Grapes Do What Comes Naturally*. Cambridge: Da Capo Press, 2011.
Garrard, Greg. *Ecocriticism*. London: Routledge, 2012.
Holmes, Richard. *The Age of Wonder: The Romantic Generation and the Discovery of the Beauty and the Terror of Science*. New York: Vintage, 2010.
Menand, Louis. *The Marketplace of Ideas: Reform and Resistance in the American University*. New York: W.W. Norton, 2010.
Morton, Timothy. *Ecology Without Nature: Rethinking Environmental Aesthetics*. Cambridge, MA: Harvard University Press, 2007.

O'Connor, Maureen. "Sommeliers Are Obsessed with Natural Wines. But Do They Actually Taste Good?" "Grub Street." *New York Magazine*, July 23, 2018. www.grubstreet.com/2018/07/sommeliers-are-obsessed-with-natural-wine-but-is-it-good.html.

Phillips, Dana. *The Truth of Ecology: Nature, Culture, and Literature in America*. Oxford: Oxford University Press, 2003.

Pollan, Michael. *The Omnivore's Dilemma: A Natural History of Four Meals*. New York: Penguin, 2006.

Snow, C.P. *The Two Cultures and the Scientific Revolution*. New York: Cambridge University Press, 1961.

Sussman, Zachary. "Wine Doesn't Make Itself." *Punch*, March 14, 2018.

Sweet, Timothy. *American Georgics: Economy and Environment in Early American Literature*. Philadelphia: University of Pennsylvania Press, 2002.

5

POSTMODERN VITICULTURE

Morgan Twain-Peterson might be said to pass for a prodigy in a world that does not tend to produce many. Whereas in Europe farming the family estate can extend for many, many generations, with young people growing up in the trade, estates in California tend to be much younger, and for a variety of reasons—both financial and cultural—this pattern has yet to appear with anywhere near the same frequency. To some extent, Morgan is an exception. His father, Joel Peterson, helped found Ravenswood, and when it sold for a large sum, both he and Morgan became owners of the Bedrock Vineyard, which also gave its name to Morgan's own label. As I waited for Morgan to arrive and meandered among the few ramshackle buildings at the end of the driveway, I seemed to be the only one there on a beautiful sunny day, Tax Day. Soon Morgan arrived, breathless from rushing and hoarse from the early onset of allergies. He was dressed in a way that fitted both a vineyard and some trendy Brooklyn bar.

At around 152 acres, the Bedrock Vineyard is one of the largest historical vineyards in California. As I read its history, I had trouble wrapping my head around the fact that the vineyard had been planted by General Tecumseh Sherman and General Joe Hooker. According to Morgan's website, it dates to 1854. In the 1880s it was owned by Senator George Hearst, father of William Randolph and the central villain in David Milch's magnificent *Deadwood*. There's also a chance that Walt Whitman's brother might have had possession of the place at one time. Some of the vines are believed to date from Hearst's replanting. Morgan took me out to the center of the vineyard near a picnic table that served for tastings at that time. I felt myself mesmerized following Morgan's index finger as he narrated:

> these are younger vines that have been inter-planted as the vines have died off. But you know, for instance, that's quite an old vine right there, the one behind it is very old. David Gates, at Ridge, has this saying, if you can see

DOI: 10.4324/9781003399810-6

through a vine, you know it's really old. That's some very old Syrah up there. And this is my favorite time of year, because we seed this crimson clover to scavenge nitrogen and fix it in the soil, and it's in bloom right now, and also all the lupine is out and the Persian clover, and it's a pretty time of year out here.

Everywhere I seemed to turn, the spiraling, knotty own-rooted vines seemed transparent. The rich and varied colors spread across my vision like I had walked into a Seurat painting. At such moments, it just seems right to want to preserve this landscape, to keep these old vines alive as long as you can even if we simply admire the sublimity of their long life and even more if you believe, as many do, that older vines produce more complex and flavorful wines (some of the arguments for this are that the older vines have roots that dig further into the soil and can hence translate that soil complexity more fully—this is up for debate—and, that since the vines struggle to produce grapes, what they do produce has greater concentration).

Suddenly emotional, I immediately wanted to know how they farmed this land and asked if he used biodynamic farming methods, which I had recently heard so much about. Morgan abruptly wheeled around and nearly spat out a response:

biodynamic's a religion. And it's just patent bullshit. You know, we farm using a lot of the standards of agro-ecology, which is something that was developed by Miguel Altieri, he's a professor at UC Berkeley, but it goes back to some tenets established by Fukuoka in Japan, and it's basically sort of like scientific biodynamics. The thing with biodynamics is that there's just so much stuff that

FIGURE 5.1 Bedrock Vineyard—Carignane vines

makes absolutely no sense. And the fact is that there's actually stuff in the practices, like spraying silica into the air, that is actually potentially injurious to your vineyard workers and whoever else is out there breathing that stuff. That's not exactly good for you. And so there's a lot of mysticism involved with it.

Morgan would not be the last person to raise the spectre of the potential harm of these sprays. As Jared Brandt of Donkey and Goat suggested to me, if you can't be in a vineyard for over 24 hours after you spray, how can that be good for anyone or anything?

In asking Morgan why he chose organic farming over biodynamic farming, I had clearly touched on something that he had both considered for a long time and that he felt very strongly about. His responses provide a capsule of the debate that surrounds this approach in the wine world. Morgan conceded that

the focus of biodynamics on the vineyards, and really walking your fields and making sure that you see what's going on and thinking about the vineyard as a very complex system, and treating the soil as the most critical thing, which is something that a lot of conventional farmers don't do. And using the softest possible products, and those that are the safest for your workers and your guys, that's all really important.

Like many others, Morgan applauded the fact that biodynamic farming encouraged—or arguably forced—a heightened attention to the vineyard. However, when it comes down to it, Morgan declared, "I prefer not to work on mysticism; I prefer to work on science." Considering how passionate he was and how thorough his objections were, I wondered aloud if he had ever discussed it with one of the major proponents of biodynamic farming in Sonoma, Ted Lemon. No, Morgan confessed, but said he would be visiting Littorai, Ted's winery, the following week. I hoped they would get a chance to talk.

★   ★   ★   ★

I had known about Littorai for some time. My wife and I had done a tasting there with Ted Lemon's then assistant winemaker, a rather mellow Californian, just as their new, environmentally friendly winery space had gone into operation. I had returned a few times, as the tasting had grown more routinized, but I had always been impressed with the wines. Lemon, following the model of his early wine job in Burgundy, focused on pinot noir and chardonnay, and those wines always seemed remarkably Burgundian for New World wines. Of course, now I look back on how I made those judgments about other wineries and think I had no idea what I was talking about at the time. However, Ted's wines have continued to seem Old World even after my further education.

As I began my research for this book, I realized that I needed to talk with someone about biodynamics. When I spoke with Rajat Parr, it had not been the main focus of our conversation, but I recalled him telling me that biodynamics seemed particularly useful in "healing" vineyards that had been intensely chemically farmed. Biodynamics had certainly become a buzzword, frequently mixed into conversations about natural wines. Alice Feiring mentions it multiple times, including toward the end of *The Battle* when she visits one of its leading French proponents, Nicolas Joly. Feiring's tone becomes serious as she provides an explanation: "Biodynamics is a holistic way of farming tied to the seasons, the moon, and the planets. Elements in the vineyard are broken down to heat, air, water, and stone. Despite a lot of psychobabble surrounding biodynamics, the movement offers much wisdom." Echoing Parr's comments to me, Feiring claims that "Biodynamics is proactive, with a focus on building the health of the vineyard."[1]

The more I researched the origins of this approach, however, the more apprehensive I became about what my conversation with Ted Lemon, who seemed to embrace the approach wholeheartedly, was going to be like. One afternoon I just started with internet searches and found myself down an extraordinary rabbit hole trying to understand the movement's creator, Rudolf Steiner. Depending on who you read, Steiner can appear as a mystic, a crackpot, an astonishing polymath, and a Zelig from the turn of the twentieth century. For someone who ended up having a strong influence on the wine world, it's amazing to find out that he did not drink. His first major work was a study of Goethe. Katherine Cole also sees Goethe as a forerunner of the early twentieth-century philosophy, phenomenology, "which emphasized the power of observation over the mathematical-deductive mechanistic models of the scientific method."[2] If you think about Goethe as Germany's preeminent poet and playwright—a figure central to German Romanticism—you might be puzzled on how this might anticipate Steiner's lectures on agriculture. However, Goethe, living at a time prior to C.P. Snow's two cultures, was also fascinated by the study of the natural world and deeply influenced by his friend Alexander Humboldt, a science pioneer who conceived of nature in terms of holistic systems. If you have heard of Waldorf Education, that would be Waldorf Steiner education. The manager of the Waldorf Cigarette company had asked Steiner to come up with an education system for his workers in Germany, and thus an education philosophy that spread to various locations in the United States, including Sonoma, had been born. And then there's anthroposophy, which Wikipedia calls a philosophy, but many call a religion, which Steiner founded when he broke from the Theosophists, a group that helped popularize seances at the turn of the century—mocked by T.S. Eliot, embraced by Arthur Conan Doyle. In addition to believing he could communicate with the dead, Steiner seems to have taken Atlantis pretty seriously as well.

Feeling a bit dazed from what I had first found, I turned to an excellent exploration of biodynamics among Oregon vintners, *Voodoo Vintners* by Katherine Cole. Steiner's lectures do not make for easy reading, due either to a translation problem or the tendency of the original to muddy up its message in mysticism. Nevertheless, Cole provides a comprehensive and lucid overview. In addition to

Feiring's point about following the seasons and the moon, Cole also underscores that biodynamic farmers should "use the raw materials on your property to nourish your crops." "Protect nature," Steiner commands, and "in return [nature] will protect your harvest. And in doing all of these things, harness the spiritual forces of the heavens."[3] Hence Morgan Twain-Peterson's conclusion that biodynamics was a religion. While following the moon is, as Cole suggests, one of the ways to distinguish the biodynamic approach from organic's, the other key element is the use of what are called the "preparations." If you are interested in a detailed description of those, you can refer to Cole's book, but these are connected to many of the practices most frequently mocked by skeptics. To get a sense of that, consider Cole's description of Preparation 500: to prepare it, you take a

> cow horn packed with the manure of lactating bovines—no bullshit—and buried two and a half to five feet underground for the winter, 'the season when the Earth is most inwardly alive', according to Steiner. It's dug up in the spring, by which point the manure looks like finely pulverized coffee grounds and smells like soft, rich earth. In minute proportions, it is added to half a bucket of water at a time. This water is stirred vigorously for an hour, in a ritualistic manner.

Then, when this is done, "it's sprayed on the soil in late spring and late autumn to encourage root growth."[4] What particularly strikes me about this description is that it has the feel of science in the sense that it's precise and reasoned and presented like a recipe, but it does not in fact derive from any scientific method. When Feiring cites the musings of Nicolas Joly, they include, "People say, 'show me the science of biodynamics.' Look, as a farmer you need water. How does it help you to know that water is H20?"[5] It's not quite intuition, but farming need not go beyond common sense, observation, and folk wisdom.

We tend to think of our more modern world as the one caught between the forces of industrialism and environmentalism, the chemical versus the organic, but, as Cole points out, Steiner grew up in world where chemical farming was becoming relevant (and in a pattern that would continue throughout the century, the industry that helped produced the weapons of war would get tied to agriculture). Cole explains that Steiner found himself repeatedly split between reason and feeling: "Torn between the opposing forces of the pastoral and the industrial, the spiritual and the sensual, Steiner developed a lifelong sense of cognitive dissonance."[6] She concludes that the German Romantic philosopher and writer—and another friend of Goethe's and Humbolt's—Fredrich Schiller's discussions of "the friction between man's sensuous side and his rational side" continued to be "a topic of public discussion and debate" in Steiner's time.[7] After meeting a healer on the train one day, Steiner became fascinated with homeopathic medicine and this— among his various interests—helped lead the way to his agricultural lectures. According to Cole, Steiner was "struck by what he was hearing from farmers that the earth, too, was sick and in need of healing."[8] With the help of Ehrenfriend

Pfieffer, who Cole suggests should be more fully recognized for his role in developing biodynamics, Steiner found "homeopathic herbal treatments for farmland" and biodynamic farming was born.[9]

★   ★   ★   ★

The day I arrived at Littorai, a mist and light rain had settled on the place. Coming off several years of drought, this rain was certainly welcome. On Ted's website for Littorai, he describes the winery's location as a farm. After you enter through the automated swinging gate, you drive past the Lemon home, a man-made pond for conserving water, vineyards, all on your right, before you arrive at the winery building itself. A sales manager let me know that Ted would be there soon, and then we talked about the cows—an indicator of Ted's biodynamic approach to farming—I saw lumbering about the vineyards. She told me about looking up one day and finding several of them staring at her through the window.

Ted showed up, looking like a gentleman farmer, but one who works the land: proper boots, sweater with elbow patches, straight brown hair looking hand-brushed across his head. Before we could talk, he asked if we could check on some new plantings. In my ignorance, I had thought initially we were looking at new vines, but this was not the time of year for such things, and we were instead checking on cover crops. Ted patiently corrected my mistake and showed me what he had come to see:

> this is good, this rain. If we get really wet, a little dirt will fall in on it. Yeah, there's a fair amount of exposed seed here. See how you can see along here, see how that seed's just exposed? Now if it stays wet for a while—see how it's germinating?

Although Ted refuses to be certified by the Demeter company that controls who can use the biodynamic label for their farming practices, he follows biodynamic practices on his "farm" and any vineyard he owns or any vineyard that he can persuade the owner to farm this way. Ever since I had seen his description of his turn away from conventional farming as a crisis of faith, I had wanted to talk to him about why he had phrased it that way. Did he mean it lightly, ironically? After our visit to the cover crops being grown for the cows, we retreated to a work space in the winery and I asked Ted to describe how he had "lost faith" in conventional farming. He asserted that he had chosen "faith in earnest":

> I sort of intentionally use the word faith, and this definitely relates to the post-Enlightenment world we live in, which is that science became a faith, and science remains largely a faith for humanity, and it's causing us enormous problems, right, that we accepted this, this faith. I mean it was a belief, originally; I don't think it was a faith—but it was a belief that science, that materialism really enabled the betterment of humanity.

In short, Lemon sees conventional farming as an outcome of the Enlightenment narrative of meliorist progress: that is, with time and proper methods, humans can attain a full knowledge of the workings of the world, and human progress will be continually positive. As Lemon explains,

> it became a faith as the power of science grew—in other words, as we developed locomotives that could do these amazing things, the common man who may have had no mechanical engineering knowledge of any kind began to assume a faith that technological, materialist solutions would lead us to a better place. And that same process occurred with pure science.

For Lemon, an important distinction must be made:

> That science became knowledge as opposed to a path of knowledge—and the distinction is so important, because a path of knowledge implies that it will change, it will go different ways, whereas knowledge can be seen as on a pedestal and complete in and of itself.

I suppose that one way of understanding this would be to say that Lemon wishes to see science as a tool that can lead to further knowledge rather than an end in itself. His implied critique of the latter echoes the cautions from the world of ecocriticism that see Humanistic critics looking to ecology as a settled, unified, understanding of the world and thus can ground any Humanistic interpretation in unassailable truth. Thus, sometimes what appears to be an adherence or sympathy with a culture of reason is a culture of feeling in disguise. Without comprehension of scientific principles, one just relies on faith and feeling that science provides the right answer. It became clear to me that in most interviews with the wine press, Lemon is not given time to explain his thinking because those interviews want something much more epigrammatic. He welcomed this chance to explain his path to biodynamics at greater length. "So," Ted noted,

> I lost my personal faith that I saw lots of other people in our world continuing to assume that these answers are either available through science as we know it, or even that the path of science itself [or] that the path of science can reveal.

It was not that Lemon simply moved from one view to another, but that he needed, in a kind of deeply philosophical way, to strip himself of a set of inculcated beliefs that he felt unsatisfying. "And so, that loss of quote unquote faith is what turned me into […] a blank slate. I mean that's what made me become open to the idea of something utterly different. Not believe in it—but open to it."

$$\star \quad \star \quad \star \quad \star$$

Early in Greg Garrard's book, *Ecocriticism*, he sketches out what he considers the broad "positions" of ecocritics, which frequently have direct mirrors in the broader world of environmental activists. Of the "positions" that Garrard labels "radical," the one that has a recurring resonance to some of the winemakers I met would be that of the deep ecologists. Garrard also considers it the most "influential" among those outside of academia, so this coincidence makes sense.[10] Almost like a political party, the deep ecologists, as summarized by Garrard, hold a series of beliefs presented as something of a platform. Deep ecologists "argue for long-term population reduction throughout the world" as they see that in a variety of ways population expansion has led to environmental crises. In addition—and perhaps more centrally—deep ecologists hold a philosophical position akin to some who ascribe to object-oriented ontology or a flat ontology. This view attempts a decentering of the human subject: the placement of all matters of importance, perspective and literally "being" as coming from and revolving around humanity. Unlike the

> "shallow' approaches" [which] take an instrumental approach to nature, arguing for preservation of natural resources only for the sake of humans, deep ecology demands recognition of intrinsic value in nature. It identifies the dualistic separation of humans from nature promoted by Western philosophy and culture as the origin of environmental crisis, and demands a return to a monistic, primal identification of humans and the ecosphere.[11]

Biodynamics may not overtly assert the need for recognizing the intrinsic value in all nature, but in its push away from monoculture and hearkening back to farming by the patterns of the moon, it clearly overlaps with some of the larger emphases of deep ecology. Perhaps most overtly, they connect via an interest in spirituality. As Garrard notes, however, "Alongside the strongly spiritualistic dimension subsists, somewhat uneasily at times, the scientific ecology from which the movement takes its name."[12] Citing a major collection of deep ecological essays, Gerard observes that no actual ecologists were included and "'ecology' appears there, if at all, as a laudable background activity that need never be discussed directly, but can rather be used to validate existing 'intuitions'."[13]

It strikes me, then, that a key thread that runs from the Romantics through to the deep ecologists and picking up folks like Ted Lemon along the way has to do with the crucial importance of intuition as guided by human observation over and against the scientific method. Garrard goes on to suggest that for deep ecologists, scientific ecologists tend to fall into the "anthropocentric management"—they put the human at the center—and thus belie one of the key tenets of this approach.[14] In short, deep ecologists share a deep distrust of—critics might say lack of interest in—the very science that has lent them their name and while they may ironically wish to decenter the human they rely heavily on the very human notion of intuition. This pattern informs many of the winemakers I met who shunned conventional farming. Consider how Ted Lemon explained to me that he knew biodynamic farming would have a positive impact:

> what ticked for me, Mike, was that even within six months we began to see things that even on a small level it seemed to me that something's going right

to me. I can remember in August of 2001 we were planting The Haven, and you're at the end of August, driest time in California, and there's stuff sprouting in your vineyard, and you know, other than herbicide-resistant plants, that just doesn't happen in conventional agriculture. You just don't see stuff sprouting in the dry season. It just doesn't happen.

So signs of vitality in the soil, for instance, showed the effect of biodynamic farming. Here the proof of positive impact derives from observation in the soil and the intuitive link that these are interconnected.

We can find a similar pattern in Feiring's book when she ventures to UC Davis to face one of the villains of her narrative, the enologists and viticulture professors whose professional credentials are grounded in science. A good deal of this chapter is dedicated to her conversation with Professor Doug Adams, who notes that "the old ways were based on an intuition that science and technology now ignore."[15] When Feiring asks Adams why he doesn't teach biodynamic farming, we get to the crux of the distance between the Enlightenment world view held largely by Adams and the views held by folks like Lemon and Feiring. "I don't see," Adams argues, "how the phases of the planets and moon could have anything to do with plant physiology. I really can't find the proof. It's like saying that you want your plant to be stressed but not panicked."[16] I find it striking that Adams' rejection of biodynamics is tied, in essence, to a rejection of the pastoral tradition and the pathetic fallacy that ascribes human emotions to plants.

Adams goes on to reject Feiring's claims that biodynamically farmed grapes produce better wines by declaring, "Prove it to me."[17] Feiring concludes that ultimately scientists, then, are among the bad guys, for Feiring "believe[s] that technology, science, and business had squelched the creativity, immediacy, and urgency once inherent to winemaking. In their place was correctness and control."[18] Instead of science, Feiring, like a deep ecologist critical of the modern, favors intuition. Consider how she connects the environment to taste through intuitive steps: "The sandy soiled *looked* like crushed coral. I *felt* like I was standing in the basin of a drained-out sea. *Perhaps* that's why I *found* a sea-like savory salinity in so many older Riojan wines."[19] You can almost imagine Adams rushing in from stage left like a Monty Python sketch yelling, but where's your proof, Alice? Instead, Feiring relies on her senses and her intuition. Another winemaker, Gideon Beinstock, would agree with this approach. Like Lemon, Beinstock feels that we rely on science to tell us what we see and what we should know:

And so there is a lot going on that our brains do not perceive, do not understand fully because we don't yet have the science to exactly tell us, because we by now require exact scientific molecules and whatever for us to be convinced of what is going on. We don't trust anymore just living in a place and seeing the changing action to tell us this is what's happening. We're waiting for some research to come and tell us.

In their views towards science, then, Fiering, Lemon, and Bienstock can all appear to be modern avatars of Romanticism.

★   ★   ★   ★

Murphys in the Sierra Foothills seemed to be a one-stoplight town. If Carriage House has one, I missed it. This book has taken me to some of the more remote wine growing areas of California, but Carriage House in the North Yuba area, part of the extensive Sierra Foothills, felt among the most remote. That morning I had headed directly north out of Sacramento, and as in some kind of dreamscape, I proceeded down narrower and smaller roads before I made the turn past Carriage House's country store, gas station and, seemingly, major landmark. I pulled up next to a three-barred metal fence, like ones you might use to separate cattle. To my left, I saw a fenced-in vineyard and, as I stepped out of my rented SUV, dogs barked from each fenced-in area, a canine cacophony. Slowly, a short, bearded man of late middle age approached. This particular trip was to meet a man who has lived many lives to this point—artist, nascent philosopher, Israeli soldier, aspiring wine aficionado learning at Steve Spurrier's legendary Paris shop, poet, member of a religious group known as the Fellowship of Friends—and one frequently called a cult by both outsiders and by the man I had come to meet, Gideon Beinstock, on occasion. I felt a bit like Oedipa Maas in *The Crying of Lot 49* meeting one of those unusual characters that tend to find a home in California, and Gideon could certainly resemble a Thomas Pynchon character in the way he could speak on an erudite range of subjects, suddenly unsettle his interlocutor, and preferred to think deeply about the world rather than focus on its superficial surface. Slivers of his past reflected in his accents—a touch of Israeli, of French.

Swinging the gate with one hand and holding back a large pair of dogs with the other, Beinstock welcomed me to his home. To my left stood a small building I took to be his winery space. A bit further up on the left I spotted a small family home and below that, Beinstock's first vineyard, the oldest block of his Home Vineyard. If you had only been to the main avenues of Napa, this might strike you as the least glamorous vineyard you had ever encountered. At the end of my final trip a few months later, I drove past Domaine Carneros, an American sparkling wine house owned by Taittinger. As I looked up the slope, all I could see was an enormous chateau modeled quite overtly, according to their website, on a French building from Champagne. Many of the buildings in and around Napa, while perhaps more American in style, still seek to create an overt impressiveness, a visual symbol of the importance of the winery's stature in the way that heavier, thicker wine bottles seek to suggest the great significance of what has been placed inside. Of those sort of trappings and homages to conspicuous consumption and materialism, Beinstock could not care less.

Although I had sent him a detailed description of my project, he seemed a bit uncertain about why I had visited, and he offered me three options: a walking tour, tasting some wine, or talking. I opted for the last. To accommodate our

conversation, he grabbed two white stackable lawn chairs and arranged them as if
setting up a TV talk show stage and then began an interplay of scolding his rowdy
dogs and moving his chair to avoid the sun's glare. Beinstock lives with his wife and
family here, but he talks about going days without really conversing. In fact, he
described how both he and his wife can be working through the vineyard at the same
time without exchanging a word, lost, I suppose, in both the physical experience and
their own thoughts. Perhaps, as a result of this, when I offered Beinstock a chance to
share those thoughts they came out in long torrents, often sounding a bit like speeches
or monologues he had rehearsed in his head. Consider, for instance, how he explains
how humans have arrived at this present, apocalyptic moment:

> I look at humanity, look at what we're doing to the planet, look at everything
> around us. It's proof of the horrible limitation of our brains. In part, because
> they make these artificial separations between things. I am human; therefore,
> my interests are different than anything else's interests. That's the key to the
> destruction of our environment. So, we're missing some things. And partly
> what we're missing, I believe, is that over the millennia that our brains became
> more and more and more the sole tool of our survival or nearly the sole tool
> of our survival, we have. Our bodies have shrunk, have become weaker, both
> physically and in terms of their senses and connection to the world and
> everything around us. We trust our senses less and less and less. I mean, look at
> how much we trust all of the electronic world more and more to the exclu-
> sivity of what our own senses tell us. So it is like another step, yet. So I am
> trying to balance it. And that's why I chose this lifestyle which is sort of
> somewhat like a hermit. And I don't do it because I dislike [people]—I lived
> in Paris and in London and in San Francisco, I love living in cities, I love
> culture. But more and more my perception about my own world was that it
> was top-heavy. It is too strongly exclusive to my box, which is my head, my
> brain, and maybe some emotions, but where's my body, where's my connec-
> tion to the world that I live in? And that was missing, and so to me that is a
> very important part of my relationship to the wine.

Here, Beinstock moves through a series of interrelated phenomenon, but key is the
strand of Deep Ecological thinking: that humans have become too wrapped up in a
theory of our exceptionalism, too wrapped up in our "boxes"—a reliance on the
brain's reasoning powers—and a dismissiveness of the very senses that allow us to
intuitively understand our world. Yet, for Beinstock, the attempts to move away
from these patterns has led him to wine and a life where he spends a tremendous
amount of time intimately connecting to plant life rather than other humans.

★   ★   ★   ★

Early in my conversation with Beinstock, he told me that it was pretty much over
for humanity. For him, we had driven over the cliff and now were simply in the

short period of seeming to fly before the crash. Although we might be able to delay the end, the end had become inevitable. As humans have become a "species not having any competition," he explained, this has led us to the point that even

> if we created a utopian world government whose sole purpose would have been to save the planet, it would buy us a lot of time. It probably still has time to change, using this energy instead of that energy ... . All of the good things. Even then, we will buy ... hundreds or thousands or ten thousands of years, but we are not going to change the course.

For Beinstock, then, what humans earned by rising to a position without competition in the grand survival of the fittest was the end of our world because humans "will grow and destroy its ecosystem." Why? "Because it cannot control itself. Our lizard brain is wired to do the word of god, procreate and cover the earth!" In the calm light of the morning many days later, those pronouncements seem somewhat reasonable. Certainly, we can find warnings every day that the planet is heading towards an irreversible crisis brought on by the actions of humanity. Yet this doomsaying also links to what Garrard identifies as one of the central tropes employed by ecocriticism and environmentalists, namely the apocalypse. In fact, Garrard explains that many critics, including Lawrence Buell, have noted the pervasiveness of the apocalyptic trope, as it can be found in *Silent Spring* but also in the works of Al Gore. "Even the commonplace notion of the 'environmental crisis' is inflected by it," Garrard contends.[20] While there is a history of environmentalists attempting to use the apocalyptic as a means of invoking change, we can see in Beinstock a more traditional, apocalyptic thinker in the sense that our fate is sealed, though he accepts it with more of a shrug.

Nevertheless, Garrard suggests that the apocalypse has a tendency to be reductive in its work as shaper of environmental narrative: "Apocalypse provides an emotionally charged frame of reference within which complex, long-term issues are reduced to monocausal crises involving groups, such as Greenpeace versus whalers."[21] The problems of thinking about the environment in terms of apocalypse surface in a variety of ways: "It tends to polarize responses, prodding sceptics towards scoffing dismissal and potentially inciting believers to confrontation and even violence," and additionally "the rhetoric of catastrophe tends to 'produce' the crisis it describes, as in the Malthusain depiction of extreme poverty as 'famine'."[22] In short, the language of apocalypse can both create its own crisis and create a neo-religious crisis dividing us into believers and non-believers. It is also one clear way in which climate change has been placed within a humanly understood frame. In his influential examination of climate change entitled *The Great Derangement*, Amitav Ghosh declares, "let us make no mistake: the climate crisis is also a crisis of culture, and thus of the imagination."[23]

★   ★   ★   ★

The most obvious way in which something like climate change has been the kind of failure to which Ghosh points can be put simply: it's a problem so large that we cannot as humans wrap our heads around it. Ecocritic Timothy Morton calls this a hyperobject in a book of the same name. In the later book, *Dark Ecology*, Morton puts the challenge in a slightly different way as he arrived at

> the uncanny realization that every time I turned my car ignition key I was contributing to global warming and yet was performing actions that were statistically meaningless. When I think of myself as a member of the human species, I lose the visible tactile "little me"; yet it wasn't tortoises that caused global warming.[24]

How much harm does the individual do? How much good can the individual do? Beinstock says,

> There are ways for us to minimize the harm that we cause to the planet. And that I definitely am trying to do [so]. We try to—this buzzword, biodynamic, we are not biodynamic, but the overriding principle of biodynamic agriculture is, see your ecosystem, or your farming as an ecosystem, and try to get it as self-sustained and fully balanced as possible. I believe this is pristine, that's what we're trying to do. But we cause obvious damage. It's just less than comparable, or other choices that we could have made that would be a lot heavier on the environment.

He tries, but he has no sense that anything he can do individually will ultimately make a difference. He's just part of that imaginary utopian government simply trying to slow the car down before it inevitably crashes.

Ghosh argues that the problem lies across culture and science, and that we are overly concerned with the individual and what I do in choosing to buy a hybrid over a Hummer. "At exactly the time," Ghosh declares, "when it has become clear that global warming is in every sense a collective predicament, humanity finds itself in the thrall of the dominant culture in which the idea of the collective has been exiled from politics, economics, and literature alike."[25] Why we can't wrestle with these problems, folks like Ghosh argue, is not just that our science can't account for them, but because our culture lacks the imagination to help us understand and see the problems and solutions as they need to be seen. Ghosh offers the example of John Updike's criticism of Abdel Rahman Munif's novel, *Cities of Salt*, which, according to Updike, lacks "individual moral adventure."[26] Instead, the novel focuses on "men in the aggregate." Thus, Ghosh suggests that, following Updike, "the contemporary novel has become ever more radically centered on the individual psyche while the collective—'men in the aggregate'—has receded, both in the cultural and fictional imagination."[27] Climate change might appear to be a science problem, but in many ways, Ghosh suggests, our ability to solve it is a cultural problem. It requires the attention of ecocritics who attempt to bridge those worlds.

This crisis of imaginative thinking that can allow humans to think broadly is in fact symptomatic of Lemon's view of the problems with conventional farming and the paradigm he says gives shape to that thinking. In explaining how Lemon came to biodynamics, he offers an example of how conventional farming thinks: "I had farmed conventionally for more than 20 years starting in Burgundy at a time that was really the height of chemical agriculture in Burgundy." After that, Lemon moved back to the States, still relying on those farming techniques. He continues:

coming to California, consulting in Oregon and California, and just experiencing that feeling that it was never enough. Either the current theory is insufficient—let's say you had magnesium deficiencies, so you went out and bought a bunch of magnesium and put it on. Well, then the theory comes along that that's not going to work until you get your pH up to a certain level so that the magnesium can be assimilated by the plant. So then you spend thousands of dollars getting your pH up to a certain level, and you put the magnesium on again, and guess what? You still have magnesium deficiency. So what I experienced was the limits of agronomic knowledge.

Similarly, Ghosh describes the thinking that led to a disaster in India:

they were trained to break problems down into smaller and smaller puzzles until a solution presented itself. This is a way of thinking that deliberately excludes things and forces ('externalities') that lie beyond the horizon of the matter at hand: it is a perspective that renders the interconnectedness of Gaia unthinkable.[28]

To change course, Lemon needed to think in a new way. When I said to Lemon that it sounded like "you felt you were chasing all the time," he responded,

Yeah, it was never enough, and you never [get there]—and the question that I had—in some ways it's an unfair question, a naïve question, and that's ok— was—and it's a false equivalence—what does the forest know that I don't know? In other words, other than human intervention, the mature forest in lots of ecosystems is a point of what they call dynamic equilibrium. It undergoes change, in a way that wasn't understood 50 years ago, but it is a state of equilibrium. In other words, the forest has a response capacity—maybe the dominant species change slightly over the years, but it has a certain sort of formula, and a certain sort of rhythm of how it regenerates itself.

This became something of a model for Lemon. He concluded that "the forest has achieved a dynamic equilibrium; clearly my farm is not a forest, but what's going on, what is the forest able to do that I'm obviously completely incapable of doing as a farm? There must be something else, some other way to understand it." Lemon has called this a crisis of faith. Like ecocritics such as Ghosh and Morton, there's a desire to find new ways of thinking, a breaking of modern patterns and seeing links between things rather than dividing and conquering.

★   ★   ★   ★

Reading about the more unusual parts of biodynamic practices or of Steiner's writings and belief systems—gnomes, fairies, regenerative limbs of the denizens of Atlantis, communing with the dead—I worried just what my conversation with Ted Lemon was going to be like. Yet, Ted calmly presents compelling and rational explanations for why he turned away from conventional farming. When asked about the more unusual aspects of Steiner's writings—and Ted has read extensively through them—he suggests that those might be best understood as metaphors. In my long drive with Tegan Passelaqua, he proposed that perhaps Ted's response was geared towards his audience, whom he assumed would be skeptical. After he asked me what Ted said about the gnomes, Tegan rhetorically asked, "But isn't that the same response of people when you bring up something that they talk about that's horrible in the Bible? You know? Something [that's] horrible, or it's hard to justify or agree with in modern times?" Tegan argued that there simply wasn't anything metaphoric about those gnomes. In fact,

> Steiner really believed gnomes protected each property. And I mean, you can talk about metaphorically or not, but once you get in and read it, it's like, no, he believed it. And, it's the one thing that people have the hardest [time with]. Basically, for people to get to where Ted is, they claim that—this biodynamic community, this is the biggest hurdle that people need to get through to really be able to go full boat. And it's basically like the turn around and drop off the table backwards and we'll catch you.

If you truly want to understand and implement biodynamics, you must believe, you must take the leap of faith.

However, even folks sympathetic to the anti-modern-science view of biodynamics have sometimes turned away from it. Both Beinstock and Jared Brandt, for instance, have declined a full embrace of biodynamics for philosophical and practical reasons despite being much more firmly encamped in the culture of feeling side of this dispute. Each winemaker emphasized that the followers and certifiers of biodynamics can be dogmatic and Beinstock, who left what he calls a cult, and Brandt, who grew up in Utah as a non-Mormon, point to their backgrounds and say that they do not want to embrace any dogma in their lives. Brandt, as I mentioned earlier, has deep concerns about the biodynamic practice of using copper sulfate, and Beinstock claims, counter to what some skeptics suggest, not only are the treatments effective, but they are in fact too effective for the environment his vineyards inhabit.

A day before I met with Beinstock, I traveled to Somerset, past the old Gold Rush town of Placerville, to meet another winemaker and vineyard owner up in

FIGURE 5.2 Tegan Passelaqua at Bechthold Vineyard

the Sierra Foothills. Hank Beckmeyer, like Beinstock, has had a rather unusual path to this isolated stretch of California. In a past life, Beckmeyer had played guitar in Half Japanese, a punkish experimental band whose lead singer resembles Jonathan Richman a bit. Tired of aspects of that life, Beckmeyer settled in Germany, working in production and then also in the wine trade. He married a French woman and they dreamed of returning to California to make goat cheese. Beckmeyer still has the long hair of a rock musician and has an easygoing, almost stoic demeanor that frequently mixes in a sly smile along with ironic and self-deprecating comments. When he told me about his time making cheese, however, he looked deadly serious as he confessed that it was the hardest thing he had done in his life. Cute, spritely goats, holdovers from those days, can still be sighted at La Clarine farm, though they reside in drastically smaller numbers now. While he and his wife started their cheese business, Beckmeyer also worked for an industrial winery and grew pretty disenchanted with the interventionist and recipe-following techniques he witnessed. Eventually Beckmeyer decided to go out on his own, doing things his own way, and planting own-rooted vines at his La Clarine farm and purchasing grapes from elsewhere.

I had never really thought of the risk of own-rooting until Beckmeyer first walked me around La Clarine and pointed to a bunch of low, own-rooted vines and said they were Tempranillo, his first plantings. Certainly that might seem like an unusual choice—there's just not much Tempranillo planted in California—but then he confessed that he didn't love the wine it had produced. A bit up the slope, he pointed to Tannat, an even more obscure grape primarily grown in Gascony, which he found much more successful.[29] Unlike vines grafted onto rootstock, you either pulled up the own-rooted vines entirely or you simply let them have their space like Beckmeyer had done. In his rejection of industrial methods, Beckmeyer had tried biodynamics. When he started to reconsider cheesemaking but at the same time was turned off by the industrial winemaking of his sidework, he found himself drawn to biodynamics:

> since we were going to grow some grapes and we had farm animals, and vegetable garden and all that stuff, and also still much of the property is wild. That farm organism thing was very appealing. And that's what initially got me curious and interested in it.

However, various aspects of biodynamics made Beckmeyer concerned. Biodynamics claimed to help heal the earth, but when did it end: "much like a person who's taking medication, eventually they're cured, or they're cured to a certain point, and you stop taking that medication." LIke Beinstock, he found the treatments too powerful for his climate and maybe for the good of the plants. As Beckmeyer explains,

> I had made the comment that people who don't stop taking their medication even when they're well, they're junkies, is what they are, they're drug dependent. And that didn't go over well with a couple people. And I said, if you take it as fact that these substances that you're spraying or using in your compost or whatever are very powerful, that's what you think is real, then these are things to be really careful of—about overdoing things.

So, as Beckmeyer grew concerned that biodynamics was essentially making his vines into junkies and that in some ways it had replaced one model of humans striving to control nature with another, he found an alternative:

> at about that time anyway I had discovered this guy Masanobu Fukuoka and it seemed to me like, oh, ok, that's an idea that's taking the whole farm concept but also like, taking out the idea of the we know better about a lot of things that we really know nothing about, and basically just letting the land be what the land is. And if you want kind of a classical kind of definition of terroir, that's it, right?

Unsurprisingly, Fukuoka's foundational text, *The One-Straw Revolution,* appeared in the US around the same time as Rachel Carson's *Silent Spring.* Perhaps because of its origins in the East, Fukuoka's approach may feel less overtly religious than Steiner's, but it does derive from a similar loss of faith in modern science. In his book Fukuoka explains that he was a scientist himself, but had come to realize that in fact "I understood nothing."[30] And while the book may not preach a new religion, it reads a bit like the story of someone who has discovered the way. He talks about his "intention of spreading the word" and being "ignored as an eccentric."[31] His main insight was that "crops grow themselves and should not have to be grown." However, his initial approach, which he calls "abandonment," failed miserably.[32] His descriptions of what has happened resemble those of Steiner and his acolytes. We have made "the land"—because of our disruption of "natural balance"—"dependent" on farmers. Sounding like a modern-day Rousseau, Fukuoka repeatedly suggests that "The [only] ones who see true nature are infants. They see without thinking, straight and clear."[33] With education comes what he calls "an idea of nature" and hence a distancing from the real thing.[34] What he ultimately preaches does not seem radically different from biodynamics: no plowing, "no chemical fertilizer or prepared compost," "no weeding by tillage or herbicides," and "no dependence on chemicals."[35] What he doesn't do, however, is substitute treatments or sprays for those modern chemicals. Because of that, this model is preferable to Beckmeyer, but, as he noted, Fukuoka is largely describing growing rice in Japan. In that way, what he provides is a model and an inspiration but Beckmeyer needs to find his own version that works for his small plot of land in the Sierra Foothills.

★   ★   ★   ★

Before interviewing Ted Lemon and Morgan Twain-Peterson, as I went down my internet rabbit hole researching, I came across a blog started by one of the brothers behind Smith-Madrone winery on Spring Mountain. The title of the blog, "Biodynamics is a Hoax," dates back to 2011 and tells you where the author stands. In his final post, "Why I Resent Biodynamic Farming!" Stuart Smith argues that the followers of biodynamics have poisoned the culture. He repeatedly uses the word, "superior" to describe the attitude of the biodynamics crowd as he does in his thesis statement: "By publicly claiming superiority they, de facto, belittle and ridicule everyone else's farming methods and wine quality for not being Biodynamic." After citing a variety of evidence of this attitude from Demeter and biodynamic winemakers, Smith asserts that "Biodynamic farmers do not have a monopoly on being environmentally sensitive farmers and I'm sick of hearing this lie." Stuart Smith points to the fact that biodynamic, organic farming and natural wine are not just about farming and winemaking, but how we understand our relationship to the environment as shaped by cultural forces, particularly through narrative. Smith is tired of being the villain in this story.

One of the more relevant aspects of Stuart Smith's blog for this book was his engagement with Clark Smith, the unrelated author of *Postmodern Winemaking*.[36] Clark Smith frequently posted comments on Stuart's blog and offered his full view of the debate in his own essay, "Biodynamics and the Limits of Rationalism."[37] In doing so, Clark Smith returns us fully to Blanning's framing of postmodernism as the next cycle in the culture of feeling and its dialectic relationship with a culture of reason. For Clark Smith asserts quite clearly that "Postmodern winemaking respects the fundamental mysteries of nature and the human soul." Despite promoting the winemaking innovations provided by science, Clark remains skeptical of science for there will always be "areas of fundamental mystery for which science can never provide useful answers." How should winemakers proceed in such circumstances? They "must be able to perceive without understanding." Clark Smith is not really interested in defending biodynamics per se, but wishes to argue that the arguments for rationalism that seek to debunk biodynamics are faulty. His essay ranges over a variety of defenses, often by way of analogy, but as Smith approaches his conclusion he gets at the postmodern heart of his claims: "Objective truth is a child's myth, and the nature of reality is a question the profs will always dodge. Science isn't a security blanket. The more it illuminates, the more darkness is unconcealed." In this battle of the Smiths, Stuart refused to give Clark the last word and posted his own retort in "Postmodernism, Rationalism, and Biodynamics," in which Smith says he "reject[s] virtually everything written in this article as utter nonsense because I reject the notion that science is limiting." Instead, he argues that science should be used to test the methods of biodynamics. I had raised this very question with Lemon, when we discussed how he hopes to influence others with his approach. I suggested that proving that these techniques work via science would help that, but Lemon rejected this approach, for to use the modern science on biodynamics would be to embrace a paradigm that biodynamics has rejected. Of course, this is also a convenient way to leave a commitment to biodynamics as a matter of faith and an overt rejection of a culture of reason, whereas others use appeals to both, or are seemingly contradictory like Clark Smith.

★   ★   ★   ★

Throughout this discussion, the hero and villain problem has been lurking. Those like Stuart Smith who don't fall in line with a clear anti-modern agricultural approach repeatedly stand as the opposition to those who seek to save the land, and consumers can feel that they are actually helping the planet by purchasing these wines. Perhaps those very same consumers feel the argument that these alternative farming practices also help "translate" the vineyard to them. In his book *Practical Ecocriticism*, Glenn A. Love suggests that we continue to be haunted by the problematic influence of the pastoral, a tradition that "take[s] on a heretofore unprecedented significance at a period when the comfortably mythopoeic green world or pastoral is beset by profound threats of pollution, despoliation, and diminishment," not to mention climate change.[38] Love goes on to explain his use of the term, "green world," a phrase first popularized by the famous literary critic, Northrop Frye. Frye argues that Shakespeare introduces the trope of the green world in his romantic comedies. It is a place, usually in nature, like the Forest of Arden in *A Midsummer's Night Dream*, that helps bring the couples together in a kind of organic rebirth cycle. Love suggests that, at its heart, the green world is really a version of the pastoral. He analyzes another Shakespeare play, *As You Like It*, to make his point, noting that "amid sylvan groves and rural characters—idealized images of country existence—the sophisticates attain a critical vision of the salutary, simple life that will presumably sustain them as they return at the end to the great world on the horizon."[39] We can make a direct link here to Pollan's "supermarket pastoral" for, after all, we may attempt a kind of metaphoric connection to that idealized place, Schoener's sentimentalized vineyard, via the purchase and consumption of this wine and want that wine's origins to feel as pristine, as one with nature rather than in opposition to nature, as possible. Love asserts that the other problem is that all of these conceptions of nature remain built from "humanistic assumption" and how the pastoral "human centered-values" essentially "impose," in Love's words, meaning "upon the city and country."[40]

★   ★   ★   ★

Like Stuart Smith who rejects the postmodern and perhaps its biodynamic fellow travelers, Glen Love asserts the need for ecocriticism to be a cultural approach grounded in science in opposition to many of the more postmodern approaches, like the deep ecologists, that have emerged in the humanities in the last forty or more years. Love cites Kate Soper to make his own case, suggesting that his problem with the postmodern lies with her understanding that "it is one thing to challenge various cultural representations of nature, another to represent nature as if it were a convention of culture."[41] The issue, then, lies in the postmodern emphasis on the way in which culture creates the reality in which we live (though this may be an oversimplified version of the postmodern). This view resembles the belief I discussed in chapter 2 that derives from Whorf of seeing language as a conceptual grid through which we understand reality. Love says the postmodern position

> hold[s] that nature constantly changes, that is has changed to the point where there is nothing "natural" left, and so—unspoken or spoken conclusion— there is no reason to consider nature as anything but another venue for what we do: control it, change it, use it up.[42]

According to Love, those who see the world this way "in addition to ignoring biology" take positions that "play into the hands of the destroyers."[43] Rather than those who embrace science—particularly modern science—being the villains, now the postmodernists and those deep ecologists[44] who ignore science take on that role. Love claims that, in part, for humanists to become more fully on the right side of things they must move past the naive assumption of "anthropocentric thinking," one built into the pastoral, that "society is complex while nature is simple."

Of course, in these various staked out positions, a real danger is simplification. Much of the debate in the wine world, and certainly one echoed in the world of literary studies, is often tied to the ways that labels help us organize things and ultimately take complex issues and middle grounds and sweep them into more easily seen oppositions and at the extreme, Manichean enemies, perhaps fighting over the fate of the planet. Celia Welch, one of the most sought-after winemaking consultants in Napa Valley, argues that the solutions to the environmental impact of the wine industry—or more broadly agriculture—are not as simple as following the ways of biodynamics or seeking organic certification by following the government's organic farming practices.

★   ★   ★   ★

We sat across from each other in what could have been a corporate boardroom anywhere in America except for the hand-picked wine bottles displayed on a table to our left. I was in St. Helena, a small town in Napa that serves both as a local industry hub and a tourist site. Celia Welch, who sat across from me, had been a winemaker for decades in Napa. Although she owns her own label, Corra, she is probably best known for making one of Napa's most in-demand and highest priced cult wines, Scarecrow. Our conversation revealed that Welch is used to being in charge. She gradually grew more and more open in expressing her views, but she never heeded any of my awkward attempts to lead her to a particular assertion. Like many of the winemakers I spoke to, Welch received her training at UC Davis, the leading viticulture and enology school in the country. Despite the stereotypes about UC Davis graduates, the reality is that a wide variety of winemakers have walked in and out of those doors. Nevertheless, Welch does fall closer to the stereotype of a winemaker who follows modern science and the methods that the program teaches which included "a full year of general chemistry, organic chemistry, biochemistry, microbiology, two quarters of physics, and then you get into the winemaking applied science, and its microbiology of winemaking, chemistry of winemaking, analysis of winemaking." What Davis does not do, Welch asserts, is

> teach style; they teach the scientific method of being able to come up with a concept or formula and make it reproducible. So the key to scientific research is reproducibility by one's peers, and their concept is, if you want to be able to consistently make something, whether it's for consistency's sake, as in the case of big winery vats—you know, Gallo wants their Hearty Burgundy to always taste the same over the decades—or whether it's a small batch that turns out exceptionally well, you need to be able to know what you did in order to repeat your success.

When I asked Welch how much she still relies on those lessons, she quickly responded, "Every single day. There is not a day that I don't make a decision that is somehow based on the science that I learned." However, for Welch, this training does not translate into winemaking as a rote or mechanical process. Instead, she suggests, "the closest thing I can liken winemaking to is being a jazz musician. You've got a sound foundation in music, and you learn when to break the rules. And you know that you're breaking them, and you break them for a reason." This reminded me of something Matthew Rorick, certainly one of the more iconoclastic graduates of Davis, told me: "there's no getting around the fact that you have to clean the barrels." In other words, no matter how experimental Rorick gets, there remain certain lessons—derived in scientific knowledge—that continue to inform his work.

Perhaps because of Welch's background and perspective, she holds very different views of both organic and biodynamic viticulture to their adherents. Part of her critique implies how both terms fall into the supermarket pastoral. Organic and biodynamic

> are very lovely sounding and highly marketable terms that are little understood by the customer. Every time I've had somebody who's not in agriculture try to tell me what organic means to them, they say "not sprayed." And there's a perception that organic means there hasn't been anything done to that product. Or that it's been done with only very, very benign ingredients. It's cleaner. And when I point out to them that uranium is organic, there's this look of confusion. And arsenic is also organic. I mean, organic and benign are two completely different concepts.

Welch suggests here that most consumers view the words themselves as implying an unmitigated good that seems to follow along the lines of Love's critique of the pastoral: that we have made nature simple and so anything that speaks to nature can be sentimentally assumed to be good. For Welch, the issue with organic certification has to do with the way the problems get solved. Rather than being concerned with how the total process might affect the environment, the emphasis is on the end product used in the vineyard. Organic certification lacks a holistic conception of nature.

Welch could sense the limits of my science education and began passionately diagraming various chemical compounds on a scrap of paper. In order to get certified, you must use a substance that,

> Even though it is identical at the molecular level, it's not organic because it was not derived from an organic substance, because we didn't mine it. So that's where as a chemist I start to have problems with the organic certification process, because not only does it have to be an organic substance, but it also has to be an organic substance derived organically.

Feeling I was starting to catch on, I blurted "Which, you're suggesting is potentially worse for the environment, if you have to mine a mountain or something along those lines?" I was on the right track, as Welch continued,

> If you have to strip-mine to get this thing, I've got a problem with that. If you have to fly it in from New Hampshire, when it's available in the East Bay, there's a CO^2 footprint that we have to talk about. And that's a big thing. Now let's talk about this versus the molecule that's like this that's got hydrogen bonds [...], so it's an organic molecule, but it's a spray. Now we're talking

about a synthetic thing that some pharmaceutical company has come up with. And, this will kill.

In the simplistic narrative in which the adherents of organic farming and biodynamic methods represent the good, those who do not can be reductively viewed as the bad. However, Welch makes a compelling point for just how complex the problems are. Because she does not strictly follow organic practices and remains skeptical of biodynamics does not mean she gleefully dumps chemicals into vineyards. Instead, Welch feels that the solutions provided by organic practices may not always solve the greater problem. Some of the organic substances can, from her view, be too powerful or too weak and create other problems:

> Here's an organic substance that also kills arachnids that are a hundred times bigger than that. So this is a lot less specific. And this is active for about seven days. This one is active for 30 days. So you're spraying your vineyard with this four times more often.

If the vineyard requires more frequent spraying of the organic substance, then

> That tractor that has to go up and down every row using diesel to do so. And how did you get the tractor to the vineyard? You put it on the flatbed truck and you drove it to the vineyard. So, now think about that CO^2 footprint and how it's exploding, and what it's doing to the fact that it's killing small insects in addition to the very small mildew thing.

These comments suggest that each side in this dispute uses rhetoric to convince an audience that they are right, but that rightness might depend on what you think is most important. Therefore, Welch concludes,

> I can advocate organic when it means fewer insecticides on fruits that grow close to the ground like lettuce and strawberries that are really prone to a lot of insect damage—because I don't really want to eat a lot of insecticide. I know that as a human being it's probably not good for me to eat poisons that kill insects. But my feeling is that the biggest threat to human existence is global warming. That keeps me up at night.

★   ★   ★   ★

On one of my last days in California, I made the drive back to Sebastopol to the Barlow, an odd mix of tasting rooms, shops, and industrial workspace where I also met Michael Browne in the shiny new Kosta Browne facility. I had come to talk with Martha Stoumen, whose eponymous label has only been going for a few years. In fact, she works in Pax Mahle's winery, hidden behind his tasting room. Because I had become fascinated with the question of whether winemaking could contribute to effective environmental advocacy, I had wanted to speak with Martha, who I had heard suggest this possibility in an interview she had given to Levi Dalton. When we met, Martha had her straight dark hair pulled back, and she was expecting a child during the upcoming harvest season. While relatively small in stature, Martha is also charismatic and articulate. As we talked, it became clear that she welcomed a chance to explain and perhaps even just reason out her own philosophies. Unlike some winemakers, Martha seems to welcome being considered a natural winemaker. However, Martha argues for seeing a direct link between natural winemaking and viticulture. When asked how she explains natural wine, she remarked that she

> really tr[ies] as soon as possible to get back to the farming. Because for me, I think the environmental farming aspect is the most important. And then I do believe there should be more transparency for the consumer about what's going into their wine at the end of the day. But how you actually make your wine, if you want to add yeast, or you don't want to add commercial yeast, it's not like it's making a less healthy wine. It's not more harmful for the consumer, if your wine's been fermented [with commercial yeast].

"As opposed to pesticides, or things like that," I interjected.

> Exactly. And not only more harmful for the consumer but more harmful for the planet. So I don't mind being a little bit more up on the soapbox when it comes to farming, but with the winemaking, that's a little bit more the winemaker's own decision involved. I think being transparent is good, and when we're more transparent about winemaking, I think we educate people so they don't just say, oh, you filter, that must be bad, and it's like, well actually filtration—maybe it's not considered strictly natural winemaking, but it's not harmful at all for anybody.

Martha's point is that consumers seem to sometimes confuse winemaking techniques that get labeled as not part of the natural approach as somehow also problematic for either consumers or the Earth.

Martha's career is a fascinating one, almost dizzyingly confusing. After graduating from UCLA, she went on to work on an Italian farm, one of the first times her minor in Italian began to pay off and also the first time she was exposed to viticulture and winemaking. Back in the US working at Cakebread, she operated largely from the point of view of what some might call recipe winemaking, though she also notes that they did natural yeast trials there as well. Though her degree perhaps pointed her towards environmental policy work, she decided not to go in that direction, but she "wanted to do something that had some sort of environmental impact in a positive way." When I asked her how she came to reject the kind of winemaking she first learned, she explained:

> why try to over-engineer this thing that's already kind of presented to us in nature in certain ways? We have to of course make sure it doesn't turn to vinegar, but a grape is a little winemaking package ready to go. Why try to

wipe the yeast and add commercial yeast and then add powdered tannin or acid because you know, we've potentially depleted soils in certain ways over time.

In some ways, it came down to "why try re-engineer nature when it's already giving us really the tools to work with," and to the question of expressing the land:

> if you are a winemaker who's focused on terroir, I think at the end of the day using whatever microbes are in your environment is just a further expression of that. You know, you want to express your soil, and your climate, and what the year gave you in terms of, you know, what's the diary of that vintage, was it a cool vintage, was it a warm vintage?

This desire led Martha to a variety of locations: working for Giusto Occhipinti in Sicily, who has been one of the biggest influences on her career, one of the largest biodynamic vineyards in New Zealand, as well as back to UC Davis to get her degree in enology, and other experiences in Germany and the Rhone. At one point, as a means of pooling resources that would allow her to farm leased land in the US, Martha belonged to a sort of wine collective. Now, she has tried to continue that practice but on her own.

As Martha and I talked about various elements of natural winemaking, including the importance of not turning to commercial yeast, her commitments to the environment, culture, and history of California, I tried to pull the various threads of her approach and beliefs together. She offered her hope that large wineries might follow the lead of smaller producers like herself, that there might be the equivalent of an Earthbound Organics for wine, which could represent a significant step in the right direction even if the wines might not be as good as those of artisanal producers, just as, she says, Earthbound can't match the farmer's market.

FIGURE 5.3 Promoting environmentalism in Sonoma, California

I kind of half-jokingly blurted out, so can winemakers help save the world? She chuckled and said,

> I don't know if save the world is the right phrasing, but I think, yeah, we can all certainly make an impact, no matter what we're doing, what our jobs are, there are always small incremental changes that we can make to help preserve our planet.

Is this then Morton's vision of someone obsessing over starting a car, of Ghosh's critique that we focus too much on the individual when we need to think as a collective, or is it the postmodern answer to the critique of large, overwhelming descriptions of history, of the failed Enlightenment project: that we need to instead focus on local narratives, or, in this case, local environments? Of course, in Martha's aspirations there does lie the possibility for collective action: there is the hope that the small wineries can change the practices of the larger, and thus of all individuals working together to make changes. Nevertheless, we can also recognize that each proponent of the "right" way to do things relies on the same loaded language of the wine reviewers, using rhetorical appeals based on a culture of feeling or culture of reason, to make a case for their "rightness."

Notes

1 Alice Feiring, *The Battle for Wine and Love, or How I Saved the World From Parkerization* (Boston: Marinerr Books, 2008), 225.
2 Katherine Cole, *Voodoo Vintners: Oregon's Astonishing Biodynamic Winegrowers* (Corvallis: Oregon State University Press, 2011), 34.
3 Ibid., 16.
4 Ibid., 5.
5 Feiring, *The Battle for Wine and Love*, 236.
6 Cole, *Voodoo Vintners*, 29.
7 Ibid., 29.
8 Ibid., 38.
9 Ibid., 39.
10 Greg Garrard, *Ecocriticism* (London, Routledge, 2012), 23.
11 Ibid., 24.
12 Ibid., 25.
13 Ibid., 26.
14 Ibid.
15 Feiring, *The Battle for Wine and Love*, 55.
16 Ibid., 58.
17 Ibid., 59.
18 Ibid., 61.
19 Ibid., 100, emphasis mine.
20 Garrard, *Ecocriticism*, 101–102.
21 Ibid., 114.
22 Ibid.
23 Amitav Ghosh, The Great Derangement: Climate Change and the Unthinkable (Chicago: University of Chicago Press, 2016), 9.
24 Timothy Morton, *Dark Ecology: For a Logic of Future Coexistence* (New York: Columbia University Press, 2016), 19.

25 Ghosh, *The Great Derangement*, 80.
26 Ibid., 77.
27 Ibid., 78.
28 Ghosh, *The Great Derangement*, 56.
29 According to the 2017 California Grape Acreage report, there are less than 1,000 acres of both Tempranillo and Tannat planted in California. In contrast there are over 91,000 acres of Cabernet Sauvignon planted.
30 Masanobu Fukuoka, *The One-Straw Revolution: An Introduction to Natural Farming*, trans. Larry Korn, Chris Pearce, and Tsune Kurosawa (New York: New York Review of Books, 1978), 8.
31 Ibid., 12.
32 Ibid., 13.
33 Ibid., 25–26.
34 Ibid., 25.
35 Ibid., 33–34.
36 Clark Smith, *Postmodern Winemaking; Rethinking the Modern Science of an Ancient Craft* (Berkeley: University of California Press, 2013).
37 Clark Smith, "Biodynamics and the Limits of Rationalism," *Wines, Vines, Analytics*, January, 2011.
38 Glen A. Love, *Practical Ecocriticism: Literature, Biology and the Environment* (Charlottesville: University of Virginia Press, 2003), 66.
39 Ibid.
40 Ibid., 66–67.
41 Ibid., 7.
42 Ibid., 21.
43 Ibid.
44 Love does endorse the deep ecologists' belief in moving away from an anthropocentric view of nature, though Garrard's claim that they rely on an intuitive understanding of nature certainly complicates this position.

References

Cole, Katherine. *Voodoo Vintners: Oregon's Astonishing Biodynamic Winegrowers*. Corvallis: Oregon State University Press, 2011.

Feiring, Alice. *The Battle for Wine and Love: Or How I Saved the World from Parkerization*. Boston: Mariner, 2008.

Fukuoka, Masanobu. *The One-Straw Revolution: An Introduction to Natural Farming*, translated by Larry Korn, Chris Pearce, and Tsune Kurosawa. New York: New York Review of Books, 1978.

Garrard, Greg. *Ecocriticism*. London: Routledge, 2012.

Ghosh, Amitov. *The Great Derangement: Climate Change and the Unthinkable*. Chicago: University of Chicago Press, 2016.

Love, Glen A. *Practical Ecocriticism: Literature, Biology, and the Environment*. Charlottesville: University of Virginia Press, 2003.

Morton, Timothy. *Dark Ecology: For a Logic of Future Coexistence*. New York: Columbia University Press, 2016.

Smith, Clark. "Biodynamics and the Limits of Rationalism." *Wines, Vines, Analytics*, January 2011. https://winesvinesanalytics.com/columns/section/92/article/82315/Biodynamics-and-the-Limits-of-Rationalism.

Smith, Clark. *Postmodern Winemaking; Rethinking the Modern Science of an Ancient Craft*. Oakland: University of California Press, 2013.

6

THE NOBLE GRAPES

The Canon of Grapes and the Literary Canon

A nor'easter had settled over the island of Manhattan and its surroundings. I had ventured to the city to reconnect with Rajat Parr and finally meet Abe Schoener. During a break in my appointments, I had arranged to have lunch with Josh Greene. When I ventured into the wine-cluttered offices, Josh promptly asked someone to grab me a glass so I could try an Alicante Bouschet from Portugal that had been perplexing Josh and few of the critics. I always welcome an unexpected glass of wine, but I could feel the surge of anxiety as I had to once again judge and offer some coherent thoughts about a wine in front of experts. Maybe this echoed the way people get self-conscious about their grammar in front of literature professors.

Josh and I made our way to a local Korean restaurant. After responding to Josh's inquiries about my ongoing research, I confessed to something that had been worrying me lately. Before I began the research for my project, I now realized, much of my wine knowledge, especially once I moved to the rural midwest, had been heavily influenced by wine publications and wine critics. Since I needed to drive an hour to the nearest wine store, I could not rely much on local knowledge or shop according to curiosity or even mood. Instead, wine magazines provided most of my recommendations. While I had not abandoned all the wines I liked during that time, since I began my research I had come to understand that there was much more out there—particularly in California—than I had realized. In fact, even my earlier visits to wine country had been largely shaped by this reading, as I would seek out wineries the critics currently loved in order to try those wines. Now, having visited a much larger variety of winemakers and often having had a chance to sample their wines, I found that there were several wines that I used to like, in particular wines of a certain style, that I no longer enjoyed as much. In some cases, I felt myself actively disliking them. I would hope my friends would not bring these wines to dinner, and I would look morosely at my holdings of these wines, passing them over for something else on a regular basis now.

DOI: 10.4324/9781003399810-7

As we tackled our bibimbap, I recounted most of this to Josh, whose knowledge I had grown to respect and admire. What has happened? How has this happened? I asked. I worried about a few interrelated issues in this transformation. Had my taste changed? Had I traded one set of extrinsic influences for another? I am not sure why this notion of one's taste changing provokes so much anxiety in people, but it clearly does. On boards like Wine Berserkers, often dominated by middle-aged men of comfortable means, this regularly comes up. Someone will post how they used to love big California cabernets, but now crave more delicate wines like riesling or maybe champagne. For these folks—and maybe me too—I can see that this may be a kind of midlife crisis. Big wines get gendered, as we discussed in the early chapters of this book. Critics often speak about them in masculine language: they are big, powerful, immense. They are the beverage of choice for steak houses. Then, in midlife when all sorts of anxiety about masculinity tend to appear in many unfortunate guises, a man suddenly finds himself unable to deal with wines that seem to unconsciously reinforce his masculinity. Gender aside, the other anxiety here is that a change in taste seems apiece with a change in identity—arguably a metaphysical anxiety. What one likes perhaps helps comprise both your own and others' sense of who you are. Usually knowing the likes and dislikes, in essence the taste of others, can be read as a marker of how much one person knows another.

The second concern, that perhaps I had traded one set of extrinsic influences for another also raises similar anxieties because it suggests that our tastes are really not our own. In fact, Pierre Bourdieu makes this argument in his extremely influential doorstopper, *Distinction: A Social Critique of the Judgement of Taste*. The realization that one's taste derives from extrinsic forces like social class can lead to a full-scale existential crisis. In fact, this might be said to be a highly personal ontological problem. Did I like those other wines because I read that I was supposed to or did I really just like them? Did I like different wines now because the people I met made strong cases for why these wines were superior, preferable, or simply cooler? Was I so easily influenced by the taste of other people? I am not sure I wanted to really answer these questions.

In the short term, however, I just wanted to know what Josh thought. He saw the problem as more epistemological (knowledge) than ontological (being). "It's not that your taste has changed," he explained. "It's that you now know more, have tasted more, and you simply have a broader range of experience." This was comforting. I was still the same person. I just knew more, and by knowing more, I could make more informed decisions about what I liked. Perhaps too, since I knew more, I could more fully identify and accurately describe what in a wine I liked or disliked.

Underlying this anxiety, we can also find questions about whether taste is collective, objective, or subjective. These lines, though, need not be starkly drawn. Another factor is time: do we overcome the individual or subjective judgment of taste via the accumulation of judgments rendered by time itself? There is also a very different flipside to this: namely, is the goal in acquiring knowledge of wine—

and arts—to gain enough knowledge to enable you to appreciate the greatness of the best? Early in this book, I mentioned the fact that wine, like art, tends to produce a certain amount of insecurity in folks who do not consider themselves experts. As my experiences as a "critic" on the *Wine & Spirits* tasting panel showed me, even a fairly experienced wine drinker can express those same insecurities when faced with folks who possess greater experience. In a sequence that mirrors Bourdieu's conception of "cultural capital" from Dana Spiotta's novel, *Lightning Field*, a character describes how she coaches a newly wealthy man to discuss wine. The notion is this: if you have a great deal of money, it may allow you access to the goods and commodities of the upper-classes, but it is not money—not capital—that makes you upper-class but the acquisition of the more intangible "cultural capital", knowledge that accretes quietly, discreetly, often through growing up among the upper-classes but can get passed on through a variety of interactions that gradually allow one to express the taste of the upper-classes.

In chapter 4, I discussed how "natural wines" posed a problem to the tradition by emphasizing, celebrating, and being snobbish even about qualities in wine that had often been thought to previously undermine the status of wine. This points to the ways in which cultural capital is mobile, and it is also situational. What might pass for "cultural capital" in Alice Feiring's circle will not pass in the offices of *Wine Spectator*. When Josh suggested that my taste hadn't changed but I simply knew more, it might be said that I had a certain amount of cultural capital in relation to a very different element of the wine world than I had previously known. The built-in challenge of Bourdieu's very conception is that it undermines the notion of objectively "good taste." Taste is situational and socially constructed—socially necessary, but not simply something out in the world that you either innately possess or lack.

I began this book describing how I have been carrying around this blog post—labeled an "Article of Merit"—by Robert Parker in which he describes several "bright shining lies" meant to bamboozle wine consumers.[1] These include "natural wines," "low alcohol wines," and "godforsaken grapes," which came to lend its name to the title of Jason Wilson's recent book. A number of things had attracted me to this almost all-purpose rant against the many things Parker detested in the current world of wine—mostly movements going on around him but defined often in opposition to his "taste" and beliefs—but I was struck with how its language seemed inherently political. For instance, in describing how false information about these movements had spread through the internet, he remarks that "the propaganda machines of totalitarian regimes work the same way." Later, in describing the "lame and fraudulent effort to get self attention," by which he means drumming up interest in grapes not typically ascribed as noble, he calls it "the epitome of cyber-group goose-stepping." He concludes that this false propaganda for grapes like "Trousseau, Savagnin, Grand Noir, Negrette, Lignan Blanc, Peloursin, Auban, Calet, Fongoneau and Blaufrankisch [...]needs to be condemned." After this fairly extreme rhetoric, Parker wishes to rein things back a bit with a hint of conciliatory tone. "Diversity in wine," he contends, "is something that I have taken seriously ever since I wrote my first sentence about wine, but it has to be good, not flawed, and not just different." This current push, Parker suggests, is simply diversity for its own sake. What's threatened? Well, clearly Parker is, but he also says that "this group of absolutists" has led a campaign of "near-complete rejection of some of the finest grapes and the wines they produce."

What struck me initially about Parker politicizing his response and using words like "diversity" was that it invoked in my mind the heated debates regarding the literary canon that dominated much of the discourse of literary studies in the late 1980s and has continued to play some kind of role ever since. Wine writers infrequently use the term canon themselves. A recent article by former English major Esther Mobley refers to the "contemporary wine canon," but it is more common to refer to the "noble grapes," which, depending on the writer, seems to be between six and twenty grape varieties. The six-grape model seems the most consistent and comprises five French grapes, cabernet, merlot, chardonnay, pinot noir, and syrah, and riesling from Germany. Why these? Well, at least in part the argument seems to go that these grapes gained early traction by being associated with the luxury of the French court—riesling excepted—and thus also became the first prominent "international grapes"—those planted most widely outside of the grapes' native soils. Undoubtedly, these are the primary grapes to which Parker refers when he mentions the "finest grapes and the wines they produce." Again, German riesling excepted, these high points all have French origins, namely the top wines from Burgundy, Bordeaux, and the Rhone. Why the argument for more noble grapes has traction has to do with highly regarded wines from other countries that also make wines that have widespread esteem among wine people, such as the nebbiolos made in Barolo. What of the ignoble? Well, to a certain extent, Parker seems to argue that history has shown that these grapes have never produced "the finest wines." "Stop and think it over," Parker implores, "when in the centuries of wine consumption has a pleasurable or delicious wine been dismissed in favor of a self-flagellating beverage that has no flavor and no character?"

Putting aside matters of tone and the implied insult in shifting the category from wine to beverage, Parker seems to be asserting that "the finest wines" come from the "finest grapes" and those wines have come down to us in the very way that Samuel Johnson, whose view echoes those of his contemporary David Hume, first used in his famous *Rambler* essay, No. 92, to define the literary classic:

> the books which have stood the test of time, and been admired through all the changes which the mind of man has suffered from the various revolutions of knowledge, and the prevalence of contrary customs, have a better claim to our regard than any modern can boast, because the long continuance of their reputation proves that they are adequate to our faculties, and agreeable to nature.[2]

Some version or other of Johnson's definition has largely functioned, often unexamined, as a measure of the texts that have come to be thought of as comprising the literary canon. This might also be said to resemble the way that Matt Kramer wished that interpretation return to a form of judgment, as I discussed in chapter 2. That literary canon, though, has perhaps not been as stable and tidy as most had assumed until the very notion of the canon itself became the subject of challenge in the 1980s.

★   ★   ★   ★

Before we return to the noble grape debate—though Parker would not give it such a dignified title—that his "Article of Merit" has escalated, let us take a little time to examine the nature of the debates within literary circles, for it is my hope in this chapter to use those debates to understand the arguments in favor of the "noble" grapes and those in favor of adding more diversity to the wine world or championing indigenous grapes. In doing so, we will once more need to return to questions of wine and art as well as wine and aesthetics. The debates about the literary canon in the United States, and sometimes referred to here as part of the "culture wars," have been written about extensively. They may have started with any number of moments, including William Bennett's report during the Reagan era, "To Reclaim a Legacy: A Report on Humanities in Higher Education" (1984), while others might cite Allan Bloom's *The Closing of the American Mind* (1987) or E.D. Hirsch's *Cultural Literacy* (1987), both of which came out a few years later. Another such moment occurred a few years later when Roger Kimball attacked Eve Sedgwick's essay, "Jane Austen and the Masturbating Girl," in his book *Tenured Radicals*. Each in their own way were conservatives growing afraid that literary studies had veered sharply left and that the humanities had abandoned what Matthew Arnold once called "the best that had been thought and said." The debates within American universities over the canon had started well before these outbursts in the culture wars, and, to some extent, continue today, often in essays like that by Eric Bennett in the *Chronicle of Higher Education*, "Dear Humanities: We Are the Problem." In essays like Bennett's, authors make the outcome of these curricular battles complicit in the current political landscape in part because the attacks on the canon and the rise of political literary criticism has left us without a common culture. Other versions of this essay ascribe the decline in the humanities in higher education to similar faults and often including the turn towards literary theory.

In an essay entitled "Diversity," Louis Menand discusses the eponymous term's importance in relation to literary studies. He does so by recounting the rise of general education requirements in American universities and the accompanying arguments for meritocracy, particularly as these movements gained traction at Harvard in the years after World War II. Menand points out that when the designers of this new Harvard curriculum, which included the famous literary critic I.A. Richards, set to work, they were concerned with "diversity," but that diversity was almost exclusively focused on class difference. As Menand explains, one solution they arrived at was teaching the "great books" and of most relevance here,

"The Great Texts of Literature." All students would take classes with a shared reading list and these would provide what was needed for "the present [...] centrifugal culture in extreme need of unifying forces".[3] These great books that could provide a "binding experience"[4] might be one way of defining the literary canon. As John Guillory explains, the term, canon, derives in part from its notion of measurement and from what stayed and what became excommunicated from the Bible. However, while there have earlier major overhauls to what we might consider the literary canon—such as the introduction of works in English as a subject of study in the United States (replacing works in Greek and Latin), the canon became a subject of controversy in a very visible sense only after the population of the student body was no longer overwhelmingly white and male.

Menand offers a definition of the canon as it came to be understood in the twentieth-century university:

> Within the specialty of literary studies, the canon consisted of those works that repay investigation under the aegis of 'literature as literature'—those works that exhibit (however it is defined) the essential 'literary' quality. And within the broader socializing mission of the university, the canon consisted of the books that can be regarded as cultural glue—the books that articulate the common assumptions of our way of life, and thereby speak to all future citizens.[5]

However, the canon, which is now frequently derided as the traditional home of dead white men, came to be challenged as the population of the student body ceased to necessarily reflect the relative homogeneity of the canon and, as Menand argues, the Cold War conditions that helped push for the "binding" role of the canon dissipated with the decline of the Soviet Union in the 1980s. At roughly the same time, multiculturalism—in many forms—gained momentum in the American university, and there arose calls from within and without the university to "open the canon."

In short, the canon had become political. People took sides. Many critics of the canon saw it as representing forces that didn't bring people together but instead discriminated against women, people of color, and the LGBTQ community. Some referred to the canon as the *master* canon, emphasizing its role not as the pinnacle of "what has been thought and said" but rather maintaining traditions that oppressed. The variety of suggestions for revising the canon included seeking to represent those who have been "excluded" from the canon, to reconsider the very foundations upon which this canon was formed—the judgments that elevated these authors and texts—and seeking to approach these canonical texts by pointing out the kind of oppressive messages they conveyed. Many of the conservatives that got wind of this saw it as a destruction of the common culture, the ties that bind a culture together. They defended the works in the canon as the high points of civilization, as the carriers of the core principles of Western culture, and simply as great works. Calls to discard, criticize, or open the canon were viewed by more conservative minds both inside and outside the academy as a threat, a lowering of aesthetic standards and leading to a disintegration of Western culture.

Although this was no doubt a distressing time to be a humanities professor, it also was an exciting time, for even your critics were claiming that what you did mattered. Writing at the time in the book *Beyond the Culture Wars*, Gerald Graff described the result as "today's education crisis" in which "the academic curriculum has become a preeminent arena of cultural conflict because it is a microcosm, as it should be, of the clash of cultures and values in America as a whole."[6] While not siding with the conservative critiques, Graff notes that by letting faculty members abide by a "live-and-let-live philosophy" they have lent ammunition to conservatives who rightly note "the incoherence of the curriculum that is content to endlessly multiplying courses and subjects like boutiques in the mall."[7] The implication here is that rather than actually making choices—either reconsidering the canon as a whole or defending it as whole—the humanities solution was simply to add more and more courses. Thus, keep your canonical literary survey courses just as they are, but add courses that focus on women and a variety of ethnic-American traditions. While Graff argued to put the conflicts at the very center of the humanities—for instance, continuing to teach Joseph Conrad's *Heart of Darkness* but at the same time teaching one of his most vociferous critics, Chinua Achebe—depending on your view, either the American "mall" curriculum has continued more or less unabated or the multiculturalist challenges have been said to have won the day. Even in Graff's time he was at pains to disprove broad ill-informed generalizations, like the notion that Alice Walker was being taught more frequently than Shakespeare.

One of the most prominent critics of the very debate itself to emerge at this time was John Guillory, whose *Cultural Capital: The Problem of Literary Canon Formation* seeks, in part, to show that both the conservative and the liberal have misunderstood how the canon has and continues to be formed, and that many of the assumptions that underlie the canon debate are at best misleading and at worst simply false. Guillory's analysis is long and in depth, but it will be helpful to consider some of its key points as it has echoes in and through these discussions in the wine world about what makes a great wine—and thus which wines are classics, or as wine people often like to call them, benchmarks. At the core of the debate, Guillory explains, is a kind of equation of the plight of representation in the larger culture, particularly its political institutions, as viewed through the lens of "liberal pluralism."[8] Having had limited success in redressing these entrenched political problems in that sphere, Guillory contends, the battle shifted to "the liberal academy."[9] He goes on to point out that canon, as a common term, is relatively recent and has largely replaced the term classic; it also explicitly links the ways in which the literary world has been formed to the process by which the Bible evolved. What might be broadly called the liberal critiques of the canon, an umbrella term that encapsulates critiques from the perspectives of race, class, and gender, among others, share an emphasis on seeing the process in terms of "exclusion" rather than "selection."[10] One solution to this problem has been to construct separate canons out of the noncanonical. Louis Menand refers to this as replacing one "monolith" with many "monoliths."[11] This response, according to Guillory, attempts to change the canon by viewing it as "a kind of mirror in which social groups either see themselves, or do not see themselves, reflected."[12] In that case, the cure is to add texts—and authors, since authors and their social group origins now become key—to provide such a mirror. While Guillory is sympathetic to this desire, he does not think the canon has been formed by inclusion or exclusion, and he's highly skeptical of the kind of essentialism that leads particular authors to stand in and represent entire social groups. Nevertheless, there is no denying the powerful effect of never seeing yourself reflected in the works taught in literature classes.

Exclusion, according to Guillory, is not how the canon has been formed nor has it been a conspiracy to keep any particular group like women out. Instead, he argues that it is better to see the authors within the canon as reflective of those who have had the most access to literacy, "for literacy is a question of the distribution of cultural goods rather than the representation of cultural image."[13] In periods of time where, for instance, it was overwhelmingly well educated, wealthy, white men who had the most access to "literacy," the works that will be canonized will likely not include many women. However, that does not mean that the decision was made by some literary illuminati group on a mountaintop near Zurich—though it does leave quite a bit of space to examine the cultural traditions that limited access to literacy. For Guillory, then, "the historical process of canon formation, even especially at the moment of institutional judgment, is too complex to be reduced to determination by the single factor of the social identity of the author."[14]

However, he also dismisses notions like those espoused by Barbara Herrnstein Smith in *Contingencies of Value* that canonical texts typically represent the value systems of the dominant social forces at any given time. In fact, Guillory finds it remarkable that both sides of the political spectrum seem to agree on this point to some extent, for it's exactly the fact that these texts represent the core values of the culture that folks like William Bennet argued when they were aghast at their decline in the academy (which I would say, along with Graff, is quite an exaggeration). If there are values that are taught from these texts, Guillory suggests, it is done via how they are taught, and often at lower levels of education, rather than necessarily something abiding in the texts themselves.[15] In addition to his academic treatise on the subject, Guillory composed a much shorter discussion aimed at students. Here he is more direct and accessible in his points. Often the more conservative position rests on an almost untenable tautology, that "some works are just great, and have simply been recognized as such."[16] This falls apart, Guillory contends, when "two intelligent readers disagree about the greatness of a particular work" showing that greatness cannot simply be self-evident. However, he notes that in the solution to the canon that includes opening the canon, "the liberal critique" "must smuggle in a concept of real literary value in order if it wants to claim that some works—formerly noncanonical works—are just as good as the canonical works."[17] Here he disagrees with Herrnstein Smith without naming her, though she also has an essay on value in the very same collection. Guillory accuses her of being a value "relativist" by which he means that she is skeptical of any value that is labeled intrinsic.

For her part, Herrnstein Smith suggests that the more overtly economic understandings of value have relevance for art, though it has been "the traditionalist—idealist, humanist, genteel—tendency to isolate art and literature, from consideration in economic terms," which thus leads to "mystifying the nature—or more accurately the dynamics—of their value."[18] Writing for students, Herrnstein Smith defines value as "relative [amount of] positivity."[19] The question is, does the same logic that says on a hot day we may value a single cold sports drink when we are in a remote, open space, more than we would a fridge full of such drinks on a cold, snowy day, apply to how we decide the value of art? With great hesitancy, she sketches out "this special kind of value"—let's say literary value—

> the possession of which is sometimes said to mark off genuine works of literature from all other texts [... and] is also commonly associated with a text's inherent capacity to produce some purely sensory/ perceptual gratification, independent of any kind of interest, or some purely passive and intellectual gratification, independent of any practical, active, or material response to the text.[20]

Here, Herrnstein Smith has brought us fully around to Kant once more, for what she is talking about is the kind of "disinterested" appreciation produced by the beautiful as Kant saw it.

However, in this same essay, she reveals her skepticism of this idea and intrinsic value in art altogether as she outlines the "skeptical scrutiny" that doubts "whether anything is left over when all those forms of value and sources of interest are subtracted" and "whether any of those crucial distinctions can actually be drawn as clearly and firmly as desired" or even whether it's even possible to do so if we tried.[21] The implication for the canon debate is that there can be no cogent discussion of the canonical status of works based on intrinsic value because all such judgments are tainted by the extrinsic. This need not lead to a conspiracy, but its results might look that way. Guillory, building from Bourdieu, has something to say about this too, but for now let us consider how these arguments defending the canonical or criticizing it or, in Guillory's case, arguing for seeing canonization as a complex, historical process that cannot be reduced to a single cause may help shed light on questions of what makes a wine great, who gets to decide, and whether some grapes simply cannot make a great wine.

In the bubbling up of these questions of aesthetics—of whether the value of wine comes from intrinsic or extrinsic sources, of the notion that if we are going to identify certain wines as great how are we going to arrive at a definition of greatness, of whether the wines produced from grapes not typically associated with greatness should be recognized, if in fact the world of wine needs to be diversified—we are finding ourselves returning to the fundamental questions of whether wine can be looked at as akin to art and we are looking at the shape of the rhetoric and controversies that surround the canon debates. These are not perfect corre-spondences: certainly the urgency of seeing the value in the novels of Toni Mor-rison does not equate to the urgency of giving trousseau from the Jura its due. There is not an institution that houses and shapes the world of wine like the academy does for literary studies and other fine arts, and wine is much more overtly tied to the marketplace than canonical literature. Nevertheless, I will con-tend that these debates about the canon can both help understand the shape of this controversy in the wine world and also help illustrate the ways in which wine can function culturally in the way art does whether or not one wishes to see it as such.

★   ★   ★   ★

Back on a highway, having met Darrell Corti, been lectured on the inanity of Parker's contentions, admired extraordinarily expensive balsamic vinegar, and gotten advice on what to buy for dinner, Tegan and I continued our conversation. He had just told me his exasperation with someone telling him his wines were simply too clean and his exclusion from a natural wine tasting event. Why does the wine need to be "dirty"? I asked.

> That is the only way you can really know that it's natural. You know what I mean, because if a woman's breasts are too perfect, then they must be fake. And you know, I mean, was God an artist? I don't know what people think, because I was about to say that I'm the creator of these wines, and if you're the creator, maybe it's a chauvinist thing to say, but if you're a creator of a woman, wouldn't you want her breasts to be perfect? If that's your job to create, whatever you think that might be. I mean, that would be this great thing, just like a wine, if people had their Barbie dolls, and you said, make the perfect woman. And to get—just like, make the perfect wine from this vine-yard, everyone's going to make a different version.

I was a bit taken aback by the direction Tegan's analogy had taken, and he seemed to read that on my face. "The reason I said that," he explained, "is, I'm the creator of these wines, I want them to be in my mind as perfect as they can be."

Would this perfection need to be in the eye of the creator or the beholder? Tegan seemed to raise the notion that everyone idealized perfection but that per-fection itself was subjective. Tegan's remarks put me in mind of longstanding debates about whether perfection was a measure of beauty, of greatness. Thinking through his comments, I responded that

> there's actually a kind of long dialectic in art about this, you know; there was a time in the nineteenth century, for example, when a lot of these English critics, like a guy John Ruskin, began praising Gothic architecture, and part of the praising was the irregularities in it. And part of that also was this sort of

sense of the human hand being visible in there, that a certain kind of perfection seems to suggest a machine, or something along those lines.

Ruskin's aesthetic views most certainly had sociological implications, and his objections to mechanized perfection is part of his objection to what he sees as the dehumanizing aspects of industrialization. This question about artistic perfection intrigued a number of nineteenth-century figures. Robert Browning's poem, "Andrea Del Sarto," written in the painter's voice, speaks to his jealousy of Raphael tinged with his complaints about Raphael's faulty lines and poorly drawn hands. Ruskin championed the work of John M.W. Turner, whose work diverged from mimetic representation and clearly anticipated the work of the French Impressionists. In "Stone of Venice," it becomes quite clear that Ruskin's architectural criticism is in fact social criticism. Although he does not always directly address it this way, Ruskin tends to view the production of perfect objects—buildings, glass beads, or mimetic images—as instances of mechanical perfection, of the rise of industrialization and the alienation of the worker. The perfectly cast Renaissance cathedrals were achieved by making humans become tools, and instead we must "honour them in their imperfection."[22] In short, those who criticized Tegan's wines, like those who tried to celebrate what others called the flaws in natural wines, clearly align with the kind of aesthetic program that Ruskin championed—one where the natural imperfections that appear in anything humans make should be celebrated as markers of the very human act of creation. We might see this as a rejection of science since it contributes to increased industrialization, and instead an embrace of the natural. While it may be an obvious way to define great art by saying that it approaches perfection, there has actually been a long counter-tradition that cherishes the signs of the human hand even with its associated imperfections. Of course, some would say that the problem with natural wines is not the revelation of the human hand, but in making a virtue of flaws. This conversation would, surprisingly, not be the last time that architectural theory would come up in discussions of greatness and wine.

*　　*　　*　　*

I am afraid of heights. I do not like to fly. I do not like to drive over bridges. When I drove over the Richmond Hill Bridge on my way down to visit Donkey and Goat's Jared Brandt in Berkeley and saw the bridge rise like a giant, twisted dragon's neck arching over the bay, I nearly had a panic attack. Driving up winding, narrow roads wound around the sides of mountains makes me skittish as well. On a sunny morning in early spring, I drove up such a road on my way to the top of Atlas Peak, cresting through the cloud bank and still climbing until I had to test the power of my rental car, as I turned onto the steep driveways that led me to John Kongsgaard's winery. I parked across from what had the obvious marks of a cellar door. One side overlooked the road I had driven up. The other showed me a vineyard. From either side, I could see quite a long way. John would later explain

FIGURE 6.1 View from Kongsgaard

that I had been looking towards the Sierra Foothills on one side, and San Francisco and the bay on the other.

Gazing up past the cellar doors, I saw John come down the path from the house that seemed to sit on the mountain top. Via text message, Abe Schoener, whom John had mentored, told me to just let John lead the conversation. Although at over six feet tall, with wavy gray hair and a sonorous voice, John could be intimidating if he wanted—he described running a large winery at one time as being like a general standing on a tank—his manner was warm and inviting. He made me feel immediately comfortable as a dog came wagging my way.

In the Kongsgaard cellar, John showed me around. Before my visit, I had learned about John's passion for classical music. He and his wife have organized the Napa Music Festival for many years, and, on this very morning, a quartet had taken up residence in his home. As he wandered the facility, he pointed out that his fermentation tanks were not numbered, but instead labeled by reproduced sheet music, including one with Leonard Bernstein's annotations. A portrait of Gustav Mahler decorated another wall.

Music and art infuse Kongsgaard's life and work. I decided to use his love of music as a means to get him to discuss greatness: "How would you compare a piece of music that you consider to be great with a wine that you consider to be great?" While he initially hesitated, saying I had asked him a "philosophy of art question," it quickly became clear that he had thought about this comparison:

> from, let's say, Classical and Romantic repertory, like from Mozart and Hayden to—let's go all the way to Mahler. That music is harmonic. I'm not talking about the edges where it's you know, the super modern, super dissonant music, which I admire, even commission, but if you take those pieces out, then the great pieces of art, whether it's music or painting, if you go and look at a Titian, it's kind of like listening to a Beethoven symphony or

FIGURE 6.2 One of the Kongsgaard tanks

drinking a great Montrachet or Judge when it hits it—so, what are those things? They're balanced; they're uplifting. You look at that greatest painting or you are in the concert hall and somebody really nails the Beethoven 7th slow movement, you have this sense of awe that I think you can feel [...]. And it's balance, and it's... I don't know how you analyze it, but it's thrilling. My old teacher Winiarski, Warren ... . I worked for him, I really treasured my apprenticeship with him, and Alex, my son, and I were out working at a vineyard with him, and we were talking about wine, and Warren's a real philosopher, so he was saying, what are you guys after? It's like, oh god, here goes Warren with a loaded question. And it caused me to think hard, and I said, I want the wine to be thrilling. Warren doesn't want that, he wants the wine to be completely balanced and just kind of whisper its greatness to you. But it's fine with me if our wine's a little bit shocking. It kind of takes you off guard, you know?

I responded, "So some Mahler is okay? When you're describing your notion of greatness versus Warren's, so is greatness in that part subjective essentially? Like, your aesthetic priority, like your individual ... ." "Yeah. Yeah, of course," John jumped in.

I always admire—or generally admire Warren's wines. But they're—maybe they're kind of mega-harmonious. And they could be a little more startling. How do you do that? How does that mean you do one more pump-over or something? It's—how you get a wine to be the way it is a whole complex matrix of decisions. And you, you know, the fun of it, the fun thing about wine is that it's science and art and total bullshit.

Later in our conversation, we returned to this notion of greatness as John shared some of his wines with me. As I carried our glasses and John hoisted the enormous bent pipette winemakers call a barrel thief, we headed down a path towards barrels that contained some of John's most famous wine, the Judge Vineyard chardonnay along with a chardonnay produced up on the mountain from vines lost to the recent wildfires. We returned to a table and sipped them side by side. Both were terrific. I felt the loss of those vines and felt lucky to sip what they produced before their death. The Judge haunted my sense memory for days, the minerality lingering on my tongue well after the liquid had disappeared. He then opened one of his rarer wines, an albariño made from grapes he had convinced his friend Lee Hudson to grow for him. And then we returned to art and architecture. "I think you can look at the model of architecture, and say that cathedrals and capitol buildings are the greatest expression of civic architecture and religious architecture," he began. "And if you like architecture like everybody that likes literature and wine should like architecture, and you go to France, you're going to go all the way to Chartres to look at that church, because it's like, phew, that's an astonishing building."

However, he noted,

it's also interesting to go visit the Romanesque village churches when you're in France. They're in some ways as stirring, but as much as the Chartres? No. You're really in the vernacular. And the vernacular is so interesting to me. And if I had one last day of architecture looking, I'd probably go somewhere in central Spain and see this little tiny perfect building that was built without an architect. It was just from the tradition. I mean just this: there's nothing more to it; there are no buttresses. It's a lump of rock, and it's just shockingly perfect. So that's not Chartres, or the Washington D.C. Capitol Building.

John's analysis suggested the complexities of defining the subjects of greatness and also this undercurrent of ultimate experience that might be used to define such greatness.

He then took the analogy squarely back to wine:

So I have really room in my aesthetic curiosity, and what can really stir me can go all the way down to something that's more humble. So that said, of course we make chardonnay and cabernet because we're interested in, you know, what's the literary version of the greatest novel and greatest epic poem.

He might have said because those are the noble, the canonical grapes.

> So we're in it for the epic stuff, and we make these wines in the image of the greatest, and we really see ourselves competing, that's not even the right word, joining in the discussion at the very highest level. And you can do that with chardonnay, with cabernet, blends, probably syrah. These are all the wines in Europe that have really expensive antecedents.

And what of the other grapes that do not fit that profile?

> Do we make viognier and albariño and sauvignon blanc? Yeah. And are they as great? I don't know. Now you have the difference between Chartres and the Romanesque lump of rock. That's kind of my answer. I think you can have your breath taken away by an albariño. Not quite the same way as you can with chardonnay.

Is this Herrnstein Smith's "relative positivity?" I felt John was trying to escape me after all that, so, while I had him so close, I blurted out, "What's the gap?" The gap between the chardonnays and cabernets and the viognier and the albariño? "Yeah, what's the gap, I don't know. That's a science question you asked to a literary guy. You know, it's a big question. Your deathbed wine would certainly not be an albariño. Even the best one. Fair enough?"

★   ★   ★   ★

You might ask yourself why it seemed self-evident that, for your final meal, you would not uncork an albariño. John suggests it is not something you can reason, but something you just feel. Part of me intuitively got what John had to say, but part of me continued to mull over the implications weeks afterward. Does the notion lie in the very wine itself? Is a wine whose taste experience is, at its best, like a vertical shot—one blast forward, in a line, like a tower—simply not as serious, as meaningful as a wine that seems to touch a variety of taste buds, that can be subtle, or powerful but is experienced more gradually, perhaps more subtly? If we accept such judgments, where does this division and this hierarchy come from? Is this a convention of human taste that is natural or is this part of the way in which humans acquire a notion of proper taste and simply apply it as if it were a natural category? Is this a version of the genre debate in literature that builds a clear hierarchy of serious fiction as opposed to entertainment, something the writer Graham Greene rather self-consciously used to divide his own works?

In the debates about the literary canon itself, this notion of genre and aesthetics has also been a part of the feminist critique of the canon. It has evolved in a few form, including 1) that the milieu of women's fiction in a patriarchy has been underappreciated, or, perhaps as some have suggested, the occupations and preoccupations of men are favored in art in a patriarchy because even women are taught to see the world through men's point of view, and 2) as critics like Tamara Jeffers MacDonald suggests of the Romantic Comedy, texts whose primary audience is supposed to be women—some pop music, romance novels, love stories—are seen as being at the bottom of the culture's aesthetic scale. Lillian S. Robinson has suggested that feminist critics have frequently gotten stuck while trying to champion previously unrecognized women writers as they "are torn between defending the quality of their discoveries and radically redefining literary quality itself."[23] Annette Kolodony describes the problem as being "unable to distinguish as primary the importance of what we read as opposed to how we have learned to read it. For, simply put, we read well, and with pleasure, what we already know how to read."[24] Robinson sees the issue as an unwillingness to fully endorse the gendered aesthetics that remain in place, whereas Kolodony suggests the ways in which that aesthetic and milieu stands as a barrier for the appreciation of texts written by women, even by women readers as they have been taught to read from a patriarchal perspective.

You might think that this notion of gendered aesthetic hierarchy has no place in the world of wine, but consider that there are wines that have been either aimed at women or associated with women consumers. These would be wines like white zinfandel, which is really a heavily marketed sweet rosé, or wines associated with the disparaging phrase, cougar juice. In particular, Rombauer chardonnay, a fairly rich, oak-forward take on the grape, gets associated with this phrase (a quick google search will get you there). Although white zinfandel and Rombauer chardonnay have made their producers a great deal of money, neither is taken very seriously by wine snobs. In fact, one can easily find disparagements of both. Similarly, in Burgundy, the supposedly "masculine wines" of the Cote du Nuit are prized more highly (with the corresponding majority of Grand Cru pinot noir sites) than their more "feminine" counterparts in the Cote du Beaune. While you might want to argue that certain wines associated with men—such as heavily oaked and big-flavored Napa cabernet—also can get criticized by the more snobbish or Eurocentric of wine consumers, it is enough to point out that there is no agist, derogatory term for those wines that singles out men.

There's another way in which Herrnstein Smith's arguments about relative value—which can be seen in part as the value of something in the moment based on an individual's (or group's) needs, desires, or uses—has resonance here. If we hearken back to Michael Broadbent's notions of certain wines demanding deep concentration or appreciation, then we see that the seeming value of some of these other wines is easy consumption—a pinch of sugar or oak helps the medicine go down—and that simultaneously eliminates them from the consideration of greatness. In this we see echoes of the discussion of natural wines from the previous chapter where the notion of glou glou, easy consumption, almost too easy consumption, gets connected to certain versions of natural wine. It puts me in mind of a beer advertising slogan I would hear when I was young: Schaefer, the one beer to have when you're having more than one. Such a slogan has not led to a reconsideration of the aesthetic merits of Schaefer in the craft beer scene! Yet this notion of high alcohol or easy access to the alcohol can be turned against many wines.

★   ★   ★   ★

In much the same way that I wanted to know whether any winemaker might finally embrace the label of artist, I had enormous curiosity about how winemakers would respond to Parker's attacks on a wide range of varieties and how wine-makers would offer their own definitions of greatness. Chris Brockway is a genial, easy-going winemaker whose Broc Cellars in urban Berkeley produces many wines from grapes Parker would be anxious to dismiss. As I sat with him across his wine tasting bar, he offered me the rare opportunity to taste unblended counoise as well as valdiguie (once known as Napa gamay). After I read an excerpt from Parker, I could see that it had gotten a bit under Chris' skin:

> it's just coming from such a different place that I'm not even sure I can understand it, because it seems to take all the joy out of wine, and discovery—once again, everything has to fit into the same thing, and you can say the complete opposite about every wine that he likes. And, the more he likes it, the less drinkable [it is]. I don't see a lot of hundred-point Parker wines around, but when I see somebody with one, they usually drink about that much …

and he gestured by pulling his thumb and forefinger together.

> It's like, nobody can drink it. You know, well, you'd be too drunk, first of all, and second of all, it's just like too much on the palate. And if you have any sensitivity to oak and alcohol, how are you going to be able to drink any of these wines, as opposed to enjoying something, and I think it's just like completely missing the whole point of what wine is. And obviously people have different interpretations, but … .

As he trailed off, I jumped in to ask, "a great wine for you—how would you define that?" He got more hesitant and seemed unsure of how much to commit:

> it's easy to overlook enjoyment, and then when you start talking about great wines, there's great wines that would fall into a lot of different people's interpretations, like Clos Rougeard cab franc would be one, Thierry Alle-mand's syrah. I think those are wines that achieve greatness given the year and things like that, but then also fall into a natural wine, but when you start getting out of, I guess, the mainstream varieties, then I think it gets a little tougher to talk about the wine in that way, because you're talking about enjoyment and things you like to drink, and it's not a trophy, this thing where you hold it up.

In his comments, Chris seemed caught between defining greatness based on how you feel—joy, pleasure—when consuming the wine, or believing it should be something closer to Broadbent's ideas of wines that require thinking and contemplation.

So, do you think the term is coming with a certain kind of baggage? "Yeah, I think it's just a tough term to describe when somebody obviously has so much enjoyment in drinking certain styles of wine. Are you only going to drink the greatest wines all the time, every day? I don't know … do you want to?" At some point, Chris and I started to try to distinguish between wines that were fun to drink and wines that were great. Fun started to seem as vexed a term as great. I get it. There are some novels that I consider great—however, conflicted I am about how I would define them as such—and some that I consider fun to read, but sometimes they overlap. But those overlapping texts always seem to require a defense of some sort. I can tell someone that I think that Joyce's *Ulysses* is a great novel and, while it will not come across as my most impressive pronouncement neither is it likely to invite much controversy. If I tell someone I consider Dashiell Hammett's *The Maltese Falcon* great, most want to know why. A hard-boiled detective novel requires an explanation in a way that an epic, experimental modernist novel by an author whose work has been written about more than anyone in English except Shakespeare does not. Thus, we might consider greatness as not something to recognize, but something that requires discernment and interpretation, both of the quality of the object (literature or wine) and the category (genre or grape variety).

With this fun versus great dichotomy now on my mind, I decided to ask Hardy Wallace about it. "A great wine is …," he hesitated,

> not that it's not good when it goes into the bottle, but that is going to evolve and develop, and get more interesting, and tell that soil story of where it's from more and more clearly as it goes on over whatever the course of its life might be. Might be five years, might be ten years, might be twenty years, thirty years, but that wine has the ability I think to greatly improve in that course of its life, and tell its story better and better and better as it goes on.

An albariño is meant to be consumed now. Is that then why it does not qualify for one's death bed? Putting aside whether such bottles have limits on their expression of terroir, Hardy's thoughts then return us to this fundamental question of standing the test of time. It's not just the notion, in wine, that year in and year out this wine is outstanding and is thus a great wine, but that the very bottle itself stands the test of time.

This notion of age and time clearly informed Abe Schoener's view of greatness as well. As Abe had said as he sipped his martini in the Ludlow's bar in lower Manhattan, he remarked that

> the serviceable wines have no capacity to induce anything like the experience of the sublime, or to make you, even in an unreflective way consider

materiality and eternality at the same time. And so for me, that's the value of really beautiful wines that have the capacity to age and that one experiences at a certain point in their lifetime, that at the same time, they make you think of eternality and materiality and its transitory nature, and for me those things are tied to tragedy and also to something like the notion of doom.

You will recall that the sublime suggests awe, as when the individual experiences a sense of being overwhelmed by the natural world, described by the many Romantic poets who recorded their encounters with Mont Blanc. Doom, however, seemed to be particular to Abe's own conception, and I asked him to explain further:

> the first sip of a forty-year-old barolo can make me think of beauty, but it also makes me think of doom, because I know that I might never have this wine again, because of the nature of my life and my material [self]. But it's also true that we know enough that maybe this is the best fucking bottle of this wine on the face of the earth right now, and if I ever try to taste another one it's going to disappoint me. And so the doom is built into the experience: how good the experience is tied into the notion that this thing that I experience is doomed.

For Abe, then, doom was tied to the sublime: that baked-into-the-moment of experience of greatness in wine—and here it seems fundamentally clear that Abe dismisses the notion of the wine experience's transience as a disqualifier for seeing wine as art—was also an encounter with our own mortality, the sense that on some level all of us are doomed; perhaps the uniqueness of the experience also suggests that notion of mortality. Clearly, Abe's view derives from a culture of feeling.

Surprisingly, however, considering Abe's own eclectic interests in grape varieties like verdelho, he is somewhat sympathetic to Parker, as can be seen in thoughts I had earlier referenced. Abe sums up his view this way:

> What I think is really special about Parker is he put hedonism at the center. And the only difference between me and Parker is we disagree on what are the sources of pleasure. But not that it should be at the center. So when I say, judge it on its ability to conjure up the tragic, I don't mean that in opposition to pleasure, that's specific—as Aristotle points out, that is a specific form of pleasure. Parker has a different pleasure in mind. But we both agree that in the long run it's about pleasure.

He may be right about this in terms of Parker's entire career and the wines that have become associated with his own taste (whether that is inaccurate as Parker himself claims), but it is worth noting that Parker dismisses many of the wines made from grapes that someone like Brockway would particularly associate with fun and which would very much seem to be akin to pleasure. Thus, identifying greatness requires interpretation: it is not simply a notion of *being* great.

★   ★   ★   ★

I want to contextualize this notion of a wine's greatness being associated with a wine that can evolve and improve with time. In a late section of *Cultural Capital*, Guillory provides a gloss on some of Bourdieu's views of value and the way that cultural capital itself gets distributed between different taste categories. He divides "aesthetic judgment" into the "elite aesthetic of the dominant classes," sometimes referred to as the "aesthetic disposition," and the "'popular' aesthetic of the dominated."[25] Guillory suggests that Bourdieu's view is that "aesthetic value" is "nothing more or other than cultural capital."[26] Expressing a certain kind of taste, valuing say the First Growths of Bordeaux is an expression of one's cultural capital, one that moves towards the dominating classes of the society and one economically signified by its value in economic capital.

These ideas then inform the way in which people appraise a variety of cultural products, from art to wine. Crucially, the way in which this works for Bourdieu, according to Guillory's application of his idea, has particular resonance for arguments that a great wine can be determined in part by how well it can be appreciated after its making. "To say that the aesthetic disposition determines the relative cultural capital granted to any particular work," Guillory explains,

> is to say that the act of judgment is the assignment, or even the recognition, of cultural capital. Judgment is the act by which the aesthetic disposition expresses or externalizes itself, according to criteria which are relatively internalized, that is, neither capable of being fully rationalized, nor materially caused in the manner of biological disposition.[27]

While this may seem obscure, the key idea here is that taste seems like it is our own—because we have "internalized" what our taste should be—and we thus apply it in the process of making aesthetic judgements, but it is not "natural" in any way. When you grow up in a particular socio-economic class you internalize certain aesthetic values; however, just like you can acquire real capital, you can also acquire cultural capital. It may not come as easily or feel quite as "natural" but this is how we come to "appreciate" the "greatest" wines when we have not grown up in a culture that teaches us how and why to appreciate them.

In reviewing Bourdieu's work, which included a great many surveys, Guillory notes that explanations for how people made their judgments "appear to be derived in a surprisingly direct way from the themes of aesthetic discourse, as though the members of the dominant classes had at least a passing familiarity with Kant."[28] While Bourdieu's subjects were French, the results point to the remarkable influence of Kant, so much so that I would imagine reaching a similar conclusion if Bourdieu's methods were duplicated with Americans. In short, people do not need to have read Kant to appear as if they have. Two key parts of the "criteria" that Bourdieu cites have rather direct relevance here: "disinterestedness" and "deferred pleasure."[29] As I have suggested, Kant's notions of beauty lying in disinterest tends to be a hurdle to considering wine as art; if you are a wine drinker, how do you ever judge wine with disinterest?

Nevertheless, Bourdieu helps us understand how so many arguments for "great wines" focus on wines that require us to defer our pleasure. Modern techniques have arguably made some wines that fit this category more immediately accessible, but some of the most treasured wines of the world have been those that are simply not very appealing when they are young. I remember that when I was first getting into wine, a waiter explained to me that I should never drink any quality Italian wine like barolo before it was ten years old. Similarly, it is a commonplace that the best wines of Bordeaux or Port need twenty years rest before their pleasures can be fully expressed. Even if those wines do offer some pleasures when they are young, those pleasurable flavors are often discounted by reviewers as "primary." As Guillory explains, "Bourdieu quite rightly points to the fact that the pleasure of aesthetic judgment manifests itself curiously as a kind of unpleasure."[30] How might this be applied to wine? Well, in part, the notion might allow us to consider that the more direct the wine's pleasures are, the less likely that wine is to be valued among those who judge. To refer to a literary example, Joyce's work might be said to have been written with the intention that a reader reread it; Hammett had little desire to put those kinds of challenges in front of the reader. Consumers of First Growths will typically say things like, I cannot wait to taste this again in another ten years; it is as if their greatest pleasures are always on the horizon. If anything, what Abe Schoener calls "serviceable wines" are always geared towards giving you what they have to offer as soon as possible. You need not despair, however, because there is always more where that comes from—either a next vintage or through sheer quantity of production.

★   ★   ★   ★

While I was traveling around California with a print-out of Parker's blog post, it turned out that another writer, Jason Wilson, was doing something similar, though primarily in Europe while writing *Godforsaken Grapes*, which borrows its title directly from Parker. As you recall, Parker himself introduced the term diversity in his discussion. While that can imply biodiversity—and clearly on some level it does—it speaks much more directly to a wider variety of wines produced from a wider variety of grapes. Throughout his book, Wilson pays attention to two interrelated categories, noble grapes and serious wines, which clearly stand in opposition to Brockway's notion of "fun wines." While someone like Guillory can critique the premise upon which the liberal critique of the canon rests, we can all understand why, built on that premise, folks would want to see greater diversity in terms of authors in the canon. Since Guillory sees canon formation through a historical lens and argues that the canon consists of works reflecting those who have the most access to literacy, he claims that, as the canon continues to modernize, it will grow more diverse because access to literacy has grown more diverse. With adding diversity to the canon, the argument goes that we need more diversity to reflect the population. What, however, is the argument for why we need more diversity in our grape varieties or wine options?

I turned to Wilson's book hoping to find some of those answers. After noting his companion's "hate" for calling some grapes "noble," Wilson explains that "What bothers people [… about the term] is that while 1,368 wine grape varieties may exist, the sad truth is that 80 percent of the world's wine is produced from only twenty grapes. Many of the other 1,348 varieties face extinction".[31] The word "extinction" is clearly loaded, designed to draw a reader's sympathies. Who wants to see a grape variety go extinct? However, are we in danger of anthropomorphizing grape varieties when we talk about them this way? In an article by Kevin Wardell entitled "Why More California Winemakers Are Embracing Varietal Diversity," written for *750 Daily*, he notes the rise of a wine event dedicated to grape diversity entitled Seven Percent Solution, a title of course borrowed from Arthur Conan Doyle. The name derived from the fact that at one point, "7 percent of plantings encompassed more than 90 different varieties, many of which were being championed by small growers and winemakers," whereas the other 93 percent came from eight varieties.[32] Wardell explains that while the larger group has expanded by one more grape variety, most importantly the 7 percent has now risen to 12. He's quick to point out, however, that not all of these grapes are obscure; grenache, for instance, has been heavily planted in both Spain and France's Rhone Valley but sparingly in California. Some of the reasons offered by Wardell for the rise in diversity are that these new varieties are increasing in value, that consumers want to experiment, and that in some ways the broader diversity corresponds to the current food trends.

While I find all of these possible, I wondered if there are deeper reasons. Wilson explains that he is "excited about having new experiences and learning new things," but he also suggests that these varieties—and for him, unlike the folks in California, the emphasis is on the indigenous grapes of a particular place—"carry with them a taste of place and culture."[33] Although he concedes that there may be some that celebrate these grapes as "an embrace of obscurity for obscurity's sake," that, because of their connections to culture, the celebration of them can "also serve a higher purpose."[34] At different times, however, Wilson has to wrestle with aesthetics. For example, in his push for grapes that lack the prestige of the notable, he asserts that "drinkable" would be "just about the highest virtue of wine."[35] It's hard to argue with that, but it resembles Brockway's contention that the "100-point wine" resists drinking. It's Bourdieu's "unpleasure."

In many ways, Wilson's book can be thought of as a quest. Like others in the wine world, he wants to taste as many varieties as he can. The driver of that quest seems largely to be experience and curiosity—and perhaps a desire to not miss out on something great. Wilson is a fine writer, and his passion for these grapes can easily spread to the reader. In many ways, though, Wilson finds himself wrestling with the preexisting "aesthetic distinctions" that exist for wine. As I have mentioned, one can acquire the taste to appreciate fine wine, and so Wilson notes that wine "is an aspirational ladder you must work hard to climb, and at the top of the ladder are the so-called Serious Wines."[36] Later he summarizes Parker's—again filling the villain role—definition of "Serious Wines" as those that "pleased the intellect as well as the palate, offering intense flavors, aromas, and always improved with aging."[37] When I had tried to propose my own system of dividing the wine world into wines of sensual pleasure and wines of intellectual pleasure, echoing the culture of reason and feeling dialectic, a winemaker asked me if I was saying he made dumb wines. Clearly, then, wines should aspire to both.

Wilson veers into the question of whether wine can be seen as art at one point. Although Wilson insists wine is not art, he routinely speaks of wine in similar terms. In one moment, he claims that if wine is art, it's nineteenth-century art because of critics with "their judgemental faux certainty and numerical scores and false logic that ranks and categorizes which wines are deemed 'best'."[38] Later, however, he will say that his objection to seeing wine as art "is that, no matter how great a wine, I've almost never encountered one that conveys the complex emotions like fear and loss or grief in the way that a great painting or a piece of music can"— just before confessing that a wine has just had such an emotional impact on him.[39] Where Wilson does keep coming back to viewing wine in ways that at least echo what art can do—besides emotion—is in its connection to culture, place, and history, which is a recurring claim made by the European winemakers he interviews. How, though, does this work in a place like California? After all, none of the grapes grown to make wine are indigenous to California. It was a question I raised with several winemakers who were invested in the Seven Percent, including two of the originators of that event, Duncan Arnot Meyers and Nathan Roberts of Arnot-Roberts.

★   ★   ★   ★

Healdsburg has become a charming town. It rests towards the northern end of Sonoma, and has a quaint town square, one now adorned with high-end restaurants and tasting rooms. Like many areas in contemporary California wine country, it seems to house multiple worlds simultaneously. Conveniently, I could walk the short distance from the bed-and-breakfast where I was staying to Duncan and Nathan's industrial winery space. With each step I moved from a place where tourists shuffle through the lives of service workers to an area where non-service work took place. I walked to the rear of a long, rectangular building, passing several other businesses before finding their residence, Duncan standing at the end of the entryway, a smile of greeting on his face. Rajat Parr had sent me here. When I had interviewed him in Lompoc for the first time, he had a bottle of Arnot-Roberts ribolla giallo lying on a table, and it had caught my eye all afternoon. At the end of our conversation, Raj grabbed the bottle and said, you should talk to these guys.

I had found out that when Jon Bonné worked for *The Chronicle*, he had named them winemakers of the year, Asimov had chronicled their quest to make trousseau (more on that in a moment), and Feiring had lauded them as two of the rare faces of natural wine in California. Asimov's story really intrigued me. It detailed how they had located trousseau in California—a grape once planted in Napa's most famous cabernet vineyard, To Kalon—after it had seemingly disappeared. This may very well have been the start of how either my context or taste started to change in such a way that I found myself asking Josh Greene to help me understand what had happened. If I had trousseau before, it was blended into port under the vivid moniker, bastardo. I confess to you now that I told Duncan I had never had trousseau with the hope he would share some, and he was kind enough to not only do so, but to share many of his wines with me. In fact, I awkwardly returned from this interview on foot carrying a case box.

Before we even tasted the trousseau, he shocked me by pouring a rosé made from touriga nacional. My head spun: Where did they find this grape out here? How did they know another of the famed port grapes would make excellent rosé, singing with acidity and a distinctive salinity? A chardonnay from the Santa Cruz mountains followed and its gravelly texture and powerful lemon flavors lingered in my mind for a long time afterward. Then, the trousseau. I wanted to know how they got so intrigued by this grape. By this time, I had pulled my crumpled copy of Parker's rant out of my pocket and our discussion was underway. Duncan took me over to a shelf lined with already consumed bottles and began to explain: "And trousseau comes from that region, and it's a very light-bodied red, and we fell in love with Jacques Pouffeney. This is the guy. I love his name anyway, right? Pouffeney," and he gestured at one of the bottles.

> We had some wines from this producer that really just spoke to us. They're energetic, lively, aromatic, fresh. They have structure and great acidity. They're not expensive. They're a relative value compared to a lot of other wines in the world. They go great with food, they age well, they're minimally manipulated in the cellar, they're made in a very hands-off way, generally, just this region is sort of this way.

Duncan speaks quickly and energetically, but his passion seemed to emerge from the very proximity of this original bottle. Still, I asked, many people admire wines from many places, but they don't always pursue making them as strongly as Duncan and Nathan have. "We decided to make this wine because we fell in love with it and we trusted our palates, and we just decided to make it and hope that there were a few people out there that felt the same way," he responded. The production of trousseau had thus come out of curiosity and passion, but not explicitly from a desire to diversify the wine world. In fact, they make wines from three of the noble grapes on a regular basis—though their takes on those grapes certainly conform to Old World models rather than New. Still, it seemed risky to me to make a wine that few had heard of and even fewer had made in California.

> We had no idea what the reception to the wine would be, and from the first couple of people that I tasted the wine with, their response was quite positive,

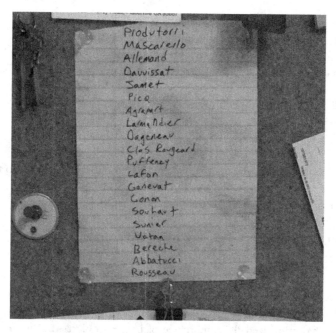

FIGURE 6.3 Duncan and Nathan's list of aspirational producers

so I knew that we had something there, so we just needed to get it into the right people's hands.

So I asked, by way of Parker's dismissal of the grape, whether you can make a "great wine" from it. At this point, Nathan joined in and they approached this question, not necessarily from their own view, but from that of the critics who seem to be what Wilson called the gatekeepers on "Serious Wines." "Yeah. Galloni does not want to give us more than a 91 for a trousseau. Which is fine, no, it's cool, it doesn't bother me, but it seems like he has a predisposition to have a ceiling on that," Duncan observed. To further clarify, Nathan continued,

> The numbers part of criticism just really adds another element, another layer onto it that makes it so much more confusing. They have these groups of scores, like this to that means it's outstanding, this to that is excellent but it's like a movie critic that only likes comedies. He's not going to give a drama a high score, because he only likes to watch comedies. You know there's no objective way of reviewing anything; you have to come into it with what your personal preference is, and that's just the way it is.

They went on to explain that it might be better to think about wines being in distinct categories rather than trying to compare trousseau to a First Growth Bordeaux. On the face of it, this makes a lot of sense. If you have never had it, trousseau looks almost more like a rosé than a red wine. Some of its signature tastes might be strawberry, watermelon, and citrus peel. How does it make sense to directly compare a wine like that to a brooding, blue and black fruit, highly tannic, opaque red wine? Still, the noble grapes are not identical in the kinds of wines they produce, so I circled back to whether a trousseau can be "great" or "serious." Nathan linked our two threads together, noting that

> it's not really a wine for serious cellaring, you know. I mean, it's great if you have a 15-year-old trousseau that's held up well, great, could be good to drink, but it's not really for the most part a wine that people can do that with, and I think that's one thing that kind of knocks it down. It just boxes it into a different place, puts it into a different box than these other wines.

Trousseaus do not produce a pleasure that needs deferring.

★　　★　　★　　★

Clearly, one way in which the debates over the literary canon and what I have been calling the canon of grapes resemble one another is that there has been one group that has prioritized the importance of how an object—literature or wine—can age. Exactly how and why these objects age, however, may seem very different on the face of it. For whether we will be reading a novel written today in another hundred years seems to be in an entirely different category than whether a wine will be better in twenty years than it will be today. One school of thought with wine is that all wines of course age, and in doing so, they change. The question is whether your palate enjoys the taste of older wines. Rajat Parr explained this view when I wondered about the aging ability of his wines. Jason Wilson raises the idea that wine culture has prioritized the notion that noble wines age well, but has not applied a fully experimental approach to testing that ability in lesser-known or -appreciated wines. Perhaps it is a matter of winemaking style or the properties of the grape itself. These issues might then seem quite foreign to the aging of literature. However, we don't have to push too far to realize that there is much art—often disparagingly labeled popular—that seems to be designed, like trousseau, for immediate consumption rather than long-term aging.

In fact, in literature the test of time approach is built out of an underlying notion that the very best art will ultimately "transcend" the circumstances of their creation. In fact, if literature is to be considered great, it should. The implications of the New Criticism that sought to wall off a work of literature from the circumstances of its creation and instead focus on its formal qualities seems to rest very much on this understanding of greatness. A text that cannot be so divested is probably not worthy of close reading in the first place. Of course, as I discussed earlier in this volume, many schools of literary interpretation have pushed back against these beliefs. While New Historicism has particularly challenged the notion of whether a work of literature could be properly interpreted without historical context, Jane Tompkins took up this issue in particular with regard to "literary masterpieces." Tompkins argues, in contrast to these notions of classics transcending time, that

> literary evaluation can never be anything but a political matter. My assumption is not that "interest and passion" should be eliminated from literary evalua-tion—this is neither possible nor desirable—but that works have that have attained the status of classic, and are therefore believed to embody universal values, are in fact embodying only the interests of whatever parties or factions are responsible for maintaining them in their preeminent position.[40]

In this way, Tompkins suggests that the status of a literary work is "maintained" by interested parties—let's say a group of academics—because of the desires or inter-ests of this group.

One example Tompkins uses is Nathaniel Hawthorne. She points out two things that may actually complicate her argument but illustrate her point: 1) that what critics initially praised about Hawthorne's work was radically different than what critics in later periods praised or dwelt upon, but also that 2) in many cases, those interests were connected to the praising of very different works written by Hawthorne. The short stories we anthologize now differ from those celebrated in the nineteenth century. Herrnstein Smith has talked about the ways in which a text, once elevated in status, has a variety of factors that tend to help it maintain that status, but we can also note that writers clearly do fall out of favor and become read less and less. Overall, Tompkins' argument suggests that perhaps the "test of time" is a kind of myth rather than some kind of objective criteria.

Could the same be said about wine? One way in which wine would seemingly differ from the role of the canon is that the canon traditionally has served as an object of study in schools. Academics publish scholarship about them, teach them to students, and ask their students to write essays about their meanings or perhaps their merits. How they are taught and for what ends might complicate what if any "values" are transmitted, but students rarely encounter such texts simply out of their own choice. Wine, in contrast, might seem to fall into a completely different category. However, if we are talking about wines that would typically be in the "canon" they may be encountered in somewhat similar ways, as a step on what Wilson called wine's "aspirational ladder." In other words, while wine may not have firm, clear institutional centers that "maintain" the noble wines, there is a way in which they are part of the education for anyone wishing to be a knowledgeable wine person, just as many conservative critics like E.D. Hirsch have argued that canonical texts should be read by any person who aspires to be cultured.

★   ★   ★   ★

As I have thought about and researched this topic, I have struggled to answer one question in particular that has nagged at me: does it really matter whether wine is diversified? Or to put it another way, why should it matter? There seems at first to be no clear constituency that would like to see itself reflected in the canon of grapes in quite the same way that there would be clear groups who would like to see their identity in some way reflected in the literary canon—whether that is an accurate view of it or not. Yes, I am attracted to the notion that the wine world should be diverse. To be honest, I now love trousseau, and I am grateful that my research introduced it to me. I do have some of Jason Wilson's curiosity for new flavors and new experiences in wine. I have trouble understanding the people that pop open a bottle of Napa cabernet every evening whether they're having sushi or beef Wellington. But do we need that diversity for less personal, self-serving reasons?

In Wilson's book, the answer is that particularly indigenous grapes in Europe help represent, perhaps synecdochally, the history and culture of the areas from which these grapes derive. The continued growing of these grapes, and the making of these wines, then, provides a direct link to the past. It keeps that history alive. What of California, a place without indigenous grapes? In terms of the production of wine, California's history is certainly briefer than that of Switzerland. However, Martha Stoumen told me about how she came to see the similarities: "A lot of these places that I was drawn to, especially in the Old World, were really focused on native grape varietals and really trying to culturally just preserve what they had, historically," she explains. After talking with Giusto Occhipinti, who focuses on indigenous Sicilian grapes, Martha felt that "in California, at that time, I didn't feel

FIGURE 6.4 Martha Stoumen harvest photo
Photo credit: Andrew Thomas Lee; courtesy of Martha.

like we had much of a grape growing culture." However, she has come to realize that "we actually do. There's a lot of history to dig into in California. It doesn't go back as far, but we're not a clean slate culturally in terms of winemaking."

However, unlike many other winemaking cultures, the United States had a severe break in its history in the form of Prohibition, when a great deal of the local knowledge about viticulture and enology got lost.[41] What a book like Thomas Pinney's *A History of Wine in America* teaches us, though, is that the history of wine in America is a diverse one. That diversity reflected both the desire to find out what grapes would do well on American soil and where they would do best, but also very much the history of immigration and settlement of California.

As we drove around areas like Contra Costa County, Tegan Passelaqua made a point about this history as he explained why he calls one of his wines mataro:

> So the Portuguese came here because they were fisherman, you know. So here's this big salmon run, with the fisherman, [and] there's this whole community of fishing history, but they also planted grape vines. So the vines they planted were carignan—they call it "kerrigan" out here—and mataro, and I've always called my wines mataro. And people think it's like this contentious thing, and I'm like, these vines were planted as mataro; they weren't planted as mourvedre. It's actually still the main legal name for the grape in California. If you look at the grape crush report, mataro's the legal name, mourvedre is an allowed synonym. But in Spain it's mataro; in Australia it's mataro.

Tegan's point, then, is not only that he wants to celebrate this grape, which would fall into the original Seven Percent Solution, but that its very name matters as a way of preserving the direct link with the people who brought it here. Calling it by its more common French name, mourvedre, works to essentially erase that cultural connection.

Martha has some similar perspectives about these grapes and history. She reflects on the fact that

> we're learning some of the stuff we didn't even know in California, where a lot of these grapes have originated from, and they're not native, but also they have their own history, they've been here long enough, so you know, zinfandel, carignan [...] certainly those grapes come from other places, but were they ever created as kind of these more traditional blends together? And no, the answer is no, so that's like a distinctly California thing.

In fact, for Martha, the story of the grapes really does provide a direct cultural link, though it's an American version, for those grapes stand "as a reflection of the California or the American story, which is a bunch of different immigrants are coming from all over, and they're all bringing something, and then it's getting mixed together."

★   ★   ★   ★

Many of the winemakers I met who were interested in the "ignoble" varieties also clearly had a strong interest in history. Not only is Morgan Twain-Peterson's Bedrock Vineyard directly connected to well-known historical figures, he nearly became a history professor himself and was pursuing a postgraduate degree in American studies before returning to wine. Like Morgan, his fellow Historical Vineyard Society member, Tegan Passalaqua. told me: "I like old cars, I like old bicycles. I think there's also something, there's a belief in me that the way things were built 50–100 years ago were more thoughtful." Perhaps no person connected me to history more than Matthew Rorick, who told me to seek out Pinney's accounts of America's winemaking past.

Early in my research and as I asked questions about the "ignoble"—esoteric, noncommercial—grape varieties, several people pointed me towards Matthew. A quick google search let me know that his winery, one named for the first Dutch troops sent into battle and one which suggests an allegiance to lost causes, Forlorn Hope, refers to each of its offerings as a "rare creature." Though he pursued a postgraduate degree in anthropology, Matthew's dissertation project was in fact directly related to the history of wine, but, like Morgan Twain-Peterson, wine called him back. To talk with Matthew, I had to travel to Murphys, where Mark Twain's famous story of a "jumping frog" had been set. We stood, tilted, on a slope of the Rorick Vineyard when I had pulled out Parker's essay. He had a straw hat that he somehow managed to wear in a fashionable, cool style like Paul Newman in *Hud*. I wanted to know what made him pursue "rare creatures." Matthew at first said that it was largely curiosity, but I thought the ways that he described these wines spoke to something more. "Lost, displaced," I remarked, "it almost sounds like, to me it sounds like animal rescue a bit, or that there's something ethical or moral about trying to keep these grapes around in these spots."

"When I started doing the Forlorn Hope stuff in '05, '06, I was really just curious. It was just curiosity. I've never had this variety before, I've never worked with it, is it good? Do I like it?" he began. However, he then suggested that the desire to grow these grapes and make these wines began to move beyond that initial curiosity:

> But over time, the trajectory of the whole project [changed and], I became more and more interested in California's viticultural history, and viticultural heritage, and a lot of the things that we lost that were broken during Prohibition, and trying to re-forge a link to that. And obviously stuff like, things like vermentino, that wasn't … well, it probably was here,

he said, pointing to his vineyard.

> But people were growing a lot of it, and California wasn't known for vermentino although they could have been in the dry Sauternes that we bottled and drank all the way until just after World War II. But bringing things like mondeuse and trousseau back, that becomes very exciting to me. I don't think

it's morally wrong to plant more cabernet and chardonnay, but I don't know, California now has a viticultural tradition of cabernet and chardonnay, of course, but there were things that got lost along the way. What happens if you pick that thread back up? Let's see where it goes. That chain wasn't broken because the variety didn't work; it was broken for outside reasons, outside cultural reasons. And it's not that every variety does work: I tried green hungarian, and it's, now I see why it's very, very uncommon in California.

Although Parker omitted green hungarian from his list, it is the one grape from which, I was told repeatedly, you simply couldn't make a great wine. Of course, that was just before Tegan once poured me a glass of a suspiciously green-tinged wine from an unlabeled bottle and challenged me to guess what it was.

After Matthew made his own concession about green hungarian, I brought the question back around to Parker and aesthetics, noting "He's very intent on arguing that you simply can't make great wine from many of the grapes that you're interested in." Matthew's response was to return us to the problem of subjectivity:

in that statement he's saying that there is a thing that defines a great wine, and that varieties, whatever varieties he wants to say are not up to snuff just do not produce wine that's within those parameters of greatness. So already for me that's problematic, because how do you define a great wine? Who defines a great wine? I might find a wine amazing that you find thin, mediocre, acidic, whatever. So there's so much subjective interpretation that it becomes really difficult to judge. You might start looking at a larger sample size and saying, oh, wow, 80 percent of the people I've talked to who've tried this wine think it's great, and 20 percent are like, nah, I don't like that. So maybe this is really good wine and some people don't like it, but here you have one person saying, "I've tried a hundred wines that are from that variety, and they're never great, so that variety cannot make great wines," and well that's one person's palate.

He hesitated at first to offer his second criticism for fear that "the second thing— this is where I feel like I might get myself in trouble with my own logic." I jokingly assured him that "I'm an academic, no one's gonna read it anyway. Feel free to say what you'd like." Relieved, he continued by asking,

how do we know why the wine isn't great? Maybe *if* it's a different site. Maybe *if* you grew it on a different site in a different soil in a different climate, *if* you approached it differently in the vineyard, *if* you approached it differently in the vineyard and the winery—the variables are endless.

Ultimately, Matthew finds the whole notion, somewhat blindly endorsed by Parker, that history has shown the noble grapes to produce some of the best wines as lacking context. Just as Guillory sought to historicize the formation of the literary canon, Rorick argued that we need to think about how history and extrinsic factors shaped our sense of which wines are great rather than assuming greatness to be a matter of *being*:

> That rant, likewise, in a very convenient way doesn't take into account sociocultural factors that led to the wines from certain areas becoming more popular, whether it was just location, or economic power outside of the wine growing in that reason that brought people there, Prohibition, sure.

To further illustrate his point, Matthew shifted us back to trousseau, which, in France, traditionally comes from the Jura region.

> The Jura's never been a big trading center. It was fairly remote, fairly isolated, so the wines didn't get out and about—and why weren't they highly propagated? Was it because hundreds of years of intense viticultural selectivity led people to avoid them? Or was it just because they were in this remote place that made its own wines and drank them, and not many of them traveled out.

And of course, when they did travel out, in our time, they were found by Duncan and Nathan who wanted to make them in California and, in doing, so actually reached back to what Matthew called the chain that connected them to the planting of trousseau in the nineteenth century.

Matthew also challenges one of the great myths about the noble grapes, the delineation of the Grand Cru vineyards in Burgundy. He dismisses

> the romantic idea that over centuries the monks in Burgundy were trying to figure out which vines made the best wines. It's romantic, but it's probably far more likely that monks in Burgundy were trying to figure out which vines were not a pain in the ass to tend. Imagine growing wine grapes before you had sulfur dust? You had to find something that would ripen before it completely rotted off the vine. It would be completely mildewed if you tried to grow cabernet there. Yeah, okay, we tried that, it doesn't work. And that's assuming that they could even get a variety of varieties to try there, because those things didn't move quickly in that day, so it would be, okay, what are the varieties that we have here? We've got pinot noir, we've got chardonnay, we've got aligote, we've got gamay.

What gets lost when you think about wine the way that Parker does and believe that we have the wines that we have because they have always been recognized for and preserved for their greatness?

> I think that you lose—when you don't take a look at a lot of the other non-wine factors that play into how things became popular in a region. Those factors are important, and they're also very often overlooked because they're

not as sexy! They're not as romantically enthralling as the idea that, ah, Burgundy pinot is amazing. But it's not because people slogged and slogged. There's probably a lot of happy coincidence, and also pure practicality.

There may be a part of all of us that desires to push back against the argument that Matthew makes. However, he wants us to consider that value may reside in any number of extrinsic factors, and we can view his critique as akin to a culture of reason critique of relying on feelings to judge. If our guesses about how noble grapes came to be known as noble are accurate, then the reason did quite literally have to do with the fact that those were wines that the French exported. They also proved to be from grapes that have shown a strong ability to grow well in a number of places. Even Pinney's very nuanced history makes the case that California's rise as a wine-growing region was catalyzed by its increasing focus on many of the noble grapes, particularly chardonnay and cabernet sauvignon, which, not coincidentally, were the focus of the Judgement of Paris tasting in 1976 where California wines made from these grapes challenged French versions. This event and its media-enhanced consequence is now at the center of Napa's mythology.

Do, then, the recent movements to diversify California help demythologize that past and reconnect the links in our history, as Matthew suggests? Can we get around the fact that at some point, however skeptical we are about the ways in which greatness gets decided, or even whether we can truly say why something is great—a question that no doubt vexes literature, all of the arts, and wine—we still come back to questions of aesthetics? After all, as Abe Schoener asked: how can we eliminate pleasure? Surely, we want to enjoy the wines we drink, we want to love the literature we read? Yet, many of us remain skeptical of taste that seems too subjective: this wine speaks to me, or I see my own experience in this novel and therefore find it great. Can we, however, find ways to judge literature, art, and wine that somehow transcend the extrinsic factors that weigh in on our very sense of them? The push and pull of these views seem to echo the perennial contest between reason and feeling.

There are, of course, no easy answers to any of these questions. Many of them have vexed us since the time that we have thought to reflect upon the nature of our culture. Is wine art? For the purposes of this book, I have operated by trying to consider the question of what happens if we just believe—at least for a time—that it is. I suppose that part of my own pleasure in wine is to view it as art because there are few things that give me greater joy than art, and when a wine feels like a transcendent and moving experience, I tend to understand its pleasures and those factors as I would art. I am aware that there may be extrinsic factors, which might range from the fact that I can see the wine's label or that I am among my closest friends, but, like most people, in that very moment those factors seem at a remove from the experience. However, this book has not been about proving that we should view wine as art, but that we can learn that wine, both as an object and as a part of our culture, circulates in that culture in much the way art does, often tied up in disputes about interpretation and as part of the ongoing "dialectic" of reason and feeling. We can then learn much about how we understand our world by paying attention to the very ways in which we transmit and speak that culture when we think and talk about wine.

Notes

1 Robert Parker, "An Article of Merit," *The Wine Advocate*, January 18, 2014.
2 Samuel Johnson, "No. 92. The accommodation of sound to the sense, often chimerical," *The Rambler*, February 1751. www.johnsonessays.com/the-rambler/accommodation-often-chimerical/.
3 Qtd in Louis Menand, "Diversity," *Critical Terms for Literary Study*, ed. Frank Lentricchia and Thomas McLaughlin (Chicago: University of Chicago Press, 1995), 342.
4 Ibid., 343.
5 Ibid., 343.
6 Gerald Graff, *Beyond the Culture Wars: How Teaching the Conflicts Can Revitalize American Education* (New York: W.W. Norton, 1993), 8.
7 Ibid., 10.
8 John Guillory, *Cultural Capital: The Problem of Literary Canon Formation* (Chicago: University of Chicago Press, 1993), 4.
9 Ibid., 6.
10 Ibid., 6–7.
11 Menand, "Diversity", 347.
12 Guillory, *Cultural Capital*, 7.
13 Ibid., 18.
14 Ibid., 17.
15 Ibid., 22–23.
16 John Guillory, "Canon," *Critical Terms for Literary Study*, ed. Frank Lentricchia and Thomas McLaughlin, 2nd ed. (Chicago: University of Chicago Press, 1995), 235.
17 Ibid.
18 Barbara Herrnstein Smith, *Contingencies of Value: Alternative Perspectives for Critical* Theory (Cambridge: Harvard University Press, 1988), 33.
19 Barbara Herrnstein Smith, "Value/Evaluation," *Critical Terms for Literary Study*, ed. Frank Lentricchia and Thomas McLaughlin, 2nd ed. (Chicago: University of Chicago Press, 1995), 179.
20 Ibid., 177.
21 Ibid., 180.
22 John Ruskin, "Stone of Venice," *Norton Anthology of English Literature*, vol. 2, ed. Stephen Greenblatt (New York: W.W. Norton, 2018), 1564.
23 Lillian S. Robinson, "Treason Our Text: Feminist Challenges to the Literary Canon," *Falling into Theory: Conflicting Views on Reading Literature*, ed. David H. Richter (Boston: Bedford/St. Martin's, 2000), 158.
24 Annette Kolodony, "Dancing Through the Minefield: Some Observations on the Theory, Practice, and Politics of Feminist Literary Criticism," *Falling into Theory: Conflicting Views on Reading Literature*, 305.
25 Guillory, *Cultural Capital*, 332.
26 Ibid.
27 Ibid.
28 Ibid., 332–333.
29 Ibid., 333.
30 Ibid.
31 Jason Wilson, *Godforsaken Grapes: A Slightly Tipsy Journey Through the World of Strange, Obscure, and Underappreciated Grapes* (New York: Abrams, 2018), 15.

32 Kevin Wardell, "Why More California Winemakers Are Embracing Varietal Diversity," *750 Daily*, May 19, 2019. https://daily.sevenfifty.com/why-more-california-winemakers-are-embracing-varietal-diversity/.
33 Wilson, *G-dforsaken Grapes*, 21.
34 Ibid.
35 Ibid., 25.
36 Ibid., 32.
37 Ibid., 41.
38 Ibid., 82.
39 Ibid., 84.
40 Jane Tompkins, "Masterpiece Theater: The Politics of Hawthorne's Literary Reputation," *Falling into Theory: Conflicting Views on Reading Literature*, 138.
41 War has, of course, had similar effects in Europe, for instance. *Wine and War: The French, the Nazis, and the Battle for France's Greatest Treasure* by Donald and Peter Kadsrup provides an account of how France continued to produce wine during the war.

References

Graff, Gerald. *Beyond the Culture Wars: How Teaching the Conflicts Can Revitalize American Education.* New York: W.W. Norton, 1993.
Guillory, John. *Cultural Capital: The Problem of Literary Canon Formation.* Chicago: University of Chicago Press, 1993.
Guillory, John. "Canon." In *Critical Terms for Literary Study*, edited by Frank Lentricchia and Thomas McLaughlin. 2nd ed. Chicago: University of Chicago Press, 1995.
Herrnstein Smith, Barbara. *Contingencies of Value: Alternative Perspectives for Critical Theory.* Cambridge: Harvard University Press, 1988.
Herrnstein Smith, Barbara. "Value/Evaluation." In *Critical Terms for Literary Study*, edited by Frank Lentricchia and Thomas McLaughlin. 2nd ed. Chicago: University of Chicago Press, 1995.
Johnson, Samuel. "No. 92. The accommodation of sound to the sense, often chimerical." *The Rambler*, February 1751. www.johnsonessays.com/the-rambler/accommodation-often-chimerical/.
Kolodny, Annette. "Dancing Through the Minefield: Some Observations on the Theory, Practice, and Politics of Feminist Literary Criticism." In *Falling into Theory: Conflicting Views on Reading Literature*, edited by David H. Richter. Boston: Bedford/St. Martin's, 2000.
Menand, Louis. "Diversity." In *Critical Terms for Literary Study*, edited by Frank Lentricchia and Thomas McLaughlin. 2nd ed. Chicago: University of Chicago Press, 1995.
Parker, Robert. "An Article of Merit." *The Wine Advocate*, January 18, 2014.
Robinson, Lillian S. "Treason Our Text: Feminist Challenges to the Literary Canon." In *Falling into Theory: Conflicting Views on Reading Literature*, edited by David H. Richter. Boston: Bedford/St. Martin's, 2000.
Ruskin, John. "Stone of Venice." In *Norton Anthology of English Literature*, vol. 2, edited by Stephen Greenblatt. New York: W.W. Norton, 2018.
Tompkins, Jane. "Masterpiece Theater: The Politics of Hawthorne's Literary Reputation." In *Falling into Theory: Conflicting Views on Reading Literature*, edited by David H. Richter. Boston: Bedford/St. Martin's, 2000.
Wardell, Kevin. "Why More California Winemakers Are Embracing Varietal Diversity." *750 Daily*, May 19, 2019. https://daily.sevenfifty.com/why-more-california-winemakers-are-embracing-varietal-diversity/.
Wilson, Jason. *Godforsaken Grapes: A Slightly Tipsy Journey Through the World of Strange, Obscure, and Underappreciated Grapes.* New York: Abrams, 2018.

INDEX

Printed in the United States
by Baker & Taylor Publisher Services